HARDMAN OF BIRMINGHAM

GOLDSMITH AND GLASSPAINTER

MICHAEL FISHER

John Hardman Jnr. 1811-1867 (JHAL)

Dedication

This book is respectfully dedicated to the staff of John Hardman & Company past and present whose skill and dedication has upheld the ideals of beauty and truth instilled by Pugin and Hardman in the design and production of stained glass, metalwork and decorative art.

HARDMAN
OF
BIRMINGHAM
GOLDSMITH AND GLASSPAINTER

MICHAEL FISHER

M.A., F.S.A.

Landmark Publishing

Published by

Ashbourne Hall, Cokayne Ave
Ashbourne, Derbyshire, DE6 1EJ England
Tel: (01335) 347349 Fax: (01335) 347303
e-mail: landmark@clara.net

1st Edition

ISBN: 978-1-84306-362-9

Print: Gutenberg Press Ltd, Malta
Design by: Mark Titterton
Edited by: Ian Howe

Front Cover: The Medieval Court at The Great Exhibition, 1851
Back Cover: Detail of the St. Dunstan window, by John Hardman & Co, 1893, now at St. Anselm's
Church Philadelphia
Page 1: John Hardman Jnr., 1811–67, photograph of c.1860 (John Hardman & Co.)
Title page: A.W.N. Pugin: design for letterhead for Hardman's new showroom in Great Charles Street,
Birmingham, 1845. Pencil drawing in private collection

CONTENTS

FOREWORD

Birmingham has few of its early Victorian manufacturers left in existence. The Jewellery Quarter, once home to the great fabricators of all things beautiful and useful, still has some fine workshops. These must be preserved at any cost. Recent talk of creating a Museum of Britishness has heightened the awareness that these highly skilled trades are disappearing. Once disbanded or catalogued by the auction rooms, they cannot be resurrected.

Keeping a Victorian behemoth afloat is at times akin to being shackled to the leg of a decaying corpse. No matter how committed, enthusiastic, or creative your work staff, without doubt, during a production period of 170 years, you will go in and out of fashion more than once. However, there are moments when there is an alignment of forces that allow great art to be produced and appreciated. From the re-creation of the spires of York Minster in Hiroshima, to the recasting of the door handles on Pugin's house, few companies can create the excitement that comes with being involved with John Hardman & Co.

But for the love of St. Jude and stray kittens, John Hardman and Company, Ltd. could have been consigned to the archive shelves of the Birmingham Museum and Art Gallery. My parents, Edgar and Margaret Phillips, believing 12 cats in the household were not enough, visited a metal merchant in search of homeless kittens. Piled high were the windows of a demolished church, in need of repair. John Hardman & Co. was recommended to do the restoration work. A relationship was struck between Patrick Feeney, the stalwart custodian of over fifty years, and my father that culminated in the eventual sale of the studio to the Phillips family. From that day on, 'Penury stalks us daily', became the family motto.

Hardman's is a living piece of British architectural history and should be inoculated against the perils of modern day commerce. In order to keep the firm viable in the 21st century, we have delved into its illustrious past for guidance. Pugin's motto 'en avant' has been reversed to 'en arriere'. Through acquisition of Hardman produced artefacts and the immersion of the workforce in 19th century archive material, we have regained the levels of skill that made Hardman's world renowned. It is through the collection, that our links with the author, Fr. Michael Fisher, were established. It was at St. Chad's, Stafford that a small exhibition of Hardman artefacts started a relationship between the author and I that has grown into our obsession for the gothic and a craving for all things Puginesque.

A retired history teacher, non stipendiary priest, devoted family man and husband to Isabel, friend, and stone carver of note Fr. Michael has promoted and transformed the image of the firm with his gruelling schedule of lectures and publications. Officially named the Hardman archivist, he has spent hours in the lofty heights of the Birmingham Library. So contagious is his enthusiasm for his subject that it has led to NADFAS setting up camp in the foothills of the archive at Lightwoods House. The future plans being to digitalize all archive material and create a photographic census of all Hardman decorative schemes extant.

What on earth could I possibly give to Fr Michael Fisher that will reflect my gratitude for the relentless energy that he has poured into the modern day John Hardman & Company? A medal. A piece of metal in the form of a coin, struck with a device, and intended to preserve the remembrance of a notable event or an illustrious person, or to serve as a reward.

John Hardman started making medals in the 1830's and continued until the 1950's. After a quick search through the auction houses, a suitable medal was found. Money collected by the Pugin memorial committee was invested to provide annually a Pugin travelling studentship worth 40 guineas. The studentship was set up in 1865, the fund being administered by the R.I.B.A., which also had the discretion of presenting a Pugin medal. The medal has the coat of arms of RIBA on one side and those of Pugin on the other. This particular medal was originally awarded to Anthony Magetson in 1907 and represented to Fr Fisher in 2004.

Similarly on the occasion of Michael's 60th birthday, he was gifted a letter sent by A.W. N. Pugin to John Knill, a generous Patron of Catholic Church building in South London, referring to the reopening of St. Giles' Church in Cheadle. The contents of Pugin's letters have become an invaluable resource to historians. But what made this letter so relevant to Michael was that it mentioned the Swan Hotel which sits directly opposite Fr. Fisher's church, the 12th Century St. Chad's, Stafford. The gift was well received, but the thought that Pugin must have seen the author's church in its unrestored state brought Michael to tears.

Today, Hardmans is emerging into a new era and is shifting the emphasis away from a purely stained glass base to one of a centre of excellence for the decorative arts. This rebirth captures the creative spirit espoused by Pugin and Hardman who used their talents to create some of the greatest decorative art of the neo-gothic period. Pugin often furnished Hardman with ancient ecclesiastical ornament for use as medieval inspiration in the workshops. Similar motivational surroundings are now on display at Lightwoods House promoting the skills which the founders helped rediscover. Lectures and tours are common place to groups as diverse as the blind, Brummagem beekeepers, unruly youths, scholars and hobbyists.

The bicentennial milestone will soon be upon us. Is it possible for a company based on the purity of bespoke design to survive modern times?

Health and safety now advocates that all employees in contact with lead must have their blood tested on a regular basis. Signs on the hot water tap must state that hot water will come out of this tap. The use of hydrofluoric acid in the workspace is accompanied by such tight regulation that this technique will soon disappear from our shores. No food or drink is allowed in work areas and barrier cream now substitutes for gloves where individuals are not latex tolerant. Conservation guidelines do not allow for modern bonded timber products to be used in workshops because they 'off-gas'. Thermal shock must be taken into consideration when stained glass panels are removed from the studio into the outside world.

This is a far cry from my youthful impressions of this most traditional of studios. Aromatic fumes from oil of tar and clove oil used as a medium in glass painting. Huge plumes of white powders billowing from the cement room. The addictive smell of burning pig tallow acting as flux on solder joints. Stirring cups of tea with lead cames and throwing the bottom third on the floor to keep the dust down. There would be black lead finger-prints on my sandwiches that I would nibble around and discard. Recycling was melting down organ pipes onto corrugated cardboard to make solder sticks. A stark contrast to the sanitized working conditions of today, where facial hair renders protective masks ineffective and the use of lead cames may soon be outlawed.

Whatever changes are required, Hardmans must remain a functioning studio. This publication illustrates the importance of the contribution that John Hardman & Co. has made to the world's cultural heritage.

In 2038 the firm will host its 200th birthday party. Michael Fisher will be 95, I will be 73, and the archive may well be fully catalogued. I will keep a chair for my friend and business partner Colin Thomas and my mother, Margaret Phillips who will be celebrating her own centennial. All must attend.

'en arriere'

Neil Phillips
Lightwoods House
Birmingham
England
B67 5DP

Detail of window for Syon Abbey (Virginia U.S.A.) by John Hardman, 2007

AUTHOR'S PREFACE

The exclamation 'Gothic For Ever!' was appended by the architect and designer Augustus Welby Pugin (1812–52) to several of his letters and other writings to express his passionate belief in Gothic as the only appropriate style for the building, furnishing and decoration of Christian churches and residences. It was taken up enthusiastically by the Birmingham firm of John Hardman as they were transformed, under Pugin's influence, from toymakers and button-makers into goldsmiths and glasspainters. It was also the last thing to be seen, inscribed in bold letters over the exit, by visitors to the exhibition, *Pugin: A Gothic Passion*, held at the Victoria and Albert Museum in 1994. That exhibition, and the one which followed in New York a year later, proved to be a turning point in public understanding and appreciation of Pugin and his revolutionary impact upon nineteenth-century art and design. Having gone through a period of unpopularity – and even vilification – in the mid-twentieth century, Gothic became once more attractive, and with it the products of John Hardman and Co. Having survived the lean years, and risen phoenix-like from the fire which devastated their Birmingham workshops in 1970, Hardman's were uniquely placed to supply an expanding market and to provide education and training in the traditional skills for which the firm had been renowned since the 1830s. In 1972 the studio moved to its present location, Lightwoods House, some four miles west of Birmingham city centre.

Set within an attractive park fronting the A456 Hagley Road, Lightwoods is a Georgian house dating from 1791; built of mellow russet brick with stone quoins and window-surrounds, and a triangular pediment over the projecting central section and front entrance. Though much altered since its early days as a family home, the building retains its grand staircase illuminated by a Venetian window, some original carved stone chimneypieces, and deeply moulded plaster cornices to several of the ceilings. Within the house today is a working studio in which all the processes of designing and making stained glass are carried on, and an extensive collection of historic Hardman metalwork, glass and archive material dating back to the early years of the firm. 'A beastly place to display Gothic', so Pugin might have thought, having famously said that about the Crystal Palace at the time of the Great Exhibition. To Pugin, neo-Classicism was synonymous with paganism, thus putting it beyond the pale of his 'true principles'. Yet, as one of Pugin's ardent admirers, Sir Ninian Comper, so ably demonstrated in many of his buildings, the Gothic and the Classical may harmoniously be combined. So at Lightwoods House, a richly carved Gothic lampadarium – a beam from which sanctuary lamps are suspended – hangs comfortably amid the luscious plaster mouldings of a Georgian ceiling, while exhibits of neo-medieval candelabra, brass lecterns and jewelled altar-vessels sparkle in the light flooding in from sash windows. 'What an extraordinary thing that they should be living in a room without mullions', Pugin might have remarked, as he once did when visiting the college-rooms of an Oxford friend.

The Pugin connection is just one of the factors which make this story so intriguing, and indeed unique in the history of the Victorian Gothic Revival. Pugin's vision of a Gothic England demanded a complete integration of architecture and the visual arts unknown since the Middle Ages, and success depended upon the ability of others to execute his designs for the full range of ecclesiastical furnishings. Of the four major firms who worked

Lightwoods House

Lightwoods House: the Collections Room, 2006

for Pugin, only Hardman's has survived into the twenty-first century. The others – Crace, Minton and Myers – have long since gone. Moreover, the close personal friendship of Pugin and John Hardman, and the marriage of his eldest daughter to John Hardman Powell, ensured that Pugin's principles of design were sustained long after his death. Rival firms of glassmakers who caught the Gothic flame – such as Burlison & Grylls, Clayton and Bell, Morris & Co. – have all gone too, leaving Hardman's as the only stained-glass firm working in unbroken continuity with nineteenth-century tradition and using its historic archive to inspire and create new work which goes beyond mere imitation of the past.

To say that nothing at all has been written about Hardman's would be grossly unfair to Fr Brian Doolan, former Dean of St Chad's cathedral, Birmingham, whose booklet, *The Pugins and the Hardmans* (Archdiocese of Birmingham Historical Commission 2004) was a pioneering study of the firm's achievements and of the relationship between the two families who were at the heart of the Gothic and Catholic Revivals of the nineteenth century. Otherwise, however, details of the Hardman enterprise are fragmentary and difficult to find, except insofar as they form part of more general publications such as Atterbury & Wainwright, *Pugin: A Gothic Passion* (1994), and Brian Andrews, *Creating a Gothic Paradise: Pugin at the Antipodes* (2002). A significant section of Stanley Shepherd's definitive study of Pugin's stained glass (University of Birmingham PhD thesis, 1997) is in the process of being prepared for publication, and that will include much about the glassmaking side of the Hardman enterprise in its very early days. David Meara's, *A.W.N. Pugin and the Revival of Memorial Brasses* (1991) analyses that aspect of the Pugin – Hardman enterprise. On Pugin himself, tribute is due to Phoebe Stanton (1914–2003), whose use of the Hardman Archive contributed significantly to her doctoral research, undertaken at a time when Pugin's architecture was severely underrated and misunderstood. Rosemary Hill's long-awaited biography, *God's Architect* (2007) fleshes out as never before Pugin's dynamic personality which propelled Hardman from relative obscurity as a Birmingham button-maker and placed him centre-stage in the revival of medieval art.

This particular study presents a broad sweep of the firm's history and activities from 1838 to the present day, illustrated with some of the finest examples of their work. The scope of the Hardman enterprise is breathtaking: everything from christening cups to coffin handles; from chair-nails to the jewelled embellishments of the Royal throne in the House of Lords; from a single-light panel in a front door to full sets of windows for cathedrals and major churches. The extent of Hardman's overseas activities is equally amazing, from its early supplies of metalwork and glass to Tasmania in the 1840s to the furnishing and glazing of great American churches such as Albany cathedral and Corpus Christi Church, Baltimore, which continued through to the 1930s. It is indeed overseas commissions which account for much of the firm's work today in the design and making of new windows. Margaret Belcher's, *The collected letters of A.W.N. Pugin*, are an invaluable tool in the hands of the researcher.

My own involvement with Hardman's began in 1999 when, as the historian on the Alton Towers Heritage Committee, I first met the firm's proprietor, Neil Phillips, in connection with the restoration of nineteenth-century Pugin glass at Alton. I was invited to visit Lightwoods House to see the collections of archive material, metalwork and glass, and before long I found myself drawn into the firm as part-time archivist and researcher. This has involved the handling of enquiries both from within the firm and from members of the public about work carried out by Hardman's at various times, and delving into the very extensive archives to find the answers. A considerable part of this book has been based on such case studies involving a particular building or commission, as illustrative of Hardman's work in that field. The amazing story of Thomas Stuart Kennedy (Chapter 5) emerged from the shadows because of two or three metalwork drawings in the Lightwoods collection bearing the name 'Kennedy' and a date, but nothing more. The ensuing search for further information in the daybooks and correspondence files in the Birmingham City Archive brought to life one of Hardman's most important clients of the 1860s, who was also a noted mountaineer and an inventor, whose wife's family were close friends of the Pugins in Ramsgate, and who commissioned Edward Welby Pugin to build a new family home for him. An enquiry from a student at Vassar College (New York) about the Cornaro window in the college library opened up another trail of discovery, and as a consequence the fascinating story of that window is told here in Chapter 7. Many more such stories must lie hidden in the records which occupy over a hundred metres of shelf-space in the Birmingham City Archive, let alone what is held in other repositories including the Birmingham Museum & Art Gallery, and the Lightwoods Collection. Most of this source material is readily accessible, and I have included here an Appendix giving a resumé of what is in the various deposits, and some guidance as to how to use the archive material, for the benefit of those who may wish to pursue enquiries of their own.

This study has also been informed by my earlier research into Pugin's work in Staffordshire, which of course involved Hardman's. This accounts for what some may see as a slight Staffordshire bias, but then Staffordshire formed a significant part of the Catholic Midlands where Pugin and Hardman were most prolific. I might even claim John Hardman himself for Staffordshire, because Handsworth, where he had his family home, was in those days a part of my home county, but Birmingham was where he established his workshops, and it was the industrial skills of Birmingham that he harnessed to the manufacture of fine metalwork and stained glass.

While it has been impossible to ignore the New Palace of Westminster and St Chad's cathedral, Birmingham, as the most spectacular Pugin–Hardman collaborations, or the planting of true-principles Gothic on Australian soil, it has to be recognised that these subjects have already been well documented in publications such as Sir Robert Cooke, *The Palace of Westminster* (1987), Michael Port (ed.), *The Houses of Parliament* (1976), Brian Andrews (op.cit.), and the cathedral clergy's *History of St. Chad's Cathedral, Birmingham, 1841–1904* (1904). I have, therefore, given rather less space than might have been expected to these aspects of Hardmans' work, and more to those which have hitherto received little or no attention, such as their extensive activities in the United States, and the role of John Hardman Powell who succeeded Pugin as chief designer.

That the Hardman firm survived after its main competitors went out of business was due in no small measure to Edgar and Margaret Phillips, who took over the business in 1974, and to their son, Neil, who was equally determined that this significant piece of Birmingham's industrial and cultural history should not disappear. Though Gothic-revival art was no longer popular in the post-Vatican II Catholic Church, the skills which had helped to create it at Hardman's were kept very much alive in the belief that one day it would return, as indeed it has. This book could not have come to publication without the active support and encouragement of Neil Phillips, whose untiring enthusiasm, dedication, and widespread travels on behalf of the firm stand him in comparison with Pugin who once described himself as 'a Locomotive being always flyin' about'. No one was better placed than Neil to write the Foreword, and I was delighted when he agreed to do so.

Today the Hardman Studio is attracting many new commissions from both the United Kingdom and overseas, and providing facilities for education and training in all aspects of glass design and manufacture; while the vast archive of papers, cartoons, drawings and watercolours offers an unparalleled resource for study and research. Lightwoods House already attracts groups of visitors from organisations such as the National Trust Association, NADFAS, The Art Fund and the Victorian Society, who come to view the collections and to see the art of glassmaking in action. The Studio forms an integral part of Birmingham's developing Pugin–Hardman heritage trail which embraces St Chad's cathedral, St Mary's College, Oscott, and the fully restored Convent of Mercy right opposite the former Hardman house at Handsworth. I hope that the publication of this book will assist the future development of Lightwoods House as a working museum, studio and educational resource centre with all the facilities necessary for the conservation and display of the Hardman collections.

Michael Fisher
St. Chad's Day, 2nd March 2008

THE HARDMAN FAMILY TREE

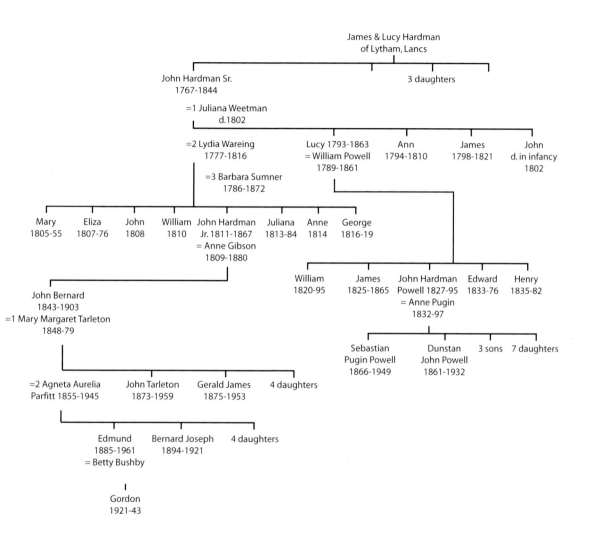

James & Lucy Hardman
of Lytham, Lancs

John Hardman Sr.
1767-1844

3 daughters

=1 Juliana Weetman
d.1802

=2 Lydia Wareing
1777-1816

Lucy 1793-1863
= William Powell
1789-1861

Ann
1794-1810

James
1798-1821

John
d. in infancy
1802

=3 Barbara Sumner
1786-1872

Mary
1805-55

Eliza
1807-76

John
1808

William
1810

John Hardman
Jr. 1811-1867
= Anne Gibson
1809-1880

Juliana
1813-84

Anne
1814

George
1816-19

William
1820-95

James
1825-1865

John Hardman
Powell 1827-95
= Anne Pugin
1832-97

Edward
1833-76

Henry
1835-82

John Bernard
1843-1903
=1 Mary Margaret Tarleton
1848-79

Sebastian
Pugin Powell
1866-1949

Dunstan
John Powell
1861-1932

3 sons

7 daughters

=2 Agneta Aurelia
Parfitt 1855-1945

John Tarleton
1873-1959

Gerald James
1875-1953

4 daughters

Edmund
1885-1961
= Betty Bushby

Bernard Joseph
1894-1921

4 daughters

Gordon
1921-43

(with acknowledgements to Fr Brian Doolan and Sr. Barbara Jeffery R.S.M.)

ACKNOWLEDGEMENTS

During the course of my research I have received valuable help from the staff of the Birmingham City Archives, and the Birmingham Museum & Art Gallery. Stanley Shepherd kindly allowed me to borrow his unpublished Ph.D. thesis on Pugin's stained glass. Sue Fryer, a daughter of Patrick Feeny, generously supplied a copy of her father's memoir on his fifty years with John Hardman & Co., and other useful information. Mrs Sarah Houle, President of the Pugin Society and a direct descendant of John Hardman Powell and Anne Pugin, has given invaluable help, the Society's Patron, Lady Wedgwood, is a constant source of encouragement and support in all matters relating to Pugin, as is Doctor Margaret Belcher, the editor of Pugin's published letters. Mrs. Catriona Blaker, custodian of the Society's photographic archive, has searched out several of the illustrations for this book. My wife Isobel has shown infinite patience as Hardman moved into the spare room to join Pugin who has been there for a number of years. I am grateful to the following for answering particular queries, tracking down vital information, enabling me to visit various locations and to take photographs, or supplying pictures: Brian Andrews (The Pugin Foundation, Tasmania), Fr Sandy Brown (St Giles's Cheadle), David Burton (Chirk Castle), Lucy Cohen (Vassar College, N.Y.), Mark Collins (Archivist, Parliamentary Estates Directorate), Rev. J. Collis (Jesus College Cambridge), Sir Patrick Cormack, M.P., Fr. Brian Doolan & Fr Pat. Browne (St. Chad's cathedral), Elizabeth Dancey (Birmingham NADFAS), Fr. Robert Fayers (St. Paul's, Brighton), Andrew Ford,. Bernard Phelan, Dr. J. Mordaunt Crook, Anne Clinch, Janet Douglas, Anne Grant, The Revd. Frank Hodges (Corpus Christi Church, Baltimore), Sister Barbara Jeffery (St. Mary's Convent, Handsworth), Michele Lefevre (Local Studies Manager, Leeds Central Library), Jane Hedley, Maurice O'Keeffe, Andrew McLean (archivist, Mount Stuart, Isle of Bute), Fr. David Myers, Mrs. J. Mainey, Miriam Power (archivist, Westminster Cathedral). Valerie Roseblade, Canon E.J. Woods.

Photographic acknowledgements, where approporiate, are given in the captions to individual pictures, but I would like also to record my thanks here to Deryck Clark, Dr. John Davis, Jane Dew, the Dossin Great Lakes Museum (Detroit), Abram Engelman, George Garbutt, Jane Hedley, Simon Huguet, Martine Hamilton Knight, Phil Sayer, Andrew Ford, Chris Singleton, Andrew McLean, Graham Miller, Louisa Nielsen, Trader Al Shimonoseki (Japan).

All other photographs are by the author.

Michael Fisher

1. PUGIN'S CANDLESTICK MAKER

Birmingham in the early nineteenth century was, according to A. W. N. Pugin, 'that most detestable of places – where Greek buildings & Smoking chimneys – radicals and disenters [*sic*] are blended together'.[1] It was not, however, completely beyond redemption, for Birmingham became the location of the first Catholic cathedral to be built in England since the Reformation; dedicated to St Chad and designed by Pugin. As the foundation-stone of St Chad's was laid in 1839, Pugin vowed that he would never rest satisfied until he saw 'the cross raised high above every chimney in Birmingham, and hear the sound of St. Chad's bells drowning the steam whistle and the proving of gun barrels'[2]. Pugin lived just long enough to see the creation of the new Catholic Diocese of Birmingham, centred upon St Chad's, and Dr Nicholas Wiseman, who had preached at the consecration of the cathedral, installed as Cardinal Archbishop of Westminster, following the restoration of the Hierarchy in 1850.

Pugin was not himself a Midlander. Born in London, he lived at various times in the capital, at Salisbury, and at Ramsgate where he eventually built his family home. In 1836–7, however, he came into contact with a number of prominent Midland Catholics whose position and influence ensured that Birmingham and the Catholic Midlands would be central to Pugin's work as an architect and designer, and the place where his ideas would take practical shape. These were John Talbot (1791–1852), sixteenth Earl of Shrewsbury, Ambrose Phillipps (1809–1878) of Grace Dieu, Leicestershire, Bishop Thomas Walsh (1779–1849), Vicar Apostolic of the Midland District, and John Hardman Jnr (1811–67). All of them became infected with Pugin's enthusiasm for Gothic art and architecture as a means of edifying and propagating the Catholic Faith in the years following the Catholic Emancipation Act of 1829. Shrewsbury and Phillipps were the wealthy patrons who financed Pugin's Gothic creations on and around their respective estates, Walsh was the very epitome of Pugin's ideal church-building bishop, and Hardman provided the skills and business acumen needed to furnish the Revival with the necessary

A.W.N. Pugin: the only surviving photograph, taken from a daguerrotype of about 1840 (Private Collection)

15

metalwork and other ecclesiastical furnishings made to Pugin's own designs. Furthermore, Hardman became Pugin's closest friend. About one third of the surviving Pugin correspondence consists of letters written to Hardman, and the families became related through the marriage of Pugin's eldest daughter, Anne (1832–97) to Hardman's nephew, John Hardman Powell (1827–95).

To Pugin, the smoking chimneys and steam-hammers of Birmingham were sad reflections of the decline in traditional handicrafts and the dehumanising aspects of the Industrial Revolution which he despised equally. It was nevertheless the developing industries of Birmingham which attracted the Hardmans to the town in the first place, and which afforded Pugin many advantages in the manufacture of architectural iron and brass, and the production of a wide range of church furnishings. The Hardmans came originally from Lytham, Lancashire; a Catholic family from an area in which Catholicism had remained strong throughout the decades of persecution. In the mid-1700s James and Lucy Hardman moved to Birmingham, attracted, as were many others at this time, by the prospects of employment in the rapidly expanding industries of the town. Their only son, John Hardman Snr, was born on 3 August 1767. At the age of fourteen John was apprenticed to James Baker as a 'toymaker'. In eighteenth-century Birmingham this signified not the making of children's playthings but the production of inexpensive metal jewellery made of gilded base metal and often set with real or imitation gemstones: what nowadays might be termed costume jewellery[3]. This trade also embraced the production of gilt buckles and buttons which were in great demand not only for the army and navy but also for the liveries of footmen and other domestic servants. Later, in partnership with a Mr Thomas Lewis, Hardman set up his own button-making business in Paradise Street, to the west of what is now Victoria Square, and where Birmingham's new Town Hall was to be built in 1832. John Hardman married three times. After the death in 1802 of his first wife, Juliana Weetman, he married Lydia Wareing by whom he had eight children, among whom was John Hardman Jnr, the eventual founder of the ecclesiastical metalworking firm of John Hardman & Co.

Apprenticeship indenture of John Hardman Snr. dated 1781 (JHAL)

By the early 1830s the Hardman family was living in Handsworth, which at that time was a suburb to the north-west of Birmingham and geographically in the county of Staffordshire. White's *History, Gazetteer and Directory of Staffordshire* (1834) lists John Hardman as a 'button manufacturer' resident at Woodland House, Hunter's Lane. Born in 1811, John Jnr was educated at Stonyhurst College (Lancashire) before joining his father's business at the age of eighteen. Earlier he had attended Messrs Fosters' Academy, and one of his copybooks has survived from this time. It contains a series of county maps, copied by Hardman when he was about ten years old, all inked-in and coloured. On other leaves are some individual creations in the form of boyish pencil-drawings of cottages, churches and castles.

Handsworth at this time was the home of the (now demolished) Soho Manufactory established in the 1760s by Boulton & Watt for the manufacture of a wide range of metal goods from buttons to steam-engines, and employing a workforce of around 600, but there was room for smaller establishments too. Hardman's of Paradise Street thus began as just one of many Birmingham workshops employing a small number of skilled men engaged in the brass, button, gun and jewellery industries for which the town was becoming increasingly famous. They shared in the general success and expansion of these trades, and their growing prosperity was reflected in generous benefactions to the Catholic Church. It was in this context that the Hardmans first encountered Pugin, probably through their involvement with the new seminary and college at Oscott, established by Dr Walsh to provide more and better-educated clergy to supply the growing needs of the Midland District.[4]

Among the benefactors of Oscott was the Earl of Shrewsbury, who had encountered Pugin at least as early as 1836,[5] and whose domestic chaplain, Dr Daniel Rock (1799–1871), was a noted liturgical scholar and writer, and an ardent admirer of Pugin's early publications. Pugin first visited Oscott in March 1837, after which he soon became involved with the furnishing of the chapel. On 29 May 1837 he dined at the home of John Hardman Jnr, thus marking the beginning of their lifelong friendship. On this occasion, or very shortly afterwards, the question of a new Catholic church for Birmingham was discussed, for on 10 June Pugin sent a set of drawings to Hardman. The accompanying letter expresses the hope that 'the present filthy hole' (i.e. a Georgian Classical building in Shadwell Street) will be demolished and 'a church erected [*sic*] somewhat suitable to the dignity of divine worship and the performance of the sacred mysteries', in other words a Gothic one.[6] Though this particular scheme did not come to fruition, the letter and the plans reveal the determination of Pugin and John Hardman Jnr. that Birmingham should have a properly designed Catholic church. The letter is interesting for another reason too. Along with the plans for the proposed new church, Pugin sent Hardman a 'rare and good' chalice and paten of Gothic design which he had bought for sixteen guineas. 'I think it is marvelously cheap and if regilt will have a splendid effect.' Pugin had also bought a ciborium 'ten times finer than any modern silver one'. Evidently these items were medieval: '. . . it becomes a duty in these times', Pugin wrote, 'to preserve these relicks from desecration'. Pugin's diary records a payment from Hardman for the chalice, which was to be offered to the Revd Michael McDonnell, priest of St Peter's, Broad Street, in the hope, no doubt, of better things to come. This is the first recorded instance of Pugin introducing Hardman to precisely the kind of medieval altar-plate that was needed to provide models for their revival of 'the Real Thing'.

It was at Pugin's instigation that in 1838 Hardman expanded the family business in Paradise Street to include ecclesiastical metalwork under the name of the Medieval Art Manufactory, in partnership with Jeremiah Iliffe. The first entry in the Metalwork Daybook is dated 26 June 1838, and it consists of an order from the London publishing firm of Booker & Dolman for fifty sets of metal clasps and corners for missals.[7] To begin with, the venture was little more than an extension into the ecclesiastical sphere of Hardman's existing activities in the production of small gilded metal items, although it is clear that the firm was moving somewhat upmarket from basic 'Brummagem-ware', branching out into silver- and goldsmithing, while Pugin's powerful presence ensured matchless quality of design. Ensuing early entries in the daybook are mainly for small items for churches, e.g. holy-water sprinklers and stoups, cruets and bread-boxes, but within a year the range expands to include candlesticks, crucifixes, chalices and lamps. The first order entered under Pugin's name is dated 9 January 1839 and consists of a quantity of altar furnishings including a crucifix, candlesticks and lamps.

Intriguingly, the Hardmans and the Iliffes did not immediately register a mark at the Birmingham Assay Office. It was not until 1843 that the mark 'H&I' was registered, suggesting that until this time they operated illegally in respect of silverware, running the serious risk of having unmarked items impounded and destroyed. Hardman Jnr. did not acquire a mark of his own until September 1845 when he and his partner William Powell Jnr registered the 'J.H & Co.' mark at the Birmingham Assay Office.

Pugin had had considerable experience in metalwork design, having been trained by his father, A.C. Pugin (1769–1832), and he had accumulated a wealth of first-hand knowledge through study and drawing of medieval architectural details, woodwork and metalwork, both in England and in Europe. At the age of only fifteen he produced a set of finely executed drawings for new plate for St George's chapel, Windsor, his remarkable skills having come to the attention of Bridge and Rundell, the Royal Goldsmiths. Though unexecuted, these drawings – along with the 'Coronation Cup' in the Royal Collection which has been convincingly attributed to him – show how the young Pugin drew freely on medieval architectural details for inspiration, but produced heavily ornamented bulbous designs that had no medieval precedent. His illustrated book, *Designs for Gold and Silversmiths* (Ackerman & Co., 1836) contains many examples, one of which is an elaborate monstrance, richly engraved and decorated with figures standing in niches under crocketed and pinnacled canopies, and with many spiky details which would have made the vessel difficult to use and very expensive to make. A collection of drawings made by Pugin between 1829 and 1834, now in the Hardman archive at Lightwoods House,[8] includes a much simplified version of this type of monstrance. It retains some architectural details such as flying buttresses acting as guards around the central lunette, and a crocketed spirelet, but most of the fussy detail and heavy engraving has gone. This was the kind of design, with clean lines and restrained ornament,

Monstrance drawn by A.W.N. Pugin, Designs for Gold and Silversmiths, 1836

Pencil drawing of monstrance by A.W.N. Pugin, c.1830 (JHAL)

Gilt-brass monstrance of 1894 (Hardman Collection)

that was to go into general production at Hardman's, and the Lightwoods metalwork collection contains a superb example of such a monstrance. Made in 1894, it follows Pugin's simpler design very precisely, and shows how closely his principles were still being followed by the firm more than forty years after his death.

By the time that Hardman and Pugin set up their Medieval Artworks, the Industrial Revolution had brought about major developments in the production of the basic raw materials of iron and brass. Not so very far from Birmingham was Coalbrookdale, where new techniques in the smelting and casting of iron had been perfected in the late eighteenth century. Meanwhile, in North Staffordshire, improved methods of brassmaking were being adopted in the 1830s by firms such as the Cheadle Copper and Brass Company, situated not very far from where Pugin was to build the magnificent church of St Giles'. Brass – an alloy of copper and zinc –was well-known in medieval times. Also called 'latten', it was used for monumental brasses, candlesticks, lamps and other items of ecclesiastical and domestic metalwork. Though copper-working dates back to prehistoric times, zinc, as a pure metal, has a very short history, the first zinc smelter in Britain having been established as recently as 1743, in Bristol. Until that time, brass could be made only by the trial-and-error method of inter-fusing oxidized zinc ore, calamine, into molten copper, or by the more satisfactory process of cementation. This involved making a 'sandwich' of alternate layers of sheet copper and powdered calamine, and firing it to infuse the copper with volatised calamine, thus converting it into brass. The availability, from the mid-eighteenth century, of metallic zinc, made it possible to produce brass by direct mixture of the two elements.

Invoices in the Hardman Archive reveal that by the 1840s quantities of brass and copper in various forms were being bought on a regular basis from the Cheadle Company, whose products were widely esteemed for their high quality. The orders consisted principally of rolled, i.e. sheet, brass or 'latten' which was composed of two parts copper to one part zinc; 'gilding metal' which had only a 5 per cent zinc content, brass tubes, and copper and brass wires.

Although the basic materials were readily available, two major problems faced Pugin and Hardman in the revival of English medieval metalwork. One was that there were relatively few actual examples upon which to draw. The vast wealth and variety of ecclesiastical metalwork which had graced English cathedrals, abbeys and churches in the Middle Ages had for the most been confiscated and destroyed during the reigns of Henry VIII, Edward VI and Elizabeth I. Pugin's publication, *The Present State of Ecclesiastical Architecture in England* (1843), bewails the wholesale pillage of sacred art at this time, and includes intriguing extracts from inventories of what even modest-sized churches possessed until it was all seized by 'the sacrilegious tyrant Henry and his successors in church plunder'. On the other hand, Catholicism had been corrupted by what Pugin termed 'paganism' – i.e. neo-Classicism – in terms of church-decoration, furnishings and ornaments. He found the fashionable Catholic chapels of London and other large towns to be 'uglier and more inconvenient than many Protestant chapels of ease', while country missions were often 'destitute not only of the ornaments, but the essentials for the holy sacrifice . . . the blessed Eucharist, the fountain of grace, received in a vessel of meaner material than what is generally used for the domestic table'.[9]

To fulfil his aim of returning the English Catholic Church to the plenitude of its historic artistic and liturgical usage, and equipping it with vessels and ornaments that were fit for their sacred purpose, Pugin had to study such surviving examples of medieval metalwork, both English and European, as it was possible to locate, and to supplement these with illustrations of vessels and ornaments shown in medieval illuminated manuscripts. Monumental brasses were also useful, since priests were frequently depicted holding a chalice. From these sources, Pugin was able to prepare designs for the Hardman metalworkers to follow. Many of these found their way into the metalwork catalogues published by Hardman & Co. from 1845 onwards and set the standard for the rest of the nineteenth century and beyond. Meanwhile, the fruits of Pugin's extensive researches were shared with the seminarians at Oscott where he was appointed Professor of Ecclesiastical Antiquities and where he established a museum of medieval artefacts and casts in order to enthuse new generations of clergy with 'the Real Thing' and as a point of reference for Birmingham craftsmen[10] – Pugin attached great importance to the close study of medieval objects as the only way in which to understand the principles of design and craftsmanship. When, in 1834, he purchased a richly ornamented gilt chalice of fifteenth-century date, he expressed the hope that 'by perseverance I shall be able to collect a splendid altar service of plate'[11] and he also supplemented his collection of artefacts with prints and illustrated books. Pugin's most lavish publication, *The Glossary of Ecclesiastical Ornament and Costume* (1844) contains, in addition to seventy-three chromo-lithographs and many engravings, a detailed text in which every known item of church furniture is arranged in alphabetical order, with copious references to medieval examples and authorities. The *Glossary* was most certainly an important work of reference at the Hardman works over a long period of time, and a fire-damaged copy – a survival from the fire at Newhall Hill in 1970 – is in the Lightwoods archive. Hardman's also built up their own collection of antique metalwork and woodwork. A typed list in the Lightwoods archive shows what was still kept at Newhall Hill in the 1930s, and it includes a twelfth-century processional cross, a sixteenth-century thurible, and a number of medieval carved figures.

The second major challenge facing Pugin and Hardman was the revival of the skills needed to execute the metalwork designs. Items such as book ornaments, crosses and candlesticks were relatively easy, being an extension of what Hardman's already did. Chalice-bowls, thuribles and lamps presented a problem, however, since they demanded the ability to beat up sheet metal into the requisite shape. Pugin later recalled these earlier difficulties:

> It should be remembered that the whole restoration has been a series of experiments, everything had to be cre-ated from the employer to the artizan. After three centuries of neglect, and the loss of ancient traditions, and of the very means employed by the old artists, it was no easy matter to reproduce their skilful works, in all their variety. A few years ago it was impossible to have procured the commonest articles of church furniture in any but the most debased style – not a carver in wood or stone, and in metal work such was the difficulty of procuring operatives, that I was compelled for the first altar lamp I ever produced, to employ an old German, who made jelly moulds for pastry coos, as the only person who understood beating up copper to the old forms.[12]

The first chalice made by Hardman was for the chapel at Oscott: a silver chalice and paten, richly gilt, entered in the Metalwork Daybook for 18 March 1839 at £22.2s. Plate previously made to Pugin's designs in readiness for the consecration of the chapel at the end of May 1838 had been executed by London silversmiths such as George Frederick Pinnel and Tomlinson & Davis, but from 1839 onwards all metalwork for Oscott came from Hardman's. In addition to the chalice already mentioned, entries in the daybook for March 1839 include sanctuary lamps, processional lamps, and two large silver thuribles mounted with enamels charged at £63 the pair.

The making of thuribles presented particular difficulty. Consisting of a hemispherical bowl on a foot, and with a lid often made in the form of a turret with piercings resembling window-tracery, and the whole sus-pended on chains in such a way as to enable the lid to be raised and lowered, the thurible required a con-siderable amount of beating-up and saw-piercing. In 1842 Pugin's Anglican friend, John Rouse Bloxam of Magdalen College Oxford, lent him a medieval English one from which to make a copy, but it took some time to complete, and Pugin had to explain that 'thurible makers are rare birds at present & we have only one man who can make a good job of them'.[13] Hardman's metalwork daybook for 30 June 1842 enters to Lord Shrewsbury 'a gilt thurible, new pattern, with boat & spoon' for what seems an incredibly low price of £9. Lord Shrewsbury also owned a twelfth-century copper thurible discovered in 1840 during the excavations prior to the rebuilding of Alton Castle, and it is mentioned by Pugin both in *Present State* (p. 90) and in the *Glossary* (p. 231).

The need to revive old methods of metalworking arose from the failure of new manufacturing methods to

Silver thurible, Erdington Abbey (photo: Graham Miller)

Medieval pyx. A.W.N. Pugin, True Principles, 1841

produce the same effect as handicraft methods. Stamping and pressing machines could turn out pierced and embossed brassware by the running metre, but these processes resulted in 'the substitution of monotonous repetition for beautiful variety – flatness for bold relief with all its attendant light and shadow'.[14]

First delivered as a series of lectures to students at Oscott, Pugin' s *The True Principles of Pointed or Christian Architecture* (1841) contains both a denunciation of current metalwork practices and suggestions as to how the ancient crafts should be revived. 'Like everything else,' he complains, 'silver-work has sunk to a mere trade, and art is rigidly excluded from its arrangements'.[15] Having listed a quantity of superb medieval metalwork which he had seen on a visit to Aix-la-Chapelle in 1839, Pugin then indicates several of the ancient techniques of silver-working by reference to just one of the vessels found in the sacristy at Aix. The object is a pyx – a vessel for the reservation of the Blessed Sacrament. Pugin's fine drawing of it pinpoints the different skills used by the silversmiths in its production. In addition to the self-explanatory ones of beating and engraving, chasing – a technique akin to sculpting – is used in this case to create the figure of a pelican which forms the handle of the lid. Filigree work, in which ornament is composed of wires twisted together into geometric designs, is used to make the pelican's nest, and there is also saw-piercing in which tiny drills and saws are used to cut patterns right through the metal, creating an infinite variety of geometrical patterns. In the accompanying text, Pugin mentions enamelling – the fusing at high temperature of coloured glass into engraved areas – and the embellishment of such vessels with gemstones. Pyxes of this type were still being made in the Hardman workshops in the 1860s and '70s, and the Lightwoods Archive includes some detailed drawings by John Hardman Powell of specially commissioned ones.

It is a characteristic of Hardman metalwork designed by Pugin, and continued after his death, that where ornament is applied it is almost invariably in the form of simplified leaf and flower designs, sometimes formed into geometrical patterns. Pugin firmly believed that nature was the real source of medieval art. 'It is absurd

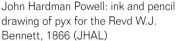

John Hardman Powell: ink and pencil drawing of pyx for the Revd W.J. Bennett, 1866 (JHAL)

A.W.N. Pugin and J.H. Powell: ink and watercolour drawing for *Floriated Ornament*, 1849 (Private collection)

to talk of Gothic leaves or Gothic figures,' he wrote; 'the types of foliage introduced in the decoration of the first medieval buildings are all to be found in nature'[16] In the case of engraved or enamelled metalwork, as distinct from three-dimensional sculpture, these natural forms needed to be stylised and flattened, and in *Floriated Ornament* (1849) Pugin published a series of thirty-nine chromolithographed designs, all based upon identified species of plants, and applicable to a wide range of two-dimensional ornament. Similar patterns had been applied to Hardman's ecclesiastical metalwork almost from the outset. Foliated patterns naturally lent themselves to such items as book-clasps and mounts. Simple engraved crosses could be formed out of four fleurs-de-lis, and there were many variations on this theme. The pointed trefoil became almost a Pugin trademark, and more complex cruciform shapes formed out of vine-leaves were particularly appropriate for the decoration of the foot of a chalice, with the more expensive ones reserved on red, green or blue champlevé enamel. The knops of chalices often had six protruding bosses of lozenge or sexfoil shape, bearing the letters I–E–S–U–S and a foliated cross, all surrounded with a border of fleurs-de-lis, and these too could be enriched with enamel. Another characteristic Pugin–Hardman motif was a squarish quatrefoil set on a hatched ground, and used in bands around the base of a chalice or around the lunette of a monstrance.

In terms of basic design, Pugin was prepared to use architectural motifs such as pinnacles and crockets to embellish items like monstrances and reliquaries for which there was medieval precedent, but he turned away from the practice of using these motifs for their own sake merely to dress up an item that was not truly Gothic in overall concept and design. Some of Pugin's very early work – for example his metalwork designs for St George's Chapel, Windsor (1827) – had fallen into this 'Georgian-gothick' category, with the massing of architectural details such as traceried windows around the bases of candlesticks, and needle-sharp pinnacles clustered around the stem. When he came to publish *The True Principles of Pointed or Christian Architecture* in 1841, Pugin publicly disowned such 'absurdities of modern metalworkers' who 'proceed from the false notion of *disguising* instead of *beautifying* articles of utility'.

Although Pugin encouraged John Hardman to advertise himself as a Goldsmith 'because it was formerly very comprehensive in its signification – & sounds well',[18] it happened in practice that around 95 per cent of Hardman's metalwork made during Pugin's lifetime was of plated base metal. It is clear from Pugin's writings that he preferred precious metal for chalices and any other items used directly in connection with the Blessed Sacrament, and while he admitted that there was precedent in seventeenth-century France for copper-gilt chalices in some of the poorer churches, and also chalices in which only the bowl was made of silver, his view as expressed in the *Glossary* was that since modern luxury now enabled precious metals to be widely used in making domestic tableware, 'it would argue a sad respect for the Holy Mysteries in those who would use inferior metals for any portion of so sacred a vessel as a Chalice'.[19] In reality, however, most of the church plate made by Hardman's was composed at least in part of copper or nickel silver, usually silver-plated or gilt. It has been observed that,

> While in public Pugin extolled the virtues of matching medieval craftsmanship to design, in private he coun-
> tenanced Hardman's development of a two-tier system of production. The upper, most expensive level largely
> conformed to Pugin's requirements . . . The lower, cheaper, level drew on materials like nickel alloy, electroplated
> to imitate silver.[20]

This was not the only area in which Hardman's established industrial practices appeared to be at odds with Pugin's published ideals of reviving ancient metalworking techniques. Hardman had little compunction about using new production methods such as those developed by the Cheadle brassworks. Large quantities of brass rod, tubing and twists were bought in for the stems and branches of candlesticks, and for rails. The bowls of chalices and ciboria could be spun rather than beaten up, and components for the bases of candlesticks such as lion-feet and angel-figures could be cast rather than chased. The result was a compromise, with Pugin himself confessing that 'It is only when mechanical invention intrudes on the confines of art, and tends to subvert the principles that it should advance, that it becomes objectionable' and that 'we should eagerly avail ourselves of the great improvements in the working of metals for constructive purposes'.[21] Meanwhile, Hardman was simply extending to ecclesiastical goods the industrial practices he already used in making convincing and inexpensive replicas of ornamental gold and silverware. It was left to the 'purists' of the later Arts and Crafts Movement to turn their backs completely on the Industrial Revolution and insist upon hand-crafting in every respect, and it was expensive. What mattered most of all to Pugin was that his well-researched designs should be accurately executed, and that the quality of the finished product should equal that of its medieval counter-part. For items made entirely of precious metals, traditional silversmithing techniques continued to be used by Hardman's. Even those made of electroplated base metal still required an element of hand-finishing, and embellishments such as jewels, enamels and fine engraving could always be added to a basic design regardless of whether it was made of precious metal or gilt-brass. There was no question, however, of sacrificing qual-ity to cheapness. In February 1845 Henry Weedall, President of Oscott, told Hardman that his beautiful work 'astonishes and delights everybody – People see the merits of the middle ages reviving, & associate together the names of Pugin & Hardman'.[22]

Not all of the new churches had wealthy patrons. For some of them cheapness was a necessity, and this is reflected in many of the smaller orders entered into the metalwork daybook; but in the matter of furnishings as well as with the buildings which he designed, Pugin was able to demonstrate that – contrary to current misconceptions – Gothic art was not necessarily more expensive than any other style. He took particular pride in his first model country church– St Marie's, Uttoxeter, Staffordshire (1838–9) – because it proved that 'a Catholic church, complete in every respect, may be erected for a very moderate sum',[23] while John Hardman stressed that items of metalwork could be made to budget, and that embellishments such as chasing or engrav-ing could be added or omitted according to what the individual client could afford to spend.[24] There were other motives for ordering inexpensive items made from base metal. In February 1845 the Revd John Kirk of Holy Cross Church, Lichfield, wrote to Hardman requesting a brass sanctuary lamp for under £5 if possible, since anything better 'could tempt the cupidity of anyone in this <u>land of thieves</u>'.[25]

Brian Andrews[26] provides an illuminating analysis of Hardman's manufacturing processes in respect of inexpensive items made from ready-made components. A simple but elegant chalice ordered in 1847 by Bishop Willson of Hobart Town was made up from a spun silver bowl and twelve other pre-fabricated elements made of plated brass. The sexfoil foot, the stem, knop and calyx, were soldered together and then attached to the bowl by a length of brass rod, threaded at the lower end. The upper end was soldered to the base of the bowl, and then this metal 'spine' ran through the centre of the other assembled components leaving the threaded end protruding through a hole in the brass base plate. A washer and nut were then put in place, and as the nut was tightened the whole assembly became completely rigid. In the case of this particular chalice, and others like it, there was a minimal amount of engraving, and then the finishing processes of plating and burnishing. The production cost is estimated at about £1.18s, and assuming the usual Hardman mark-up of about 40 per cent the retail price of the chalice would have been around £2.12s.

It was not always the poorer clients who chose the cheaper alternative to precious metals. The Revd Daniel Haigh, the wealthy benefactor of the church of SS. Thomas and Edmund at Erdington. commissioned many items made mainly of gilded base metal, though richly embellished with engraving, enamels and jewels. Even the Earl of Shrewsbury, who expended some £1,400 on large quantities of metalwork for St Giles', Cheadle, bought a good many stock items. Of the specially commissioned ones, very few were made even partly of silver. A finely engraved and enamelled chalice is a case in point. In December 1844 Pugin told Hardman to make a chalice for Cheadle to the same design as a silver-gilt one commissioned by Dr Henry Weedall, 'only the foot *copper gilt* or german silver plated & parcel gilt, for Lord S. is sure to ask me – & he will be angry if it is all silver'.[27] The 'foot' of a chalice seems here to signify everything but the actual bowl, although in

the *Glossary* Pugin identifies four components: the foot (i.e. the base only), the stem, the knop (the bulge at the centre of the stem by which the chalice is grasped) and the bowl. Weedall's chalice and paten cost £37, and the identical-looking ones for Cheadle only £25.[28] This particular design owed a good deal to medieval originals made by Italian goldsmiths in Siena. Although clearly Gothic in style, these differed from English chalices in that they were generally larger, had a deep conical-shaped bowl rather than a shallow hemispherical one, and a complex, sexfoiled foot, frequently ornamented with enamels. They usually had a calyx: a circlet of pointed leaves rising from the top of the stem to support the lower part of the bowl, and inspired by the botanical *calyx* or cup-shaped outer part of a flower, from which the word chalice is ultimately derived. Pugin was able to study several of these chalices at first hand. For his new (1840) church of Our Lady & St Thomas of Canterbury, Dudley the enamelled foot of a thirteenth-century Sienese chalice was given a new bowl at Hardman's to Pugin's design, and a complete Sienese chalice was in the collection owned by Lord Shrewsbury's domestic chaplain, Dr Daniel Rock. Among several silver-gilt chalices made in this style by Hardmans was the one commissioned by Bishop Wiseman after he left Birmingham to become vicar apostolic of the London District in 1847. Set with stones and enamels, it has a saw-pierced foot, and is very similar in design to the one later shown by Hardman at the Great Exhibition.[29]

'Sienese' chalice, St Giles's, Cheadle, 1844

When the Cheadle chalice was ordered, Pugin – sensing perhaps that such a beautiful object produced for such a modest price was likely to attract other clients – suggested to Hardman that he should make an identical one for stock: 'I think it would be a good thing to make 3 or 4 of a sort when we have a good pattern.'[30] As demand for the firm's products grew, the issue of building up stock for sale became ever more important. 'You manage very badly not to have a chalice or 2 in stock,' he told Hardman in October 1844. 'I know we shall never do any good *without a stock.*'[31]

One of the new industrial processes in which Hardman's had a direct hand was electro-gilding. Until the nineteenth century the only method of gilding silver or base metal was to apply an amalgam composed of mercury and finely powdered gold to the surface to be gilt. The mercury was then evaporated by heat, leaving the gold adhering firmly to the metal. Mercury-gilding produced a highly satisfactory and durable result, but the process was extremely injurious to the health of those operating it, and mercury gilders generally died of poisoning before the age of forty. A much safer process of plating by means of electrolysis was developed in Birmingham by the plating and gilding firm of G.R. & H. Elkington, and in 1837 the two John Hardmans entered into a partnership with Elkingtons and with another Birmingham button-making firm, Hammond &

Silver-gilt chalice made for Bishop Wiseman (Westminster Cathedral; photo: Phil Sayer)

Turner, for the specific purpose of working the Elkington electro-gilding process.[32] Therefore, from the very outset of the medieval metalworking venture, Hardman had this new gilding process at his disposal, although it has to be said that to begin with it did not produce as hard-wearing a finish as mercurial amalgam.

The Elkington method of electro-deposition was also suitable for use with nickel silver, or 'German silver' – an alloy of nickel, copper, zinc, and a tiny quantity of iron – which was manufactured in England from about 1830 and is known to have been used by Hardman's as a substitute for silver. Although German silver was somewhat intractable and generally suitable only for casting, Pugin appears to have preferred it to Britannia metal, another nineteenth-century alloy, which consisted principally of tin and antimony, with minute amounts of copper, brass and iron[33]. Sheffield plate, a 'sandwich' made of heavily plated sheet copper, was much more workable, and Hardman's appear to have used it occasionally.

There is evidence that Pugin and Hardman were involved at an early stage with the making of electrotypes in which electrolysis is used to deposit metal into a mould or onto a coated wax model. Used mainly for small objects, this alternative to casting produced very accurate copies of quite complex originals. Pugin himself describes the process in a letter to Lord Shrewsbury dated 5 June 1843 regarding a seal which the earl had ordered:

> . . . Wegall made as model in wax for the handle, of a Talbot – the electrotype was then applied to deposit a
> coating of copper over the wax. The wax was then melted out & it was intended to precipitate a thickness of silver
> inside the copper & dissolve the copper off by nitric acid . . .[34]

'Wegall' was Henry Weigall, a well-known seal-engraver based in St James's Street, London, and the 'Talbot' which was to be the subject of the handle was an extinct breed of hunting dog which appears frequently in the heraldic devices of the Talbot Earls of Shrewsbury.

It was not modern technology itself to which Pugin objected, but its misuse in the suppression of true art and the creation of shams. This was nowhere more evident than in the ironworking trade. The Industrial Revolution had made cast iron abundant and cheap, and the material was being used for a wide variety of purposes: as a substitute for wrought iron, and as a substitute for non-ferrous materials. While Pugin readily acknowledged the value of cast iron for structural purposes where strength was required, he also observed that 'it is seldom or never left as iron. It is disguised by paint, either as stone, wood or marble'.[35] When in 1837 Pugin began to work for Lord Shrewsbury at Alton Towers, he found a Georgian-gothick house bristling with such 'deceptions', where previous architects had used the skills of the Derby-based Britannia Ironworks to create elaborate cast-iron tracery for the windows of the chapel tribune, Gothic arches and railings for the tribune itself, and iron cusps, crockets and corbels for the chapel ceiling, painted dark brown so as to resemble wood. Cast-iron tracery was also applied to solid doors to create the illusion of Gothic panelling, or set into glazed doors as ornamental frames to hold the panels of glass.[36]

Yet ironsmiths no less than silversmiths had once been great artists, and Pugin was familiar with many surviving examples of outstanding wrought-iron work executed by medieval craftsmen in England and Europe, and not only their work but their methods too: the forging of twists and scrolls, the cutting of leaves and crockets, working with pliers to create variety, depth and sharpness; and the use of bolts, nails and rivets as an integral part of the design. Pugin's published and well-illustrated writings on ironwork, supplemented by actual examples, became the models from which Hardman's effected a revival; all very different from so-called 'Birmingham Gothic' in which architectural details such as crockets and finials were applied indiscriminately to cast-iron objects such as clock-cases, inkstands and fire-irons.

John Hardman Powell: ink drawing of iron casket (JHAL)

Amongst the items of medieval metalwork in Pugin's private collection was a small iron chest with an arched top which he had inherited from his father and which is now in the Victoria & Albert Museum.[37] It would appear to be French work of the fourteenth century, but with the handle and some other parts repaired or renewed – possibly by Hardman's – in the nineteenth century. At least two of these chests were made by Hardman's exactly to the original medieval pattern of the ironwork, but using figured walnut for the body, and they are currently in the Hardman metalwork collection at Lightwoods House. Another such chest, made entirely of iron and much more richly ornamented, exists in a private collection, and in the Lightwoods archive there is a drawing of it by John Hardman Powell.

Pugin was particularly interested in finely wrought door furniture. Strap-hinges designed for strength but also elegantly elaborated with scroll work soon became a part of Hardman's metalwork output, along with doorplates, handles, locks and keys, and furniture-mounts. Some of this

Iron casket in private collection

work could also be executed in brass. Larger pieces of architectural ironwork, such as forged railings, vanes, finials and brattishing for roof-ridges, were also undertaken. The Pugin–Hardman metalwork introduced into Alton Towers from 1839 onwards was different both in design and execution from that of earlier decades, some of which Pugin was able to eradicate or disguise in the process of redecorating and refurnishing parts of the house.[38]

Pugin was scathingly critical of so-called 'Gothic' grates 'which are not infrequently made to represent diminutive fronts of castellated or ecclesiastical buildings with turrets, loopholes, windows, and doorways, all in a space of forty inches'.[39] Instead, Pugin designed fire-dogs, or andirons, to support simply-constructed grates, with or without fire-backs, for the large open fireplaces which were a prominent feature of his domestic architecture. The metalwork was, of course, all executed by Hardman. The andirons generally have arched feet, and are often ornamented with brass rosettes or shields engraved with heraldic devices. Grates were frequently equipped with the necessary fire-irons: finely wrought pokers, tongs and shovels, but minus the crockets, finials, figures of saints, and other 'absurdities of modern metalworkers' who 'proceed from the false notion of *disguising* instead of *beautifying* articles of utility'.[40] The Hardman collection at Lightwoods House includes examples of andirons made by the firm to Pugin's designs, and also several drawings of complete fireplaces with alternative designs for grates and fire-dogs.

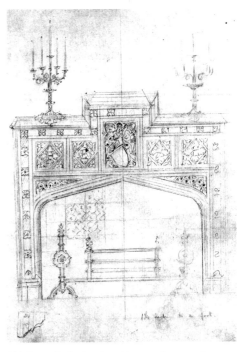

J.H. Powell: design for chimneypiece, grate, andirons and candelabra, pencil/ink (JHAL)

The success of the Pugin–Hardman revival of metalworking in Birmingham in the 1830s and '40s led one mid-Victorian writer to pronounce that '. . . the art of revived metal-working has ceased to be a matter of observation or comment. The difficulties which attended its earlier existence are now almost forgotten, and processes are now practised as a matter of routine which were then only re-discovered and mastered after sore labour and heavy sacrifice'.[41]

The early success of Hardman's medieval metalworking business is reflected in the daybooks and sales ledgers. The first metalwork daybook, covering the years 1838 to 1844, runs to 212 pages of entries; that for 1849–54 runs to 800 pages in a larger format. The files of metalwork letters tell a similar story: a few dozen for 1840–1 rising to hundreds by 1845–6. The yearly turnover rose from just over £1,000 in 1841 to more than £12,000 in 1848, and by 1851 the total workforce was around 200. Some of the operations were carried out in-house at the Paradise Street workshops, while others were entrusted to out-workers such as Edward Chivers of Church Street, the engraver John Heath, of 68, Great Charles Street, and the Elkingtons. 'If the button factory could not supply all the skills necessary, the vast pool of expertise in the Birmingham metalworking and jewellery trade could and did.'[42] It was above all the name of Pugin which helped to draw a growing number of clients once his reputation as an architect and propagandist had been established. The daybooks and the metalwork letters addressed to John Hardman show that clients often mentioned Pugin by name. Some potential clients wrote to Pugin personally, and if the intended item of metalwork needed his attention, he would sometimes produce a drawing; otherwise it would be passed over to Hardman who could supply from stock or make up an item from an established pattern – but Pugin was the ultimate source of all the designs. In October 1839 the Revd William Vaughan wrote to Hardman to order a church lamp 'of course à la Pugin',[43] and in

A.W.N. Pugin, processional cross from Designs for Gold and Silversmiths, 1836

Grace Dieu Chapel: processional cross designed by Pugin and made by Hardman c.1845

February 1843 the Revd George White, of St Edmund's College, Ware, asked Hardman to send him a list of processional crosses 'from Mr. Pugin's design'.[44] In the same year, the Revd George Spencer, writing from Oscott to order a pyx and holy-oil stocks, tells Hardman that he has a problem with the inscription and asks, 'Have you proper forms for the thing from Pugin?'[45]

Sometimes it was Pugin's publications that were the source of designs for Hardman's metalwork. In November 1843 the Revd R. Brown of Lancaster wrote to say that 'In a book of Mr. Pugin's drawings published by Ackermann & Co., 96 Strand in April 1863' he had seen 'a very pretty drawing of a processional cross, it is no.16 in the collection', and asked if Hardman had any like it. The publication referred to is *Designs for Gold & Silversmiths,* on page 16 of which there is indeed a handsome processional crucifix which has the figures of Our Lady and St John standing either side on brackets. Within six weeks Hardman's had produced one to this pattern, and Brown wrote back with the payment, saying that 'it is universally admired by all who have yet seen it'.[46] Another correspondent, Lt A. Penrose Miller of the 92nd Highlanders, wrote to Hardman requesting four of Pugin's candlesticks so that he could see '. . . the effect of a little *Puginism* upon the humble altar of Fortwilliam'[47]

By 1842 Theodore Jewitt, brother of the engraver Orlando Jewitt (1799–1869) who engraved a number of Pugin's illustrations, was acting an an agent in Oxford for articles made by Hardman's to designs by Pugin. In February of that year he wrote to Hardman asking if they made offertory basons, altar crosses 'of Mr. Pugin's design', but 'without the figure'. Jewitt seems to have been catering for a predominantly Anglican clientele. He complains to Hardman that 'The book ornaments you sent have the arms of St. Chad & the other M for Mary but I suppose they will answer for patterns. I should also like to know whether you make Book ornaments of a commoner kind, and smaller'.[48] Charles Morton & Co., of the Sheffield Plate Warehouse, Bouverie Street, London,. also expressed an interest in Hardman's book- ornaments for a mainly Anglican market. 'If we succeed in getting them into sale, it would not be for the Catholic Church but they would be required of the same description & we presume the most appropriate design would be Gothic.' They also enquire about the possibility of stocking Hardman's church plate 'which from what we learn is of a class wholly different from what we have'.[49]

Three former employees of Hardman's – Evans, Thomason and Brawn – eventually set up their own church-furnishing establishment in St Paul's Square, not very far from the Hardman works, boldly advertising that they were 'in possession of a thorough knowledge of the character of the work as developed by A.W. Pugin Esq., architect, from whose drawings they have worked'.[50] Pugin was understandably stung by this kind of plagiarism, but while he complained that imitators of his work could afford to sell cheap because 'they steal their brooms ready made', he also admitted that so long as they imitated 'true principles' Gothic and promoted sound craftsmanship then 'the movement progresses, and the right sort of thing becomes general, and that is the great point'.[51] Though for a time Hardman paid Pugin a fee of 10 per cent on work commissioned through him, Pugin was the last one to be motivated by profit, and successful though he was, he did not amass a large personal fortune. As an architect he rarely charged a full fee for the churches he designed, and to many of them he made gifts of antique furniture and statuary, as well as metalwork and glass made to his own designs.

Among the early Pugin churches which Hardman's furnished was St Mary's, Derby (1839), a large church built in the 'Perpendicular' style which Pugin was soon to abandon. Its significance was noted by Bishop Wiseman who commented that for English Catholics it marked 'the real transition from chapel to church architecture'.[52] There were also critics and controversies. On the day of the consecration, Pugin and Lord Shrewsbury (a principal benefactor) drove off in a huff on discovering that the 'revival' had not yet extended to the Gregorian music and all-male choir which they thought were proper to the occasion, confiscating the cloth-of-gold

St Mary's church, Derby (photo: S.B. Birkett)

vestments that the earl had loaned. Later, in a calmer mood, Pugin reflected on the importance of St Mary's for the Revival in general and for his own reputation. Just a year after the opening he wrote, 'When I commenced Derby I nearly stood alone. Good Dr. Walsh was my only supporter. I was generally regarded as an enthusiast and visionary who aimed at impossibilities. The case is *now altered . . .*'[53]

The priest at the time of the building of St Mary's was the Revd Thomas Sing, who had been in charge of the Derby mission since 1836, and Lord Shrewsbury was one of the principal benefactors. Some of the most substantial entries in the Hardman daybook for 1839 consist of metalwork ordered by Sing for the new church. This included a gilt tabernacle at £25, six candlesticks for the high altar 'with tubes and shields' at £18.18s, and a 'large and richly gilt antependium (altar-frontal) at £9. 'There was a church and church ornaments like nothing else', Pugin wrote in 1841,[54] but although he made sure that St Mary's was 'perfectly supplied with everything', two years onwards Pugin found 'rich and beautiful vestments thrust into a corner . . . the ornaments are left to get filthy, the lamp has never been lighted'. The full panoply of metalwork and other furnishings with which Pugin and Hardman equipped the new churches required cleaning, maintenance and proper storage when not in use, and the appointment of a sacristan to look after such things was in Pugin's opinion every bit as necessary as having a priest.[55]

Although Fr Sing had been educated at Oscott, he was ordained in 1834, three years before the 'Pugin Revolution' began to set new architectural and liturgical standards for Oscott-trained priests to take with them into their parishes. Priests of the older generation were unaccustomed to such refinements – to some they were irksome and unnecessary innovations – and in the early days Pugin often complained that his intentions for the new churches were being ignored because of clergy who did not known how to use them properly.

Hardmans' involvement with St Mary's continued throughout the nineteenth century and into the twentieth. In 1854–5 E.W. Pugin extended the building and installed a new high altar and reredos, complete with the appropriate metalwork. The daybooks for June to August 1855 include entries for six brass altar candlesticks, 'hexagon pillar, richly engraved', two five-light branch candlesticks, a concave corona lamp, and an ebony altar cross with gilt metal mounts. A wrought-iron and brass screen was constructed below the rood, at the very considerable cost of £250, and in October a metalwork pulpit was entered in the daybook at £47.10s. Both the screen and the pulpit have since been removed. New glass designed by John Hardman Powell replaced three earlier apse windows by William Warrington,[56] and Powell was also responsible for glass and sculpture in the new Pieta chapel. Pugin's grandson, Dunstan Powell (1861–1932) designed windows for the nave and Lady Chapel between 1927 and 1932 when a major restoration of St Mary's was undertaken by Hardman's.[57]

The project closest to the heart of Pugin and the Hardmans was the building and furnishing of St Chad's, Birmingham. In 1834 a committee was formed, with John Hardman as its secretary, to promote the building of 'a commodious and splendid Catholic Church in the town of Birmingham.[58] Bishop Thomas Walsh, vicar apostolic of the Midland District, was also a prime mover in the scheme to create what would be in effect a Pro-Cathedral, with an appropriate espicopal residence.[59] An architect was engaged in the shape of Thomas Rickman (1776–1841) of Liverpool and Birmingham, but the appeal raised only £138 and the scheme was shelved. By 1839 circumstances had changed. Walsh had been willed a large legacy from the estate of Charles Robert Blundell of Ince Hall, Lancashire,[60] and he committed a considerable portion of this to the building of St Chad's. Pugin – with only a few months of practical church-building experience to his credit – had now replaced Rickman as the favoured architect and the earlier abortive plans he had sent to Hardman for a small apsed church were superseded by something on a far grander scale.

The history of St Chad's cathedral has been well documented.[61] The style, based on north German hall-churches of the later Gothic period, was chosen by Pugin because it was 'both cheap and effective and Like-wise because it is totally different from any *protestant* errection [sic].[62] With its western towers and spires, steep gables, and windows filled with rich tracery and stained glass, St Chad's would stand out in sharp contrast to the 'present filthy hole' in Shadwell Street that it was set to replace, and to the Catholic church of St Peter in Broad Street, both of which were, in Pugin's view, tarred with the same 'pagan' – i.e. neoclassical – brush. Not far distant from St Chad's was the Georgian St Paul's, and there was Thomas Archer's English Baroque church of St Philip in Colmore Row. In both of these buildings 'pagan' neo-Classicism was compounded by Pugin's other *bête noire*, namely Protestantism.

If in Pugin's eyes Bishop Walsh was a latter-day equivalent of the medieval church-building bishop William Wykeham, and Lord Shrewsbury the 'grand seigneur', John Hardman Snr was compared to 'the pious & munificent' William Canynges of Bristol, the wealthy fifteenth-century merchant of Bristol who rebuilt the church of St Mary Redcliffe in splendid style.[63] Together they took the place of the more usual church-building committees with whom Pugin had very little patience.

John Hardman Snr took the initiative in this respect. Along with several others, he signed away all 'congregational' proprietary rights over the new building, the disclaimer being inscribed on a medieval-style illuminated parchment which is still preserved in the cathedral sacristy. In addition to his initial contribution of £1,000 to the building fund, Hardman made a donation of £250 at the time of the foundation, and John Hard-

St Chad's cathedral, Birmingham c.1847: watercolour by J.D. Swarbreck (St Chad's cathedral)

Hardman metalwork on display at St Chad's cathedral (photo: Deryck Clark, 2003)

man Jnr gave £50, but that was not the limit of their benefactions. The most prominent item of furnishing in St Chad's was the great rood-screen which Pugin considered to be an essential part of an English church, and for the making of which Hardman paid £600. Embellished with medieval woodcarvings, and carrying aloft the great crucifix with its fifteenth-century figure of Christ, the screen was controversial almost from the outset, with Bishop Wiseman – who arrived on the scene in 1840 as co-adjutor to Bishop Walsh – firmly opposed to its being installed in the first place because, allegedly, it would interrupt the view from the nave to the altar. Hardman wrote to Pugin in great distress, informing him of Wiseman's intentions. Pugin's response was to threaten to resign as architect of St Chad's unless Wiseman backed down, and he actually wrote out a letter of resignation.[64] According to Pugin, Hardman Snr, 'who has been the very soul of this great church', would have 'instantly retired from the active post he has so ably filled and not improbably have left Birmingham.'[65] Wiseman bowed to the pressure, withdrew his opposition, and the screen was duly built, but Pugin and Hardman never fully trusted him again. According to Pugin, Wiseman had 'no feeling for old English Antiquities. All his ideas are drawn from Modern Rome'.[66] It was 'modern Rome' that eventually prevailed, when in the re-ordering of the cathedral in 1967 the screen was ejected in spite of assurances that it would be retained.[67]

As well as supplying a good many metalwork items to the cathedral, Hardmans were also involved with Pugin's revival of medieval-style vestments,[68] and St Chad's possesses an important collection of these. As a musician, John Hardman Jnr was as enthusiastic as Pugin for the revival of Gregorian chant performed by cantors in surplices instead of 'the interminable squalling of a few female professionals and whiskered vocalists',[69] and in 1854 he established a Gregorian choir at St Chad's, endowing it with £1,000, and directing it personally. He also paid for the moving of the rood-screen into the first bay of the nave to make room for choir-stalls to the east of it. The high altar was the gift of John Hardman Snr, and other members of the family made later additions to it such as a new set of six candlesticks given in 1854 by Hardman Jnr and the Powells. A new tabernacle with finely-engraved and enamelled doors was made to John Hardman Powell's design in 1878, and the reliquary designed by Pugin to contain the bones of St Chad discovered in 1839[70] was embellished in 1931 with a carved wooden canopy and angel supporters to the design of Gerald J. Hardman (1875–1953). The whole ensemble of altar, tabernacle, reliquary and baldachino has been described as 'one of the most important mid-nineteenth-century recreations of medieval furnishings, comparable to the throne ensemble in the House of Lords'.[71]

Soon after Hardman & Co. ventured into stained-glass production in the mid-1840s, Hardman windows began to complement the earlier ones made for St Chad's to Pugin's designs by William Warrington and William Wailes. Among the most notable is the Glassmakers' window in the north aisle, given in 1853 by employees of Hardman & Co. The idea for the window came from Pugin himself, and although it was not actually made until after Pugin's death, there seems little doubt that he was involved with its design. In a letter to Hardman written in about 1851 he asks,

> . . . Can't you get your glass painters to commemorate the late departed artists in their window – in that *fine* proportioned window over the Bishop's tomb – what a fine thing with the Patron *Saints* of the *art & of the individuals* thereby it would be a very fine thing & they could have all that is already in taken out as fast as possible. it would be a magnificent gift to our communion . . .'[72]

The window depicts St Luke and St Andrew of Crete – the patron saints of glasspainters – with the figures of four of Hardman's men at work underneath. The entry for the window in the Glass Daybook names them as Edward Hendren, Thomas Grew, James Jones and Samuel Jones. It was fairly typical of Pugin – who consistently refused to allow into his churches any reference to himself as architect – that he should have wished the artists who worked to his designs to be so commemorated. The window was eventually located not over the bishop's (i.e. Walsh's) tomb, but in a two-light window further to the west. The canopied tomb, designed by

St Chad's cathedral, Birmingham: detail of Glassmakers' window

St Chad's cathedral, Birmingham: detail of the Immaculate Conception window with figure of John Hardman bottom left

Pugin and carved by George Myers, was displayed in the Medieval Court at the Great Exhibition of 1851 and eventually sited under a huge six-light window in the eastern part of the north aisle. In 1868 this window was filled with glass designed by John Hardman Powell as a memorial to his uncle, John Hardman Jnr, who had died in the previous year. The subject is the Immaculate Conception, proclaimed as a dogma of the Church as recently as 1854, and it incorporates the small kneeling figure of John Hardman vested in his cantor's cope. The last major addition to the cathedral was St Edward's chapel (1931–3), designed by Sebastian Pugin Powell, son of John Hardman Powell, with an altar and baldachino by Gerald Hardman.

The steeply sloping site upon which St Chad's was built required the construction of a massive crypt and sub-crypt to bring up the east end to the level of the cathedral frontage. The crypt was built in the Norman style to echo the architectural pedigree of medieval English cathedrals such as nearby Worcester. It was a revival in function as well as in its architectural style, designed by Pugin as a burial-place for those intimately connected with the cathedral, and one in which 'none but Catholic memorials for the dead will be allowed'.[73] The crypt contains a number of chantry chapels furnished with altars for the celebration of Requiem Mass, and the most important of these is the Hardman chantry situated under the Lady chapel and dedicated to St John the Evangelist. Below this is the vault where John Hardman Snr, John Hardman Jnr and many other members of the family were buried.[74]

The status of St Chad's as a cathedral was emphasised by the Bishop's House which was built on the opposite side of Bath Street facing the west doors of the church. Pugin set much store by this building as typifying the kind of residence proper to a Catholic bishop, including a private chapel and a great hall capable of seating about sixty people.[75] Hardman's made the altar-plate and other metalwork furnishing for this building which, sadly, was destroyed in the 1960s to make way for the Birmingham inner ring road. Some of the stained glass, and two *coronae lucis* from the Bishop's House, are currently preserved in the Hardman collection at Lightwoods House.

it was outside St Chad's in about 1842 that the adolescent John Hardman Powell had his first sighting of Pugin. an incident that he recalled vividly much later in life. Having just come out of the cathedral by a side-door, he was sauntering up the hill towards the Bishop's house when:

> . . . a man whose figure was very like that of a sailor, came running down to the door I had just left; he had a pale oval face, long dark hair, grey eyes, and lips moving rapidly in talk to himself . . . the impression left on my mind was as if a fire engine had passed me by.[76]

Little did Powell then suspect that he was soon to be tutored by Pugin's dynamic personality, to be a part of his household, and eventually a member of his family, with long-term consequences both for himself and for John Hardman & Company.

It is a curious fact that of the three major churches built in the Midland/Central District by Pugin, none was in the early-fourteenth-century style which he came to believe was 'decidedly the best period of pointed architecture'.[77] St Mary's, Derby, is in the late Perpendicular style, its tower consciously echoing that of the early-sixteenth-century tower of All Saints' parish church nearby, while at St Chad's Pugin took inspiration from Baltic and North German Gothic. The third great church, St Barnabas', Nottingham (1841–4), was different from either of these. Inspired by the ruins of the Cistercian abbey at Croxden, close to Lord Shrewsbury's home at Alton Towers, Nottingham is in the First Pointed, or 'lancet' style, and monastic in plan with the chancel entirely surrounded by an ambulatory and eastern chapels. Here it was Lord Shrewsbury's wish to 'see Croxden revived'[78] that prevailed, with Pugin confessing at a later date that although the lancet style with its narrow windows was suitable for a Cistercian Abbey in a secluded valley, it was not so suited to a crowded town centre where there was a need for larger windows and more light.[79] St Barnabas' was the largest Catholic church to have been built in England since the Reformation, and in 1850 it was elevated to cathedral status when the Diocese of Nottingham was created.

Though the Hardman family were not involved with Nottingham as principal benefactors as they had been at St Chad's, St Barnabas' proved to be of considerable importance to the firm of Hardman & Co. both in the short and long term. The priest in charge of the Nottingham mission at this time was Robert Willson (1794–1866), who was committed to the Gothic Revival, had come to know Pugin in the early 1830s, and was highly esteemed by Lord Shrewsbury. Hardman was contracted to supply metalwork to the value of £275 for St Barnabas'. This included not only the usual crosses and candlesticks for the altars, but also many fittings for gas lighting including 59 standards for the screens which enclosed the choir, and a *corona* to hang in the choir.80 Before St Barnabas' was consecrated, Willson was appointed Bishop of Hobart, and when he moved to Tasmania he took with him a quantity of church furnishings designed by Pugin and made by Hardman. Nottingham therefore played a key role in the establishment of a very important and long-lasting relationship between Hardman of Birmingham and the expanding Catholic Church in Australia.[81]

St Barnabas' cathedral, Nottingham, from A.W.N. Pugin, Present State, 1843

As at St Chad's, the Hardman connection with St Barnabas' continued over many years. In 1932 the Blessed Sacrament Chapel was redecorated by Hardman's to designs by Elphege and Oswald Pippet who worked very much in the style of Pugin.[82] Pippet's scheme included the arms of the eight Bishops of Nottingham, figures of angels with emblems prefiguring the Eucharist, and carved corbels in the shape of angels bearing shields also emblazoned with emblems of the Blessed Sacrament. In 1974 Hardman's supervised the cleaning and restoration of Pippet's decorative scheme, under the direction of Patrick Feeny.[83] At the time, this was the only part of the cathedral to have retained its full complement of stencilled decorations, the rest having been painted out in the 1960s. Re-ordering and redecoration carried out in 1993 included the uncovering and restoration of elements of the original Pugin decoration in other parts of the cathedral.

For Pugin and Hardman, the Gothic Revival was not simply a matter of architecture, church furnishings, decorations and liturgical choreography. It had a strong social message which embraced education and the care of the poor, matters which had been the concern of the Catholic Church in the Middle Ages. As they saw it, many of the social evils brought about by the Industrial Revolution should be redressed by the Church, demonstrating what Catholic art and Catholic charity could do together to improve body, mind and spirit, in contrast to the demeaning and dehumanising treatment meted out in the workhouses of the Protestant State. As well as supporting the schools attached to St Chad's, John Hardman Snr gave an endowment of £1,000 for the maintenance of Catholic schools in Birmingham.[84] In 1840 he gave land opposite the family home in Hunter's Lane, Handsworth, as the site of a new convent for the Sisters of Mercy. The Sisterhood originated in Ireland in the late 1820s, and their principal work was teaching in schools, visiting the sick, and helping in missionary work among the poor. Pugin was the architect – having already built the first English Mercy Convent in Bermondsey in 1839: 'the first regular conventual buildings erected in this country since the change

St Barnabas' cathedral, Nottingham: the Blessed Sacrament Chapel after restoration of decorative work, 1994 (photo: Martine Hamilton Knight)

John Hardman Snr. Portrait by J.R. Herbert
(St Mary's convent, Handsworth)

Candelabrum made for John Hardman incorporating
his coat of arms (Hardman Collection)

of religion'.[85] In addition to his gift of land, John Hardman financed the buildings and furnishings at Handsworth to the tune of £5,535, and Lord Shrewsbury contributed £2,000. The best-known portrait of Hardman Snr, by J.R. Herbert, shows him kneeling by the window of his house, with a view towards the convent in the background. Two of his daughters joined the convent: Juliana, who was appointed first Mother Superior – a post which she held for thirty-five years – and Mary, who became superior of the orphanage which the nuns opened at Maryvale.

J.R. Herbert's portrait of John Hardman Snr. includes a coat-of-arms which appears also on the frame which Pugin designed for it: *gules a bar dancetty or between two flaunches erminois*. No record has been found at the college of Arms of John Hardman's establishing a right to arms either by descent or by a grant, so one assumes that – like Pugin – he adopted a shield of arms informally. The shield also appears on a large three-branched brass candelabrum which was clearly made for Hardman's personal use, and which was displayed prominently at the Birmingham Exhibition of Manufacturers in 1849.

The Hardman family home in Hunter's Lane underwent extensive alterations and additions in 1842, Pugin – naturally – being the architect. According to John Hardman Powell, it was Pugin who 'Christianised' it not just by Gothic additions but also by the change of name from Woodlands House to St John's.[86] Plans and sections were sent to John Hardman Jnr in December 1842, and the total cost of £292 suggests that the alterations were considerable. In about 1834 Hardman had married Anne Gibson (1809–80). By 1842 they had five children ranging from between seven years of age to a few months, and there were to be four more. Not surprisingly therefore, Pugin's additions included a 'Capital nursery & children's bedroom', and 'a very good servants room at top'.[87] Their eldest daughter, Mary, followed in her aunts' footsteps as a Sister of Mercy, while their only surviving son, John Bernard (1843–1903), eventually succeeded his father as head of Hardman & Co.

For both Pugin and Hardman, 1844–5 was a bittersweet year. In August 1844 John Hardman Snr died after a long illness, and was buried at St Chad's in the crypt chapel of St John which Bishop Walsh had granted to him as a free gift in perpetuity in recognition of his services and benefactions to the Church. His widow, Barbara, moved across the road into St Mary's convent, where she died in 1872. Within two weeks of John Hardman's death, Pugin's second wife, Louisa, died quite suddenly in London leaving him a widower for the second time, and with six children to look after. It is an indication of the close friendship between the two families that Louisa was buried in the Hardman vault at St Chad's.[88] A third funeral took place in May 1845, following the death of Hardman's five-year-old daughter Juliana.

For the Company, however, 1844–5 was a year of good fortune and promise. It was towards the end of 1844 that Pugin agreed to take on his one and only apprentice in the shape of Hardman's nephew, John Hardman Powell. In February 1845 Pugin discussed with Hardman the possibility of their venturing into the manufacture of stained glass, and by the end of the year they were installing their first windows.[89] In 1845 Hardman's set up new workshops and a showroom at 166 Great Charles Street, Birmingham, and printed their first catalogues and trade cards. The domestic market for 'medieval' metalwork and stained glass was expanding within both the Catholic and Anglican Churches, Pugin's role at the New Palace of Westminster ensured that Hardman's received some of their most important secular commissions, and an overseas market was beginning to open up. Just seven years on from its inception, Hardman & Co. had come of age.

In the long term, the most significant of these developments was the arrival of John Hardman Powell (1827–95). Though frequently complaining about his punishing workload, Pugin had consistently refused either to employ a clerk to do the more routine parts of his drawings, or to take on a pupil. However, towards the end of 1844, he agreed to take on seventeen-year-old Powell, fifth son of William and Lucy Powell, Lucy (1793–1863) being John Hardman's half-sister, and William (1789–1861) being Hardman's partner in the metalworking firm. The idea seems to have been put to Pugin by Hardman himself, and it is another reflection of the close friendship between them that Pugin agreed to an apprenticeship, though not without conditions. Powell was to go and live at Pugin's home in Ramsgate, and to stay until he was twenty-one. 'It would be well for you to speak seriously to him before he comes,' Pugin told Hardman, 'for he is the only person I have ever consented to take as a pupil although as you know I have been offered a good deal of money to do so'.[90]

It took some time for Powell to settle in at The Grange. He had bouts of sleepwalking during which he sometimes injured himself, so that Pugin took to locking the bedroom door.[91] Another source of irritation was the amount of time Powell spent in letter-writing, and Pugin asked Hardman to do what he could to curtail it: '. . . he writes long letters like a girl about nothing . . . it is a dead waste of time & annoys me'.[92] Then there was the question of the bad drawing habits Powell had acquired during a brief period of working at Elkington's metalworking factory in Birmingham. Pugin nevertheless persevered, at a time when he was, for personal reasons, restless and unhappy, and sometimes ill through overwork. He could have been no easy taskmaster at the best of times, and this was not the best of times. A letter written to John Hardman in mid-February 1845 seems to say it all:

> . . . do not take any notice but I gave Powell a good dressing Last week & I think he is a deal better for it. he has got a most careless habit of drawing without thinking the Least of what he is doing. I had taken immense pains that morning in explaining to him the principles of tracery & a Quarter of an hour afterwards he did just the same as If I had never spoken a word. he says he acquired the habit of working without thinking at *Elkingtons* – & cant get out of it. it is a sad thing for he really can do well when he tries . . . am now often sunk to the Lowest depth of despondency – & can never get poor Louisa out of my mind. the minutest circumstances connected with her illness & death recur to me continue with a force & reality that is dreadful . . . [93]

In spite of all the difficulties, Pugin could see that Powell had great talent and potential as a draughtsman and designer, and he involved him with both drawing and the making of models for metalwork items including the railings for the House of Lords and the brass screen for the Blessed Sacrament chapel at St Giles', Cheadle. Powell also made an admirable sacristan. caring for the furnishings and ornaments of the private chapel which was central to life at The Grange. By the end of 1845 Powell was also assisting with the cartooning of windows, and was competent enough to be left in charge at the Grange while Pugin was away.94 There is evidence that Powell was involved in the preparation of the plates for *Floriated Ornament* (1849), particularly the detailed colouring-in of the designs for this lavish publication which sets out Pugin's thesis that nature, in the form of leaves and flowers, is the real source of art.

A few weeks before his twenty-first birthday in 1848, Powell moved back to Birmingham, having already decided to do so as soon as the seven-year arrangement with Pugin came to an end. It was only a temporary hiatus, for Powell moved back to Ramsgate during the summer, and in October 1850 he married Anne (1832–97), Pugin's eldest daughter, thus bringing the Pugin and Hardman families even closer together. They moved into a house at St Lawrence on the outskirts of the town, and Powell decided to do most of his drawing there, much to the annoyance of Pugin, who, having equipped The Grange with facilities specially for Powell, expressed his displeasure to Hardman, '. . . while he is ostensibly with me I shall insist on his working in my place . . . if he intends to go why not like an honest man say so & not back out by inches'.95

Powell nevertheless stayed with Pugin, and after Pugin's death in September 1852 he stepped into his master's shoes as chief designer of the whole range of Hardman's undertakings. The Lightwoods archive contains

John Hardman Powell (photograph in private collection)

Anne Powell (photograph in private collection).

a good many of his drawings, many of them pasted on boards for continued use by employees of the firm, and some with detailed annotations. So closely did the pupil follow his master that in the early years Powell's handwriting and his drawing style are barely distinguishable from those of Pugin himself. Other collections of Powell's drawings and letters reveal a breadth of interest that goes beyond Pugin, who had indeed complained bitterly to Hardman that Powell was 'A pagan at heart' and that he had surreptitiously brought into his room at The Grange casts of pagan gods such as Venus and Apollo.[96] As well as the expected drawings of architectural details, metalwork, religious subjects and studies for stained glass, Powell's later drawings include scenes from Arthurian legends and German folk-tales such as *The Pied Piper*.

There is no doubt, however, that Pugin was the dominant influence in Powell's life. Through Powell this influence continued to shape the character of Hardman's products for many decades after Pugin's death, although – like Pugin's eldest son, Edward (1834–75) – he developed his own interpretations of Gothic style. Powell also ensured that the Pugin flame was imparted to others, including his sons Dunstan (1861–1932) and Sebastian Pugin Powell (1866–1949), who in their turn occupied leading roles at Hardman's. As architects, both Edward Pugin and Peter Paul Pugin (1851–1904) continued to use Hardman's as suppliers of architectural metalwork and church furnishings, and as late as 1907 the firm was proudly advertising itself as continuing the medieval principles 'revived and taught by Augustus Welby Pugin'.[97]

It is this sense of continuity which contributes so significantly to the uniqueness of Hardman & Co. among the leading firms who executed Pugin's designs, and much of it is due to John Hardman Powell; but that is not his only legacy. During his years at The Grange, Powell saw the many other facets of Pugin's complex and magnetic personality: the devout Christian who sanctified each working day with prayer; the generous and genial host who regaled guests at his table with lively conversation and hilarious anecdotes; the philanthropist who risked his life to save shipwrecked mariners; the loving father who in the midst of all his busyness found time to play games with his little children. It is to Hardman Powell that we owe the two memoirs, written much later in life, which answer the question, 'What was Pugin really like?' brilliantly and accurately in a way that could only have come from someone who had lived under his roof and shared his table.[98] On 14 September 1889 – the thirty-seventh anniversary of Pugin's death – Powell penned this moving tribute with which he prefaced his memoir:

> Pugin in his Home
>
> A memory offering
>
> to lay on the Tomb
>
> of his Master
>
> Augustus Welby N. Pugin
>
> whose example was noble
>
> and every word instruction
>
> by his grateful Pupil
>
> John Hardman Powell

2. COMPLETE CHURCH FURNISHERS

The broad range of Hardman's activities in the early 1840s is well illustrated in a letter sent to John Hardman by the Revd Charles Fisher, priest of the Catholic mission at Chepstow, Monmouthshire:

My dear Sir, I am glad to find by the directory[1] that you continue your manufacture of church ornaments & beg to inform me of the prices of the following – the cruets & stand in silver – the chalice in silver gilt, the thurible, sanctuary lamp & Holy Water vat in gilt metal – and the various sizes of Brass crucifixes. Can you also give me some idea as to the price of vestments & the various laces & orfrays [*sic*] you have prepared for them. I have been much pleased with the mitres & other ornaments prepared for our New Bishop Dr. Brown & hope his Lordship will on all occasions study to extend the use of the ancient & canonical style of church furniture . . . I shall be much obliged to you if, when you answer this you will send me at the same time by post a packet of altar bread, for, when I was last at Oscott, I was struck with the superiority of theirs over the London bread which is in use here – if you do not purchase it yourselves, you can profitably inform me as to the Maker in Birmingham.

Wishing you all the Compliments of the New Year
I remain, my dear Sir,
Yours very faithfully,
Charles L. Fisher[2]

If Hardman's were not already supplying altar-bread they soon turned their hand to it, and they also made special baking-irons for convents and other agencies who wished to make their own wafers stamped with the Sacred Monogram or other emblems. Altar requisites such as candles and incense were also included in their merchandise. The *Catholic Directory* for 1842 carries an advertisement for William Stone, a Catholic printer and bookseller based in Birmingham, who proudly offers altar-breads 'from designs by A.W. Pugin Esq., and which have received episcopal sanction', and it is possible that Hardman was the supplier.

Hardman's new premises at 166 Great Charles Street included a specially designed showroom for displaying the complete range of the firm's products to potential customers. Pugin made the drawings for this in January 1845 and he sent Hardman 'a Glorious plan' of the showroom, promising to follow it up with an interior view for inclusion in advertising material, and 'a book that you can send by post', i.e.

'Church Furniture Revived at Birmingham': A.W.N. Pugin, *Apology*, 1843

a catalogue.[3] He had already given a fair impression of what such a showroom might look like in his *Apology for the Revival of Christian Architecture* (1843), where a full-page engraving entitled 'Church Furniture Revived at Birmingham' shows examples of everything from chalices, candlesticks and reliquaries to statues, stained-glass windows and memorial brasses. Now that it was being translated into reality at Charles Street, Pugin wrote excitedly to Hardman that the effect would be 'transcendent', with 'space to shew everything' including a rood-screen and two small altars, aumbries for vestments and church linen, a display of brasses, altar-frontals and other textile items[4]. In November 1844 Pugin had come into contact with John Gregory Crace (1808–89) the 'Royal Decorator' of Wigmore Street, London[5] who specialised in textile fabrics and wallcoverings. Crace had made some Gothic-style fabrics to Pugin's designs suitable for vestments and hangings, and Pugin asked him to send samples in various colours for display at Great Charles Street.[6] Quantities of trade cards and letterheads, all designed by Pugin, were printed, the letterheads ornamented with illustrations of church metalwork and describing Hardman & Co. as 'Goldsmiths'. To begin with, loose pattern-sheets for items such as crosses and candlesticks were produced, but by the end of 1845 these had given way to more substantial catalogues. Two thousand copies of Hardman's catalogue of 'Sacred Vessels' were printed in November, and five hundred copies of his 'Domestic' catalogue.[7] Outside the new workshop there was to be a sign-board painted with the figure of St Eligius, the patron saint of metalworkers, and Pugin involved Hardman's nephew, John Hardman Powell, in the designing of this.[8]

For Pugin, the revival of what he often called 'The Real Thing' encompassed not only architecture and metalwork, but every kind of church furnishing, and, in matters of church order, a return to the Sarum Rite which had been the most prevalent of the medieval English liturgies in use until 1549. Turning his back on the post-medieval Tridentine Rite of 1570, and the neo-Classical trappings of contemporary Catholicism, Pugin sought to re-connect English people with their pre-Reformation Catholic heritage, convincing them in the process that the English Catholic Church was a home-grown plant, and that German-born Protestantism was the interloper. For this to succeed, such things as altar-furnishings and vestments had to revert to their medieval English form, replacing the commonly used French and Italian styles which served only to reinforce popular beliefs that Catholicism was 'foreign'. As with the revival of medieval metalwork, the revival of old-style vestments and soft furnishings required a considerable amount of research. The destruction of medieval art in all its forms in the sixteenth and seventeenth centuries had left few survivors, but such as there were – notably those owned by Lord Shrewsbury and his chaplain, Daniel Rock – provided Pugin with appropriate models, and these were supplemented by figures of vested priests depicted on monumental brasses and illuminated manuscripts. The medieval forms – and particularly that of the principal priestly vestment, the chasuble – were so very different from those in current use as to raise a storm of protest from clergy who did not see why they should step back four hundred years at the whim of a recent convert from Protestantism. Pugin found a firm ally in Bishop Walsh, who quite happily wore his voluminous chasubles, but others fought hard to have them banned, as for a time they were.[9] The Newport mission priest, Charles Fisher, thought it wise to exercise caution when, in February 1841, he wrote to Hardman about a new chasuble he wanted in time for Lent. '. . . Mr Pugin informs me that the vestments were ordered to be cut narrower & therefore do not make mine more than *2 feet* 6 across the shoulders, in order to avoid all difficulties about it'.[10] It has sometimes been said that Pugin misunderstood the medieval form of the chasuble, making it less full than it should have been, but his writings (including the *Glossary)* make it clear that this was not the case. What finally emerged was something of a compromise between the very full all-enveloping medieval shape and the drastically cut-down 'fiddleback' generally in use in the early nineteenth century. The 'Pugin' chasuble, roughly shield-shaped and reaching about halfway down the priest's arm, eventually won wide acceptance in the Roman Catholic and Anglican Churches.

Hardman' s were involved in the production of all of these things, and it began well before the opening of the Great Charles Street premises. Mrs Lucy Powell, half-sister of John Hardman Jnr and mother of John

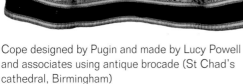

Cope designed by Pugin and made by Lucy Powell and associates using antique brocade (St Chad's cathedral, Birmingham)

Lucy Powell; oil painting in private collection

Hardman Powell, supervised the vestment-making at Hardman's from 1842, and she continued for the following twenty years. By 1845 she had moved into separate premises at 55 Frederick Street, in the Jewellery Quarter, along with her daughters. Pugin designed printed stationery for them, in a lettering style almost identical to that used for Hardman's, and advertising them as makers of 'embroidery, fringe, gold and silk laces, vestments and altar linen'. From 1844 onwards, Pugin's association with the firm of John Gregory Crace ensured that textiles woven to his own designs were available for the making of vestments and other textile items, while woven braids and appliqués (generally referred to as 'lace') were supplied by firms such as Lonsdale & Tyler of London, and Thomas Brown & Son of Manchester. Machine-embroidery was another area in which modern industrial processes took the place of the handicraft methods which Pugin would have preferred,[11] but such was the pace of the Revival that there was little alternative. On 5 March 1845 – only a fortnight before Easter – Pugin wrote to Hardman in something of a panic about things he needed at Ramsgate for Holy Week: 'You must get Mrs Powell to send me the following . . .' and the list includes a cope which he 'must have' for Palm Sunday.[12]

Medieval needlework often included metallic gold and silver threads and wires, making it both rich and heavy. In 1834 Pugin rescued for his collection of antiquities some pieces of fifteenth-century embroidery worked with silver thread which someone had taken to a silver refinery to have burnt in order to sell the metal residue.[13] Pugin's own ecclesiastical embroidery also incorporated rich bullion work and metallic fittings. For some of this he used Lonsdale & Tyler, the London-based firm of army accoutrement makers who were well accustomed to using gold and silver bullion in the making of ceremonial uniforms. It was John Hardman, however – in association no doubt with Lucy Powell – who was entrusted with the making of specialised items such as episcopal mitres[14] and antependia (altar-frontals) which combined elements of needlework, metalwork and jewellery. Several precious mitres were made for St Chad's, Birmingham, and also for individual clerics as they were elevated to the episcopacy. Based on surviving medieval examples, and those seen on memorial brasses, they increased in richness and costliness as time and experience progressed. A precious mitre made in 1844 for William Riddell on his election as co-adjutor of the northern district is entered in the Metalwork daybook at £22; one made for Bishop Brown of Wales three years later cost £36/10/–, while the richest of all was that commissioned by the Revd Daniel Haigh for Bishop Wiseman following his move to London in 1847. Entered in the Hardman daybook at an amazing £65, it is described as:

> A precious mitre of rich raised embroidery work on velvet, set with stones, jewels, enamels and beaten plates of silver, with gilt crockets running up sides & gilt cross set with pearls[15]

Hardman's supplied not only mitres, but the whole range of 'episcopal ornaments'. In 1841 a full set of accoutrements was made for Francis George Mostyn (1800–47) following his appointment as vicar apostolic of the northern district. The entry in the metalwork daybook for 29 January 1841 includes not only items made of jewelled metal, such as his pastoral staff and episcopal ring, but the full range of embroidered vestments and items of everyday wear such as purple silk stockings and a purple silk cassock.[16] There was also a cope, a heavy cloak-like garment worn by bishops and others, and fastened across the chest by a clasp known as a morse. The morse could be made of stiffened fabric, one edge of which was permanently stitched to the cope, or it could be in the form of a detachable plate of enamelled or jewelled metal. The Mostyn cope was equipped with a gilt metal one, set with stones and enamelled with the Mostyn arms and those of St Cuthbert. In 1848 a similar morse was made in gilt metal for Bishop Wiseman, and set with enamel, stones and cross-keys.[17] A

Jewelled mitre made by Hardman's for Bishop Wiseman, 1848 (Westminster Cathedral; photo: Phil Sayer)

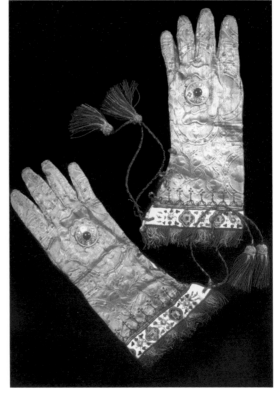

Episcopal gloves made for Bishop Wiseman, with jewelled metal ornaments by Hardman (Westminster Cathedral; photo: Phil Sayer)

coloured drawing which appears to have been the combined
work of Pugin and Hardman Powell shows designs for a set
of four morses relating to different occasions or seasons of the
Church's year. One carries emblems of Christ and the Blessed
Virgin Mary, another is enamelled with the Crucifixion, and a
third has an expressive emblem of the Holy Trinity. The fourth
– evidently designed for use at funerals – has detailed annotations stating that it is for use with a black cope, that it is to be
made of plated German silver enamelled in 'very deep blue–
purple' and that the rim is to be engraved with the first verse of
the *de profundis*, the psalm most commonly used in the Offices
for the Dead. Morses made of metal were detachable from the
cope itself, and were secured to the garment by means of hooks
and eyelets. An annotation in Pugin's hand reads, 'the hooks
must be riveted on exceedingly strong'.[18]

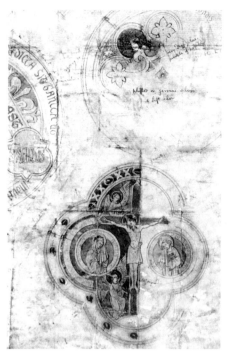

A.W.N. Pugin/J.H. Powell; design for cope-
morse, c.1850; ink/colour (JHAL)

Episcopal ornaments also included engraved seals and pectoral crosses. When Bishop Wiseman became Archbishop
of Westminster following the restoration of the Hierarchy in
1850, a set of four seals was designed for him, almost certainly
by Pugin who offered to design all the episcopal accoutrements
he needed. The detailed drawings for the seals, by John Hardman Powell, form part of the Lightwoods collection,[19] along
with designs for a number of pectoral crosses, one enamelled
with the arms of St Chad, and another intended for Edward
Ilsley (1838–1926) on his appointment as auxiliary to Bishop
Ullathorne of Birmingham in 1879. A pectoral cross also figured
in the set of episcopal ornaments made for Bishop Mostyn. On
discovering that Mostyn's sister had already placed an order
with Hardman's for most of the accoutrements, his somewhat
indignant brother, George, wishing not to be outdone, ordered
a cross and chain 'such as our bishops usually wear'. Having
seen the one made by Hardman for Bishop Brown of Wales,
Mostyn asked for the chain to be differently designed as he
thought that Brown's was 'more like a lady's chain'.[20] Pectoral
crosses were generally made with a hinged back which opened
up for the insertion of a holy relic. One such cross is kept in
the metalwork collection at Lightwoods. Made in silver-gilt
by Hardman's in 1879, it is of the usual reliquary type, but

Archiepiscopal seals designed for Wiseman
c.1850 (JHAL)

instead of a relic of the True Cross it contains an antique gold crucifix engraved with emblems of the Passion.
Beautifully engraved in Gothic letters on the case are lines from the first and last verses of the hymn *Vexilla
regis prodeunt* written by Venantius Fortunatus (c.530–609 AD) and which form a part of the Liturgy of Good
Friday. The metalwork daybook shows that the cross was made, not for a bishop, but for a layman, Charles
Hadfield, to hold the antique crucifix already in his possession.[21]

Personal jewellery formed a small but important part of the Hardman enterprise. 'Pugin' crosses and crucifixes, priced from a few pence for brass ones to several shillings for silver ones, were sold to individual
purchasers or through agents such as James Burns of Portman Street, London, who began to order quantities

Silver-gilt reliquary cross made by Hardman's for Charles Hadfield, 1879 (Hardman Collection)

The parure made for Jane Knill to Pugin's design (chromolithograph from Matthew Digby Wyatt, *The Industrial Arts of the XIX Century*, 1851–3)

John Hardman Powell: designs for bracelets, c.1855, ink/colour (JHAL)

of these items from June 1848.[22] Gild medals and badges, 'Miraculous Medals', and similar items occur frequently in the daybooks, usually ordered in bulk by churches, gild secretaries, or agents such as Burns. Some wealthy customers commissioned specially designed items of jewellery; for example John Sutton, a friend and client of Pugin,[23] bought an expensive cross-shaped brooch made of gold and set with enamels, stones and pearls.[24]

Among the most important pieces of personal jewellery made by Hardman's were those commissioned by Pugin himself: a cross and chain and a pair of earrings made for his first wife, Louisa,[25] and a parure of ten items in a fitted case made in 1848. The parure, for which Pugin paid a total of £255.9s.6d, was originally commissioned as a wedding gift for Helen Lumsdaine, to whom Pugin became engaged on 25 January. To Pugin's deep distress, the engagement was broken off a few weeks later on account of her parents' objection to her becoming a Catholic. The parure was nevertheless completed, and, with a few small alterations, it was given to Jane Knill (1825–1909), the Catholic girl whom Pugin married in August 1848. The most expensive item in the set was a large jewelled and enamelled cross and chain in solid gold, entered in the daybook at £55.11s, while the most exquisite is a gold headband set with stones and seed-pearls, and finely lettered with the words *christi crux est mea lux* (Christ's cross is my light).[26] As with most of his metalwork designs, Pugin was careful to study the relevant 'authorities', i.e. surviving examples of medieval jewellery, and when his instructions were misunderstood he complained to Hardman, '. . . I believe your jeweler is a humbug a real humbug . . . I have been looking at all the authorities'.[27] Several photographs exist of Jane Pugin wearing the parure, and looking every inch the 'first-rate Gothic woman' of Pugin's dreams, who 'perfectly understands and delights in spires, chancels, screens, stained windows, brasses, vestments etc.'[28]

John Hardman Powell continued the tradition of creating Gothic jewellery in the Pugin style, for example rings, bracelets, necklaces and seals. Several of his designs for floriated crosses and chains exist, There is also a drawing of a headband similar to that in Jane Pugin's parure, and lettered *ave maria gratia plena dominus tecum* (Hail, Mary, full of grace, the Lord is with thee), and designs for bracelets, possibly intended for family members. Powell's designs reveal a lighter touch, using delicate filigree to link the enamelled components.[29]

Personal jewellery occurs only sporadically in the Hardman metalwork daybooks. The vast majority of entries are for ecclesiastical items, and for a growing clientele of both Catholics and Anglicans. The Church of England in the 1840s was undergoing a revival in its understanding and use of long-neglected 'Ornaments of the Church and of the Ministers thereof' enjoined by the Book of Common Prayer. At the forefront was the Cambridge Camden Society, founded in 1839. Like Pugin, the Ecclesiologists, as they became known, looked back to the Middle Ages for inspiration in re-creating the English parish church, in structure and in ornament, as – in their case – it would have been immediately before and immediately after the introduction of the First Prayer Book (1549).[30] Pugin's works were avidly read by members of the Society, and Pugin had many friends among Catholic-minded Anglicans, chief of whom was the Revd John Rouse Bloxam (1807–91), a Fellow of Magdalen College, Oxford, with whom Pugin regularly corresponded and shared his ideas. Pugin designed many personal items of metalwork and furniture for Bloxam, who furnished his College rooms in medieval fashion.

Another Anglican clergyman who was in direct contact with Pugin and Hardman was the Revd Benjamin Webb, a founder-member and Secretary of the Cambridge Camden Society. In September 1843 he wrote to Hardman:

> . . . You will perhaps remember making some crosses for me from a drawing given by my friend Mr. Pugin. He once told me that you would allow me to get anything from your manufactory, although you might occasionally hesitate to supply ecclesiastical ornaments to persons not in your communion. You could greatly oblige me by sending me a pair of the small plain altar candlesticks.[31]

The enthusiasm of some Anglican clergy such as Bloxam for the revival of medieval church furnishings contrasted sharply with the indifference and active hostility of many Catholic clergy who were still content to '. . . Administer baptism out of an old physick phial; reserve the blessed Sacrament in *dirty cupboard* say mass in a vestment made out of an old gown, burn gas on the altar'.[32] Having been deprived, through the decades of persecution, of the kind of refinements now on offer from Pugin and Hardman, Catholic clergy would need time to adjust, and Pugin realised that improving standards would be an uphill struggle. 'We have a sorry soil to plant in, and that not from protestantism; actually protestants in many cases are far better inclined to Catholicism than half the soi-disant Catholics of our day'.[33] Anglicans who did embrace Pugin's vision of glorious altars, chancels and screens laid themselves open to charges of 'popery', while Catholics who shared his enthusiasm for an 'English' Catholic Church with its distinctive rituals and ornaments were suspected of pandering to the Oxford Tractarians who believed that it was possible to live a Catholic life without leaving the Church of England.[34]

The Gothic movement nonetheless gathered momentum. Few Catholic churches were built after the mid-1840s in styles other than 'Puginian' Gothic, and Gothic was the style which swept through the Church of England in the shape of new churches, additions to existing ones, and thousands of restorations. In all of these there was scope for new furnishings and ornaments of the kind designed by Pugin and made by Hardman. Few and far between are the Anglican churches so unaffected by the Catholic Revival that they did not acquire at least an altar cross, a pair of candlesticks and a new chalice, and many of them acquired a great deal more. In their sanctuary furnishings many Anglican churches became the very model of what Pugin considered to be the correct arrangements, with no more than two candlesticks on the altar itself, and two standard candlesticks on the altar step.

As for the new Catholic churches, Hardman's supplied specially designed chrismatories for the Holy Oils in place of 'the old physic phial' of yesteryear, proper tabernacles to supplant the 'dirty cupboard' for the reservation of the Blessed Sacrament; splendid vestments cut from newly woven fabrics instead of makeshift ones fashioned 'out of an old gown', and elegant candlesticks and branches for the altars instead of gas-burners. Everything was, of course, made to Pugin's designs as illustrated on the early leaflets, in the later catalogues, and in the working drawings kept at Hardman's for the instruction of the workforce. The list of goods supplied by Hardman's for St Mary's church at Brewood, Staffs, in 1843 may be taken as typical of the requirements of a small country church at this time:

Tabernacle	£12	0	0
Six candlesticks	12	12	0
Altar cross	8	0	0
Holy-water vat & sprinkler	1	12	0
Set of cruets	5	0	0
Elevation candlesticks			
with tubes and shields	8	5	0
12 consecration branches	3	0	0[35]

So accustomed had the Catholic Church become to the comparatively modern practice of having six large candlesticks on the high altar that Pugin's plea for two and no more fell largely on deaf ears. He also believed that, in accordance with medieval precedent, the Blessed Sacrament should be reserved, not on the high altar, but in a specially designated side-chapel, and in a 'tower' tabernacle of cylindrical shape. However, his plans were frequently upset as, for example, at the church of SS Mary & Thomas, Dudley, for which he had commissioned fittings from Hardman's at his own expense:

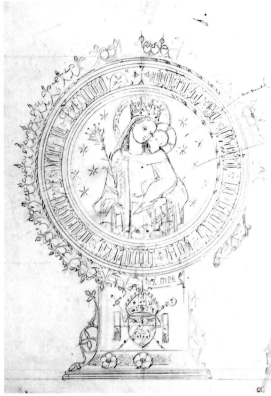

Silver-gilt reliquary made by Hardman for Bishop Wiseman, 1845 (Westminster Cathedral; photo: Phil Sayer)

A.W.N. Pugin/J.H. Powell: design for paxbrede, c.1850, pencil/ink (JHAL)

> . . . All my plans at Dudley have been completely upset. I had got 2 candlesticks on the altar – these are to be increased to *six* to suit the modern fashion. I had made a beautiful tower *engraved & enameled* for the reservation of the blessed Sacrament in a *side chapel.* this is condemned & a shewy front tabernacle of Packing case dimensions is to be placed *on the high altar* which should be left free & unencumbered . . .[36]

Bishop Wiseman was, of course, cast as the villain of the piece, and Pugin complained bitterly to his friend, Ambrose Phillipps, 'The church at Dudley is a compleat facsimile of one of the old English parish churches, and nobody seems to know how to use it'.[37]

Though not as carried away on the Puginian wave as was Bishop Walsh, Wiseman was not necessarily anti-Gothic, and he owned several pieces of metalwork designed by Pugin and made by Hardman. In addition to the 'Sienese' silver-gilt chalice made for him in 1845, he had a silver-gilt reliquary made to hold a relic of the True Cross. Set with pearls, stones and enamels, it is entered into the metalwork daybook at 12 September 1845, at a cost of £35.15s.

Reliquaries were not, of course uncommon, but Pugin's attempts to revive the Old English Liturgy included the re-introduction of a number of furnishings and ornaments which had not been in use since the mid-sixteenth century. Among these was the pax, or paxbrede, succinctly described in the *Glossary* as 'a small plate of gold, or silver, or copper gilt, enamelled, or piece of carved ivory, or wood overlaid with metal, carried round, having been kissed by the Priest, after the *Agnus Dei* in the Mass, to communicate the Kiss of Peace', and Pugin also refers to a fifteenth-century example then in the metalwork collection at Oscott. By the nineteenth century

– and indeed until the liturgical reforms of the Second Vatican Council – the passing of the peace amongst the congregation had long been discontinued, but Pugin clearly saw it as a significant part of the liturgy, and the provision of a paxbrede might hasten its revival. Surprisingly, in view of his attitude towards some of Pugin's 'revivals', a pax was ordered by Bishop Wiseman,[38] and another was made in 1851 for St George's, Southwark.[39] Two drawings for paxbredes are in the JHA Lightwoods collection. One of these depicts the Virgin and Child, and the annotations show that it is to be made of silver gilt, with an enamelled centre. Around the periphery is an inscription in Gothic letters taken from Psalm 44 (45); *diffusa est gratia in labils tuis, propterea benedixit Deus in aeternam* (graciousness is poured upon your lips because God has blessed you for evermore).

The largest collection of Hardman metalwork ever assembled in one church is almost certainly that supplied to St Giles's church, Cheadle (Staffs.), in readiness for the opening of that church in September 1846.[40] The paymaster for the entire project was the sixteenth Earl of Shrewsbury, and the total metalwork bill amounted to around £1,400, a sufficient sum, at that time, to finance the building of a complete church. Most of the work was executed in plated metal and supplied from stock items, but there were some notable exceptions. At Cheadle, Pugin succeeded in providing a magnificent side-chapel for the reservation of the Blesssed Sacrament, and the furnishings for this included a specially designed tabernacle engraved and enamelled with figures of the four Evangelists and vine-scroll ornament[41] (it is no longer at the church). At the entrance to the chapel there is a superb openwork screen of brass, the single most costly item made for St Giles's, entered in the metalwork daybook on 6 June 1846 at £251.14s. The lower part of the screen incorporates three rows of quatrefoils decorated with chalices and the *agnus dei*, and in a letter to Hardman, Pugin notes that John Hardman Powell is making the wax models for the chalices.[42] Other significant items for Cheadle include a chrismatory for the Holy Oils. Made in plated German silver, this beautifully simple vessel consists of an outer case with a hinged lid in the shape of a pitched roof with pierced cresting along the ridge, looking much like a diminutive reliquary. Inside are two cylindrical oil-stocks with engraved lids. These hold the oil of the catechumens and the holy chrism, both used in the rites of Christian Initiation. The metalwork daybook enters the chrismatory under 4 August 1846 at a cost of £5. 12s, and a separate stock to contain the oils for anointing the sick is charged at £2. In a letter to John Hardman, Pugin also refers to drawings for a paschal candlestick for the Easter Vigil ceremonies, and a Lenten herse-light, suggesting that he make three of each item – including the chrismatory – '& then we should have some stock – & they would come a deal cheaper'.[43] The Lenten herse-light consisted of a triangular candle-stand holding a number of tapers which were symbolically extinguished one by one during the Holy Week office of *Tenebrae*. Paschal candlesticks, used during the Easter

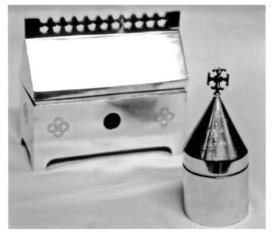

vigil ceremonies, received special attention from Pugin in the *Glossary*. Often of enormous size, they sometimes had branches in addition to the main stem for the Easter candle, and a small lectern from which the deacon would sing the *Exultet*.[44] The paschal candlestick for Cheadle was entered in the daybook at a fairly modest price of £25.

The lighting of churches was something over which Pugin took great care. In addition to the lights that were required for liturgical purposes on and around the altars, and processional torches and lanterns, lighting was needed for purely practical reasons in other parts of the building. Although Pugin was obliged to use gas-lighting in some of his churches, he did not particularly like it, and preferred to use candles

St Giles's, Cheadle: chrismatory in plated German silver, 1846

wherever possible. Candlesticks and standing candelabra could be made with numerous branches to give more light, and the reflection of candlelight upon polished brass gave an added sparkle, especially if the stems had spiral twists. Single standards could be made by Hardman's to convert into branched candelabra simply by removing the candle and inserting into the empty socket an upper section with multiple branches. A pair of altar candlesticks was made for Cheadle on this principle, with branches that could be fitted into the sockets for occasions such as Benediction.[45] A pair of five-light Benediction candlesticks with an octagonal gallery and a flared octagonal base appear somewhat different from those entered at £40 in the daybook on 3 August, but – unlike the branched candelabra – they are still at St Giles's.

St Giles's Cheadle: benediction candlestick

In spite of his stated preference for just two candlesticks on the high altar, Pugin was obliged to provide a 'big six' for Cheadle. They are of a very distinctive design, having a cross within a roundel set into the stem just above the knop, with one of Pugin's favourite mottoes, *Christi crux est mea lux* (Christ's cross is my light) engraved on the roundel, to accompany the 'richly gilt cross & figure set with chrystals [*sic*] and enamels' entered into the Hardman daybook at a cost of £34.10s. The date of this entry – 22 August 1846 – shows how perilously close to the consecration-day Hardman's were running in their completion and delivery of metalwork. Included in the same entry is the beautiful enamelled crucifix for the altar in the Lady-chapel, entered at £26, well above Pugin's original estimate of £14. A monstrance of the 'sunburst' type, made of plated metal, engraved and set with stones, was entered on 26 August, only five days before the opening of the church. Described as 'New Pattern', this too went into general production.[46]

The rood-screen at Cheadle, of which Pugin was particularly proud, was furnished not with the customary six lights, but a row of thirteen twisted brass stems with crested pans, and also two branches. To illuminate the nave, Pugin designed a set of five *coronae lucis* or chandeliers, suspended on chains from the roof. Each one had fleur-de-lis cresting and the text, *Domine da nobis lucem* (O Lord, give us light) and held twenty-four tapers. The coronae were made of iron and estimated at £100 the set.[47] The chancel was furnished with an extremely fine antique corona,[48] and for the Blessed Sacrament Chapel Pugin designed a lamp suspended from a small crown with a Latin inscription set on red enamel.

Pugin's lighting scheme in the richly coloured interior of St Giles's worked perfectly and it made a huge impression on visitors. In January 1847 the *Illustrated London News* carried the following description:

> When the church is lighted up for evening service the effect is gorgeous in the extreme; the gilded and diapered walls of the chancel glowing in the flood of yellow light of the tapers at the altar; the glistening gilded ceiling, forming a rich background to the lofty rood, with its pierced and elaborately-traceried screen; the coronae in the nave lighting up the painted and gilded pillars, their soft light fading away in the deep blue roof, whence the gilded stars sparkle with exquisite richness– form a picture, once seen, never forgotten.

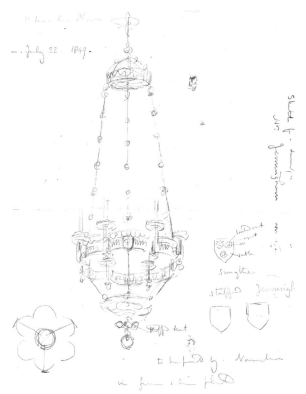

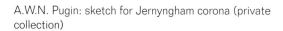

A.W.N. Pugin: sketch for Jernyngham corona (private collection)

The Jernyngham corona (private collection. Photo: Lucilla Kingsbury – Joll)

Pugin correctly predicted that St Giles's would be a model church to which 'all the learned men will flock'.[49] It became a kind of showroom in which the combined talents of all those who had executed Pugin's designs were brought together as nowhere else, apart, perhaps, from the New Palace of Westminster; and Hardman's benefited hugely from those who saw their array of metalwork and wanted similar items for their own churches. A prime example is the Anglican Ecclesiologist Thomas Gambier-Parry (1816–88) who commissioned the architect Henry Woodyer (1816–96) to build the church of Holy Innocents, Highnam (Glos.). Completed in 1851, it is about as Puginesque as it was then possible for an Anglican church to be, clearly modelled on Cheadle, and replete with Hardman metalwork and glass.

Pugin's lighting schemes were widely adopted in other churches, both Catholic and Anglican, and the Hardman catalogues devote more space to candlesticks, branches, candelabra, gas-brackets, lamps and *coronae* than to any other range of products. Iron *coronae* formed part of Pugin's restoration of the Anglican parish church at Wymeswold (Leics.).[50] Thomas Gambier-Parry ordered a set of six brass *coronae* from Hardman's for his church at Highnam,[51] and a particularly handsome one was ordered for St Mary's church, Clapham. Made of iron with brass saw-pierced cresting, it consisted of two tiers with eight candlesticks on each level and eight three-light branches.[52] In 1849 Marianne Jernyngham, a member of a prominent Catholic family, commissioned a most beautiful *corona* incorporating a sanctuary lamp suspended on chains underneath. Made of plated German silver, it has six beaten candlesticks, elaborate saw-piercing, and enamelled shields with the arms of the Stafford-Jernynghams. The engraved inscription records it as given in memory of Edward Jernyngham, and that it was intended to hang before the Blessed Sacrament. A letter from Pugin to John Hardman (d.1849) includes a drawing of the lamp with details of the heraldry, and a subsequent one contains the plea,

'Don't neglect Mrs. Jernyngham's lamp for she is the grandest woman I encountered'.[53]

Only one complete Anglican church was ever built by Pugin: St Lawrence, Tubney (Berks.), about ten miles south-west of Oxford,[54] but he was involved with the restoration and furnishing of several more, mainly at the invitation of clergy influenced by the ideas of the Ecclesiological Society, many of whom turned to Hardman's for the supply of ornaments and furnishings in the 'correct' Gothic style. Typical of these was the Revd John Frampton of St Saviours, Tetbury (Glos.), built in 1848 by Samuel Whitfield Daukes (1811–80). Frampton had served as curate to the Revd Charles Lowder – a prominent Anglo-Catholic – at St Peter's, London Docks.[55] The metalwork furnishings supplied by Hardman's reflect Frampton's own Anglo-Catholic attitudes, and although they were eventually to become quite commonplace, some of them were remarkably 'advanced' for the 1840s:

Large silver chalice & paten	£15.18s
Smaller do., parcel gilt	" "
Silver flagon, parcel gilt, engraved	12.12s
Plated almsdish	2.10s
2 brass candlesticks weith sexfoil feet	4. 4s
2 brass pulpit branches	1. 2s
Brass sanctuary lamp & chains	4.10s
2 offering basins	2. 4s
Cruet in plated metal	1. 1s[56]

The sanctuary lamp was a most unusual item for an Anglican church at this time. This, and some of the other items, reflect the centrality of Eucharistic worship at St Saviour's from the very beginning. Frampton's ordering of a 'large' chalice and a flagon reflects the Anglican custom of administering the chalice, as well as the Eucharistic Bread, to the laity, a practice long discontinued in the Catholic Church and not revived until the mid-twentieth century. Communicants tended to do more than simply moisten their lips, so a commodious chalice was needed. The flagon, as referred to here, was an Anglican peculiarity, and distinct from the 'cruets' which contained the unconsecrated wine and water. The flagon was actually placed on the altar along with the chalice and paten prior to the Prayer of Consecration, and then used to 'top up' the chalice as necessary during the Communion.[57] Hardman appears at first to have had some doubts as to the propriety of a devout Catholic making such an item. In a letter dated 24 August 1843, the architect Thomas Hellyer tells Hardman, 'I am delighted to find you have overcome your scruples as regards the flagon. I cannot see any impropriety in your having undertaken it, and altho it is needed by the rites of the Anglican Church still I think it should not deter us from endeavouring to emulate the pious zeal of our forefathers.'[58]

Some of the flagons made by Hardman's had a body of ruby glass with metal mounts and handles incorporating roundels pierced with Gothic tracery, and lids surmounted by a pelican – an emblem of Christ shedding his blood for mankind and often used on vessels connected with the Blessed Sacrament. Pugin's design appears to have been taken from a medieval 'crewett' illustrated on page 88 of the *Glossary*. One was made in 1849 for Nockalls Johnson Cottingham, son of the celebrated architect Lewis Cottingham (1787–1847). Entered in the daybook at £18.18s, it is described as 'a large and elaborately worked cruet of ruby glass, mounted with gilt metal with design, raised on lid, of pelican & young on nest etc'.[59] A similar one was made in 1851 for the Revd Edward Paget of Elford, near Lichfield.[60]

Not only did Hardman's supply metalwork to Tetbury church, they also undertook the decorative work in the chancel: an example of a relatively recent venture into an area of ecclesiastical art and design which was soon to be of considerable importance to the firm. The work at Tetbury included painting and gilding of the altar and reredos, and staining and gilding the screen and the ribs, bosses and cornices of the chancel ceiling.[61] The daybook records the name of the painter as Thomas Earley, who had been employed by Hardman's since 1845 and who carried out a number of Pugin's decorative schemes, for example at Oscott and the Drummond Chantry at Albury (Surrey).[62]

Samuel Daukes was one of many architects who adopted Pugin's ideas and built churches in his style. In 1846 Pugin told Lord Shrewsbury that 'There are so many Catholic architects now that there is not a chance of any new buildings . . . I believe I design for all of them, for I actually see my own figures and casts used'.[63] After Cheadle there was to be only one more great church for him, St George's, Southwark (1848), for which Hardman's made a rich array of metalwork to his designs. Within the Catholic Midlands, Pugin was eclipsed by Charles F. Hansom (1816–88), the younger brother of Joseph Hansom, the architect of Birmingham Town Hall. Bishop Ullathorne (1806–89), who in 1848 succeeded Walsh as Vicar Apostolic of the Central District, regarded Hansom as 'his' architect, and famously remarked that 'anything that Pugin can do, Mr. Hansom can do better'.[64]

Pugin, however, was quite happy to design metalwork and glass for Hansom, whose churches he genuinely admired as embodying his own 'true principles'.[65] One of the finest examples of a Hansom church furnished by Pugin and Hardman is SS Thomas & Edmund, Erdington, built in 1848–50 as the Catholic parish church for what was then a village on the outskirts of Birmingham. Hansom was assisted by the Revd Daniel Henry Haigh (1819–79), a scholar and antiquarian who used some of his inherited fortune to build and furnish the

Ruby-glass flagon designed by Pugin (water-colour study by Violet Prosser 1966) (JHAL)

SS. Thomas & Edmund, Erdington: Reliquary cross (photo: Graham Miller)

Chromolithograph of the Medieval Court at the Great Exhibition of 185 showing the Erdington altar with its an-gel-capped riddle-posts, hangings, and with the lampadarium suspended above (Dickinson's Views of the Great Exhibition)

church. Haigh – a former Anglica – was well acquainted with Pugin, who noted his reception into the Church (1 January 1847) in his diary. On the following day Haigh visited Pugin at his Ramsgate home, and Pugin records a visit to Erdington on 29 April 1850. The church reflects Hansom's close following of Pugin's mature style as expressed for example at St Oswald's, Liverpool (1842), St John's, Kirkham (1845) and St Giles's, Cheadle (1846), while many of the furnishings showed Haigh's sympathy with Pugin's view of an 'English' Catholic Church. This is particularly true of the altar and its surroundings. Though it was all removed in a reor-dering in 1897, the records show that the original high altar at Erdington was of the 'English' type, enclosed on three sides with curtains suspended on rods attached to riddel-posts. The metalwork daybook enters to Haigh 'six very richly decorated pillars for curtain rods, of richly wrought brass, two patterns on each standard, with wrought iron pillars inside the brasswork' and 'a rich brass brattishing with curtain rods for curtains suspended from above pillars', at a cost of £144.10s. Each of the pillars was surmounted by a cast brass angel holding a candlestick.[66]

Another of Pugin's 'revivals' introduced at Erdington was the lampadarium – a large wooden beam, carved, gilded and painted, and suspended in front of the high altar. From it were hung seven brass sanctuary lamps.[67] This reveals, among other things, that Hardman's craftsmen were capable of making large objects in carved wood as well as in metal. Lampadaria were also made for St Mary's, Oscott, and St Chad's, Birmingham. Only the one from Oscott now survives, along with its complement of lamps, at Lightwoods House.

Haigh equipped the high altar with a set of six brass candlesticks with four angels of cast bronze at the foot of each one. He provided an expensive 'sunburst' monstrance, richly engraved and set with enamels and stones, and a pair of thuribles made entirely of silver.[68] Hansom and Haigh followed Pugin by providing a chapel on the south side for the reservation of the Blessed Sacrament. The altar was equipped with a tabernacle, the doors of which were finely engraved and set with stones. A silver electrotyped *crucifixus* was made separately for attachment to the door, but this no longer exists.[69] When the high altar was remodelled in 1897, the new reredos incorporated a tabernacle, so the existing one was abandoned, and the Blessed Sacrament Chapel was renamed as St Joseph's Chapel. The altar from it now serves as a forward altar under the chancel arch. Other alterations which followed the Second Vatican Council included the demolition of Hansom's stone rood-screen.[70]

The largest metalwork item made by Hardman for Erdington was a brass lectern made in two parts. First of all there was 'A brass richly wrought bookdesk of 2 angels holding scroll' entered in the daybook at 26 August 1848. It may have been intended as a missal-stand for the high altar, but in February 1850 Haigh was charged £32 for 'A brass base for book desk no. 1843 forming lectern, of moulded base and stem with 2 branches to support desk'.[71]

Lectern and candlesticks, Jesus College Chapel, Cambridge (photo: Graham Miller)

Lecterns were among the most important large-scale brass objects produced by Hardman's. In medieval times many such lecterns had come from workshops in the Belgian region of Dinand, and Pugin was aware of many surviving examples both in England and in Europe. In England, lecterns had fared rather better, in the upheavals of the sixteenth and seventeenth centuries, than most other metalwork furnishings, possibly because, as reading-desks from which the Holy Scriptures were read, they were not generally denounced as objects of 'superstition'. Around forty examples were known to exist, and in the *Glossary* Pugin draws particular attention to those at Norwich, King's College, Cambridge, and Merton College, Oxford. The book-rest sometimes consisted of a double desk to support the antiphoners – the large-format music-books from which the cantors would sing certain of the musical parts of the Mass while standing either side of the lectern. Others were made in the form of an eagle with extended wings – a symbol of St John the Evangelist – and first introduced (according to Pugin) for chanting the Gospel at Mass. A particularly fine example of this latter kind, originally from a church in Louvain, was presented by Lord Shrewsbury to St Chad's cathedral at the time of its opening. From there it was taken to Oscott, and sold from there in 1967 to the Metropolitan Museum in New York. Described in detail by Pugin, the architectural base consists of pierced tracery and pinnacles with figures in niches, resting on three lions couchant, and with branches for candles either side of the eagle book-rest. Though Pugin greatly admired the design, he judged it to be 'rude in execution',[72] believing, no doubt, that Hardman's metalworkers could now do better. Lecterns with similar architectural bases were indeed made for St Cuthbert's College, Ushaw (Durham) and St George's, Southwark. The latter was displayed by Hardman at the Great Exhibition along with the ones from Erdington and Jesus College, Cambridge.[73] The Cambridge lectern is not of the 'eagle' type, but consists of a moulded column resting on an octagonal base supported by lions couchant, and with candle-branches rising either side of a double book-rest surmounted by brattishing and the figure of St John the Evangelist. Pugin modelled it on the King's College lectern which he greatly admired. Entered in the metalwork daybook at 4 October 1848 at a cost of £200, it was the gift of Sir John Sutton, who commissioned other work from Pugin for the college chapel, including a pair of standard candlesticks with diapered metal pillars rising from richly moulded bases resting on the familiar couchant lions.[74]

'Eagle' lecterns became increasingly popular in the later nineteenth century, particularly in Anglican churches where they were among the least controversial furnishings to be introduced in the wake of the Ecclesiological Movement. In the course of Gilbert Scott's restoration of Lichfield cathedral in the 1860s a brass eagle lectern was supplied by Hardman's, at a cost of £120, with a rope-twist pillar and three large lions at the base.[75] There is a particularly fine example from the 1880s in the Lightwoods Collection.

Hardman's lecterns and missal-stands were sometimes complemented with specially bound altar-books and Gospel-books embellished with ornamental metal corners and clasps. Book-ornaments, indeed, had been amongst the very first products of the firm in 1838. Pugin, however, took book ornamentation to new levels. Not only did he design the gold-blocked bindings for his self-illustrated publications on architecture, he also had some of his personal copies, and those intended for presentation, bound in boards covered with silk velvet and embellished with gilt-metal ornaments.[76] Pugin's bindings soon became well known. As early as 1841 the Revd William Riddell, assistant priest at Newcastle upon Tyne, wrote to John Hardman asking to discuss the binding of a missal during his visit to Birmingham for the opening of St Chad's:

> I am thinking of getting a Folio Missal bound *a la Pugin*, that is in velvet with brass corners etc. etc. Before bringing it with me I shall feel much obliged to you (if you have a few moments to spare) to let me know the cost of such a thing, and if I could get it handsomely tolerably done for £3.[77]

A missal bound in this fashion was supplied to St Giles's, Cheadle, in August 1846. Inspired by the ornaments Pugin had seen on a medieval hymnal in Mainz cathedral, the gilt corner—-pieces incorporate rampant

One of the most elaborate brass lecterns ever designed by Hardman's. With some small modifications, it was made for St. Paul's church, Brighton (by R.C. Carpenter, 1846), where Hardman also provided stained glass to Pugin's design. Undated ink and watercolour, attributed to J.H. Powell.

lions which may be taken as symbolic of St Mark the Evangelist or of the donor, the Earl of Shrewsbury. For St Chad's cathedral, Pugin promised there would be a Gospel-book 'covered with enamels ivory carving & gilt plate – set with stones', while the magnificent medieval lectern would stand in the choir furnished with 'an antiphonarium of noble dimensions heavily bound & clasped in metal'[78] for the use of the cantors. An illuminated copy of Pugin's seminal book, *Contrasts*, was put into this type of binding for presentation to the Pope.[79] Having been disposed of by the Vatican Library in modern times, it has returned to England and is now in a private collection. The Hardman metalwork collection at Lightwoods House includes the cover of a breviary said to have belonged to Pugin himself, and later passed down to members of the Hardman family.

The repair and restoration of medieval metalwork and statuary was yet another activity for which there are sporadic entries in the Hardman metalwork daybooks. In March 1844 the Revd Robert Richmond sent to Hardman a processional cross which had been kept in the Catholic chapel at Blackladies, near

Brass eagle lectern of 1885 (Hardman Collection)

Brewood (Staffs.), with instructions for its repair in readiness for the opening of the new church at Brewood. He describes it as 'a really Catholic one which perhaps has been there since before the Reformation'.[80] Pugin, who had a particular fondness for Brewood, paid for the repainting and gilding of a late-medieval statue of our Lady which currently (2007) stands in the south-east corner of the south aisle, and the provision of a new metal lily and crown to replace the existing damaged ones.[81] At this time Hardman's had at least one specialist painter capable of undertaking this kind of restoration work, which included diapering: a technique whereby parts of a statue – usually items of clothing – were gilded and then coated with the appropriate colour. A point was then used to remove small areas of paint *sgraffito*-fashion, creating intricate patterns with the gold shining through. The artist was Edward Mackay, who was a friend of Pugin, 'professor of painting' at Oscott, and responsible for the painting of statues for Nottingham cathedral and St Mary's, Southport. Hardman's had been using him to carry out fine work of this kind since 1842.[82]

In 1845 Hardman's undertook the repair and regilding of an old enamelled *feretrum*, or shrine made to contain relics of saints, for Lord Midleton,[83] but one of the most important – and best-documented – pieces of restoration work relates to a superb fifteenth-century altar-cross bought by the Earl of Shrewsbury in 1840 from Samuel Pratt, a dealer in antique furniture based in New Bond Street, London. Pugin congratulated the earl

St Mary's, Brewood, Staffs: medieval statue restored by Hardman's in 1844

Prayer-book cover with gilt-metal fittings, c.1840 (Hardman collection)

on his purchase: 'The cross you have secured at Pratt's is so exquisitely Beautiful that it may be considered dirt cheap at the price you gave, it is indeed a glorious acquisition . . . I will get up a pair of candlestis [*sic*] to match.'[84] In his *Dublin Review* article, 'On the present state of ecclesiastical architecture in England' (1842), Pugin describes the cross – having now been given to St John's church, Alton – in some detail:

> The cross is an exquisite specimen of ancient silver work of the fifteenth century, made, as the inscription round the foot relates, by one Peter, for a German bishop, who bore the charge for the love of Christ crucified. This precious relic of Christian art is parcel-gilt, and covered with ornaments and images of wonderful execution.'[85]

St John's church, Alton, it needs to be said, forms part of a complex of buildings designed by Pugin and paid for by Lord Shrewsbury as a revival of the medieval 'hospital' or almshouse, where the poor of the villages of Alton and Farley would receive treatment far superior to that of the parish workhouses set up under the 1834 Poor Law, and in splendidly decorated and furnished buildings little different in style from those in which the earl and his family lived. This social dimension of the Gothic Revival was hugely important to Pugin, and that an altar-cross as magnificent as this medieval one should have been given to a church that was primarily for the poor is typical of both earl and architect.[86] Before it could go to Alton, however, the cross needed repair and restoration at Hardman's, and this is entered to Lord Shrewsbury in the Metalwork daybook at 20 June 1842: 'A Silver Cross regilt & plated – repaired & several parts remade, £15'. In addition to that, Pugin fulfilled his promise to design a pair of candlesticks to match. These are entered at the same date at £35, and Pugin's annotated drawing for them still exists.[87] Made of plated metal set with enamels, the candlesticks have gilt knops designed to match that of the cross, and a Latin text in honour of St John the Baptist, to whom the church is dedicated.

Above: St Giles's, Cheadle: medieval Flemish
corona restored by Hardman's in 1846

Left: St John's, Alton, Staffs: fifteenth-century
altar cross restored by Hardman's, 1840

The medieval *corona* in the chancel at St Giles's, Cheadle, has already been mentioned. The earliest reference to it comes in a letter from Pugin to Hardman written in December 1844: 'The corona for the chancel I shall make out of the old iron one we have got.'[88] Considered to be Flemish, and of fifteenth-century date, the corona needed quite extensive repairs. The entry for it in the Metalwork daybook charges the not inconsiderable sum of £30 to Lord Shrewsbury.[89] The principal expense was no doubt the repair/cutting of the inscription which runs all around the hexagon: a Latin text in honour of the Cross of Christ.[90] Instead of being engraved onto solid metal, as was Pugin's normal practice, the inscription is saw- pierced – a technique sometimes referred to, in respect of lettering, as cut-card work. This made for a much lighter and more delicate result, and the restored corona was described by one contemporary observer as 'one of the most beautiful pieces of church furniture in the country'.[91]

St Giles's may have had the largest array of Hardman metalwork to be seen in any church, but for individually commissioned pieces the London churches outshone all others in terms of elaboration and the use of precious metals. Chief of these is St Mary's, Clapham (1849–51). The architect here was not Pugin, but William Wilkinson Wardell (1823–99), an architect who, like Charles Hansom, was greatly influenced by Pugin and designed churches in the Pugin style.[92] Though Wardell came into the category of architects whose plagiarisms prompted Pugin's comment, 'they steal their brooms ready made', they appear to have been on good terms, and it was for Wardell's church at Clapham that Pugin designed what is arguably his most impressive array of church plate. Some of the entries in the Hardman metalwork daybook are under the name of the Revd F. de Held, the Redemptorist priest of St Mary's, and endorsed 'W.W. Wardell'. They include the most elaborate and expensive monstrance ever made to Pugin's design. Made of silver, parcel-gilt and set with stones, and enriched with tabernacle work, it is entered at £125. A rich silver chalice and paten are entered at £50, and a silver ciborium at £75.[93]

The plate from St Mary's was among the exhibits displayed by Hardman's in the Medieval Court at the Great Exhibition of 1851. The Medieval Court, indeed, was largely the creation of Hardman and Pugin, following upon the success of their earlier contribution to the Birmingham Exposition of Arts and Manufactures held in September 1849. Crace and Minton had played lesser, but significant roles, and Pugin was pleased with the way in which the exhibition had apparently succeeded in advancing the Gothic/Catholic cause. 'It has been very hard work for many years,' he wrote, 'but it will repay all the toil. our exposition at Birmingham was very creditable, has attracted a deal of attention & done much good'.[94] Among those whose attention was so drawn was Henry Cole (1808–82), the design theorist and later first director of the South Kensington Museum. His report on the Exposition in the *Journal of Design and Manufactures* included a description and illustrations of Hardman's display, and a handsome tribute to Pugin's 'wonderfully versatile ability'.[95] Cole was a member of the organising committee of the Exhibition of Ancient and Medieval Art held at the Society of Arts in 1850 and for which Pugin loaned objects from his collection of antiquities, and – significantly – he was a key figure in the organisation of the Great Exhibition.

Three members of Pugin's group – Crace, Hardman and Minton– contributed separately to the Great Exhibition under the various specialist headings into which the work was classified; but they also pressed for a joint exhibit in which they – along with George Myers (stonecarving) – would be able to show the complete range of Gothic art, both ecclesiastical and domestic, and – possibly through the influence of Henry Cole – they secured a prime location for what was to be known as 'The Medieval Court'. Having visited the site for the first time in January 1851, Pugin was none too impressed with the Crystal Palace itself, describing it as the *Vert Monstre* and 'a beastly place to show off Gothic work',[96] but over the next few weeks he busied himself with arranging the decoration of the Court and the planning of displays. A member of Hardman's staff, Thomas Earley, was permanently based in London from March onwards and sent regular reports back to Birmingham. Earley was particularly proud to note that during a preview visit by Queen Victoria on 15 April he, 'a Dirty painter', had been privileged to hold conversation with her for some five minutes.[97] The Queen visited the Medieval Court again on 7 May, when 'she much admired all the things' and particularly a large *corona lucis* which was among several items being made by Hardman's for Sidney Herbert's new church at Wilton.[98]

The Wilton corona was one of many pieces of previously commissioned work which Hardman had to borrow or withhold for the Exhibition. Other coronae were loaned by the Earl of Shrewsbury along with items of plate intended for Alton Towers. Then there was the altar ensemble and lectern from Erdington, the lectern and candlesticks from the chapel of Jesus College, Cambridge, and the newly-made chalice, ciborium and monstrance for St Mary's, Clapham. Pugin himself loaned many metalwork items from his house and church at Ramsgate,[99] and an iron candle-stand from the Lady-chapel at Ramsgate received particular praise in the Juries' reports as 'a most elaborate piece of ironwork worthy of the ancient smiths – a striking proof that our operations when under proper directions are quite capable of representing the most beautiful works of medieval skill'.[100] As a comment on the success of their intention to revive 'the Real Thing', Pugin and Hardman could have desired no higher praise.

Other Hardman exhibits were made specifically for the Exhibition, or taken from stock, and these were either returned to the showroom afterwards or sold. A set of six silver candlesticks with twisted stems and set with crystals were displayed on the altar carved by George Myers for the new church at Pantasaph (Clwyd). These were returned to Hardman's and were known thereafter as 'the Exhibition candlesticks'.[101] Henry Cole purchased two silver chalices and some floriated branched candlesticks for the South Kensington Museum.[102] The Pugin/Hardman revival of monumental brasses was exemplified by a sample memorial made specifically for the Exhibition, depicting a priest in full vestments under a triple canopy. The 'Exhibition Brass', as it became known, was eventually used to commemorate an early – and sometimes underestimated – supporter of the Gothic Revival, Bishop John Milner (d.1826) in the church where he was buried: SS Peter & Paul, Wolverhampton. Every aspect of church furnishings and fittings was shown, including a cabinet filled with vestments made no doubt by Lucy Powell.

In addition to metalwork goods exhibited in their own right, Hardman's work was seen elsewhere in the Medieval Court as part of composite items. These included hinges, handles, escutcheons and sconces for Crace's Gothic furniture, also the metalwork parts of the Great Stove and the jardinières, all of which incorporated Minton's tiles[103] and the jewelled and enamelled brass tabernacle set into Myers' soaring stonework canopy.[104]

It is estimated the over six million people visited the Great Exhibition, and the event was widely reported. The Medieval Court covered 560 square feet of floor-space, and 1,360 feet of wall-space, the latter being used to display fabrics and wallcoverings, with panels of stained glass arranged along the whole of the north wall. Even so, the *Illustrated London News* expressed regret that 'the court is not twice as big as it is' because the sheer quantity of goods displayed meant that they were somewhat crowded together.[105] A few months later the *Illustrated London News* carried a full-page engraving, and a detailed description of the exhibits prefaced by a handsome tribute to Pugin as the overall designer:

> To Mr. Pugin, then who furnished the design for this gorgeous combination, is the highest honour due; and he has marvellously fulfilled his own intention of demonstrating the applicability of Mediaeval art in all its richness and variety to the uses of the present day.[106]

The scene was also captured in colour in Dickenson's *Views of the Great Exhibition*, and Matthew Digby Wyatt's *The Industrial Arts of the XIX Century* (London 1853) includes chromolithographs of the Pantasaph altar, the Great Stove and Jane Pugin's *parure* of jewellery. Thus the influence of the Medieval Court on the design and manufacture of Gothic art extended well beyond the duration of the Exhibition, and although Pugin died within a year of its closure, the medieval style in both ecclesiastical and domestic wares continued to gather momentum, and principally through the firm with which Pugin had been most intimately associated, namely Hardman & Co.

3. PUGIN'S GLASSPAINTER

Glasspainting in Birmingham appears to have commenced in 1784 when Francis Eginton (1737–1805) set up a workshop in Soho where he produced some notable glass including windows for Lichfield and Salisbury cathedrals, for St George's chapel, Windsor, and for William Beckford's celebrated Gothic mansion, Fonthill Abbey (Wilts.). There was also the firm of F. & C. Pemberton, and the large glass-manufacturing firm of Chance Bros. & Co. also had a painting department. None of these, however, carried out glasspainting in the true medieval manner which respected the vertical divisions and the tracery heads of windows, and had a distinctive style of figure-work. Instead the 'painterly' style had been adopted, whereby the whole expanse of the window was treated as a single canvas and figure-work was executed in the manner of the portrait-painters of the period, sometimes on large rectangular sheets of glass fitted together in an iron grid. Medieval stained glass, on the other hand, was of the 'mosaic' kind, consisting of many pieces of glass of various shapes and sizes held together by lead 'cames' which themselves contributed to the overall design of the window. There was also the question of the materials used, the thickness and texture of the glass, and the correct colours.

Eighteenth-century 'gothick' did at least rekindle an enthusiasm for the art of stained glass which had largely died out in England after the Reformation but it was the Victorian Gothic Revival which created a new demand for stained glass in the true medieval style, based upon scholarly research and the study of surviving examples. Amongst those who attempted, with some success, to effect a revival was Thomas Willement (1786–1871), followed closely by William Warrington (1796–1869) and William Wailes (1808–81), all of whom were used by Pugin to paint glass to his designs, and were important and influential figures in the Revival.[1] As far as Pugin was concerned, however, none of them was entirely satisfactory. 'The Glass painters will shorten my days,' he told Lord Shrewsbury; 'they are the greatest plagues I have.'[2]

The first hint that Hardman might add stained glass to his range of products came from Pugin himself. In the middle of February 1845 he wrote to Hardman, 'I have some great schemes in my head which I will tell you by & bye. it does me good to scheme. I am scheming a stained glass shop – but this only between ourselves.'[3] There are no more references to the project in the Pugin–Hardman correspondence until the end of September 1845, but John Hardman Powell recalls that during the summer Hardman enlisted the services of two sons of Robert Henderson, a glasspainter based in New Street, Birmingham, to assist in the preparation of stains and in the firing of glass in a kiln, or 'muffle'. They brought with them their chief painter, a Mr Hinckley, who had twenty-four years' experience. A kiln was constructed, and 'with two or three boys the work was started'.[4] According to Powell, Pugin's main reason for turning to Hardman was that he was 'wishful to have his glass executed more immediately under his own care, and the direction of one whose views for the progress of mediaeval art were entirely in accordance with his own'.[5] Given the close personal friendship that existed between them, the undoubted success of their metalworking enterprise, Hardman's shrewd business sense and Pugin's consummate skill as a designer, the venture could hardly fail. By February 1846 Pugin was able to write, 'I have quite succeeded in establishing my new manufactory for stained glass at Birmingham, I shall be able to make very fine windows with old thick glass etc. I have already several very large windows in hand.'[6]

Pugin understood stained glass to be an integral part of the overall design of a church interior, and, as with everything else, to have a practical and instructive purpose. Coloured glass complemented the painted decorative work, embroideries and encaustic tiles, and Pugin believed that the softened light admitted through stained glass 'is well calculated to awaken those emotions and thoughts, in the hearts and minds of the worshippers, which they should feel and entertain, when within the temples, and before the altars of God'.[7] With its depictions of Biblical scenes and figures of saints, stained glass was needed no less in the nineteenth century than it had been in the fourteenth, for as Pugin observed, 'while the children of this enlightened age are ignorant of the very saint by whom their country was converted to the Christian faith, they are well versed in the legends of Mother Hubbard, and Puss in Boots!'[8]

As with medieval metalworking techniques, the revival of glasspainting meant the recovery of a long-lost art. Pugin's scholarship was of paramount importance. He travelled widely in England and Europe seeking 'authorities', as he called them, in the shape of surviving medieval glass of various periods, noting not only the design of the figure-work and ornament, but also the colours and textures of the glass, and the details of leading. He also acquired many samples of old glass for glassmakers and glasspainters to study. Pugin's aim was not so much to make reproductions of medieval windows as to create new work on the same principles, taking advantage – as was the case with Pugin's ceramic and textile designs – of new materials and the advances in botanical and anatomical knowledge which had taken place in the post-medieval period. With regard to Pugin's understanding and use of colour, John Hardman Powell judged that,

> As a colourist he was supreme, not only for splendour and contrast, but on his knowledge of the juxtaposition of tones, and subtle harmonies, which even the old Artists, excepting those of the Renaissance, might have envied. Seeing the glamour produced by time in ancient Glass and that simple imitation would be crude he did not wait for this effect to come as a mere antiquary might but varied the whites and introduced transition tones, like a Genius. He always wrote himself the colouring of windows on the cartoons knowing that their chief excellence or defect must lie there.[9]

The ultimate source-book for Pugin – with glass as with other aspects of Gothic art – was always nature, and this applied to both figure-work and ornament. '*The first productions of Christian art*', he wrote in 1845, '*are the closest approximations to nature, and when they failed in proportion or anatomy, it was not a defect of principle, but of execution.*'[10] This letter, addressed to the painter J.R. Herbert, who was a master at the London School of Design, also makes the point that instead of being a mere drawing school, such an institution should train operatives in the use of the various materials: 'artist smiths in silver and iron, artist chasers in metal, artist glasspainters . . .'[11]

The processes involved in the making of a stained-glass window are complex, but they remain substantially the same as they were in Pugin's day, and most of them derive ultimately from established medieval practice. Once the subject-matter of the window has been decided upon, in consultation with the client, the first stage is the making of a sketch. The speed at which Pugin was able to produce preliminary sketches is legendary. His biographer, Benjamin Ferrey, tells of how he once met a client at St Mary's, Oxford, asked a few questions about the subject-matter of a five-light window for the church, and 'in less than a quarter of an hour made two or three masterly sketches for the subject of the window, to the astonishment of all present'.[12] Once a design has been approved, it is drawn out full-size on the cartoon table, the cartoon then becoming the working drawing.

From the cartoon the cut-line is prepared on a sheet of tracing linen, and it is from this that the individual pieces of mosaic glass are cut to their correct size and shape, allowing sufficient room between the pieces for the heart of the H-sectioned lead cames into which they are eventually to be fitted. Hydrofluoric acid may be used to eat away shapes on flashed[13] glass to reveal white or yellow glass underneath, or to give gradation of colour on pot metal. Abrading with a sharp point produces a similar effect. An enamel paint containing metallic oxide and ground glass is used to paint faces, hands, drapery folds, etc., and the pieces are then fired in a kiln to fuse the paint into the surface of the glass. Building up light and shade may involve several firings, or 'burnings'. A silver compound painted onto glass and fired produces a transparent 'silver stain' which varies in hue from pale yellow to deep orange. Finally, the mosaic pieces are assembled into panels with lead cames, the joints are soldered, and then a prepared liquid cement is rubbed into the leads with a brush. Copper ties are soldered on at intervals for fastening around the saddle-bars fixed to the masonry of the window to help bear the weight of the leaded glass and prevent movement. The panels are then ready to be taken to the building into which the window is to be fitted.

The stained-glass enterprise set up by Pugin and Hardman was split between several locations. Pugin was in sole charge of preparing sketches and drawing cartoons, and this he did from his home at The Grange, Ramsgate. In addition to the Library in which he had his drawing-table, Pugin built a Cartoon Room furnished with the large tables necessary for making working drawings. When finished, these would be sent to Birmingham with all the necessary instructions so that Hardman could oversee the actual production of the windows and their installation. This arrangement was not entirely satisfactory because Pugin was able to see the completed windows only on his sporadic visits to Birmingham or after they had been fixed on site. In 1849 he wrote to Hardman:

> Our great disadvantage is my never seeing the work in progress. I make the cartoons & that is all. but I am sure the old men [i.e. the medieval glassmakers] watched everything & I predict that we shall never produce anything very good until the furnaces are within a few yards of the easel.[14]

On his own admission, Pugin was 'such a Locomotive being always flyin about'[15] that he was never for long in any one place, as his diaries bear witness. Ramsgate was, however, the base where most of his drawing was done, and his diaries and his letter-headings testify to longer periods of time spent there from 1847, the year in which he began to build the church of St Augustine next door to the Grange. Visits to Birmingham averaged at about five per year, and Hardman visited the Grange from time to time. The thousand and more letters which passed between Pugin and Hardman fill in some of the gaps: they 'became as brothers', comments Powell,[16] who is the prime source of information about the Ramsgate end of the stained-glass operation.

By the time the cartoon room was finished, Powell had been living at the Grange for several months, and in the early stages of his apprenticeship had been assisting Pugin with metalwork drawings and the making of wax models. His habit of sleepwalking, and the drunken antics of Pugin's domestic chaplain, Dr Luigi Acquarone, meant that the atmosphere at the Grange was not always conducive to a good night's rest. 'Between him and the Dr. there is no rest', Pugin complained to Hardman, '& I shall be obliged to *go Out* to sleep at last!!!'[17]

Powell appears to have assisted Pugin with cartoons from the beginning of the stained-glass venture, and although there were some occasional lapses, he learned quickly from his master. In the summer of 1845 Pugin was confident enough to leave him in virtual charge at the Grange while on visits to various locations in England and Ireland, and on his return told Hardman that 'since I left he has worked very well & on an improved scale. his drawing of St Eligius for the Sign will be sent off tomorrow'.[18] By 1850 Powell had progressed so well that Pugin was convinced that he would be 'a sterling example of what an artist can be without going through the academy process . . . he deserves *every encouragement.* in a short time he will be an excellent artist'.[19]

In addition to Powell there was Edward (1834–75), Pugin's eldest son by his second marriage, and only eleven years old when the stained-glass operation began. He too was gradually drawn into the business, first of all by filling in cut-lines and assisting Powell with the more mechanical parts of cartooning, and then moving on to drawing, all of course under the demanding supervision of his father, who by 1851 was able to tell Hardman that Edward 'will soon become one of our best figure painters, he is now doing the groups for alteration that is putting them in sepia & if you examine them you will see what I say is true'.[20]

As the volume of work increased, Pugin needed more assistance in the cartoon room, and he asked Hardman to send from Birmingham any young men whom he considered to be sufficiently talented. Among these were Edwin Hendren, Frederick Hill and Thomas Earley, the latter having worked for Hardman as a painter and decorator. It happened that they all had good voices, and so were drawn into St Augustine's choir.[21] After some initial difficulties, Hill became a competent cartoonist. Pugin was at first impressed with Earley's work but later found him to be lacking in discipline and given to larking about, and so concluded that 'the atmosphere of Birmingham would be more congenial to him'.[22] Hendren proved to be the most successful, initially as an assistant to Powell, then playing a larger role after Pugin's death. He is named as the cartoon maker in the glassworkers' window (1853) at St Chad's, Birmingham, and he continued to work for Hardman's until his death in 1894.

Others who came to work for Pugin at Ramsgate included Enrico Casolani, a pupil of the Nazarene painter J.F. Overbeck (1789–1869) and 'a most distinguished Christian artist',[23] and there was Francis Oliphant (1818–59) who had been principal designer at William Wailes's glassworks in Newcastle upon Tyne and was probably therefore already known to Pugin before he began working on his own in London. As an experienced artist and cartoonist, Oliphant was able to negotiate his own terms of employment, and he remained for the most part in London: an unsatisfactory arrangement because Pugin was unable to supervise the drawings

Edward Hendren, artist at Hardman's for over fifty years (Hardman Collection)

Detail of window by William Wailes in the chapel at The Grange, Ramsgate: Edward Pugin as a boy, c.1844

directly. Oliphant was an important figure who worked on some of Pugin's largest and most complex windows, but Pugin also feared that because of the freelance nature of Oliphant's work, his designs might end up in the hands of other window-makers. Pugin always made it clear that he would design for nobody but Hardman, nor would he produce windows to anyone else's design.[24] This underlines the close relationship between Pugin and Hardman, and explains why, in the matter of window design and cartooning, he took a dominant role, and trusted no one fully except Powell and young Edward.

At the Birmingham end of the operation, Hardman bought most of his glass from local sources such as William Perks & Co., Smith and Pearce, and Lloyd & Summerfield, all of Birmingham; then from 1849 James Hartley & Co. of the Wear Glass Works in Sunderland became the principal supplier of glass, and Francis Emery of Cobridge, Stoke-on-Trent, of colour. It is clear, however, from Pugin's letters that he was not content with 'stock' items, and wished to have glass of the quality that the 'ancients' had produced.[25] Medieval glass was thicker and more uneven in texture and colour than that produced by more modern processes, and what in ordinary plate-glass might appear as defects and faults – such as streakiness – were, in the case of antique glass, features which helped to create interest and variety. Much credit is given to the work of Charles Winston (1814–65) in reviving the production of antique glass through systematic experiments, but it is also clear that Pugin and Hardman were experimenting too, in conjunction with Hartley's, and at a somewhat earlier date.[26] In August/September 1849 Pugin spent several days in Paris, Rouen and Évreux specifically to study the technical aspects of ancient glass, which, he confessed to Hardman, he had missed on an earlier (1837) visit because he had had no idea then that he would ever be making glass as well as designing it.[27] While at Évreux he purchased a quantity of old glass for examination, concluding that,

> . . . We have hardly one of the old colours in our glass & I expect we shall have a deal of trouble to get them but at any rate we have now the patterns . . . I have learnt an immense deal this journey . . . if we accomplish the tints we shall be at the very pinnacle of glass painting.[28]

Particular problems lay with the production of ruby glass with the characteristic brilliance and streakiness of its medieval counterpart, and white glass that was semi-opaque. James Hartley acknowledged that the modern system of manufacture, though well suited to the production of large sheets of perfectly smooth and evenly transparent glass, worked against the reproduction of antique glass which needed to be done in small pieces 'as we do our samples, this no doubt is the way the ancient glass was made, every separate piece was a study'.[29]

Hartley's experiments extended to other colours, based on samples sent to him by Hardman, and, prompted by Pugin's expertise and skill as a colourist, he made significant progress. The Birmingham firm of Lloyd & Summerfield also carried out experiments with antique glass, and they received particular praise from John Hardman Powell who, while acknowledging the achievements of Hartley's and of James Powell & Sons of Whitechapel, concluded that 'there are many colours made by our own townsmen that have not been surpassed, if equalled'.[30]

The first glass produced commercially by Hardman's is entered into the Glass Daybook at 24 November 1845, and was for St Cuthbert's College, Ushaw (Durham), the

St Cuthbert's College, Ushaw: west window, 1847 (photo: Graham Miller)

Catholic seminary for the Northern District. Pugin designed many of the buildings at Ushaw, notably the chapel which was in the Decorated style. The first Hardman glass consisted of small windows for the cloisters, and these were soon followed by large commissions for the chapel itself, the library and the refectory. Though Pugin's chapel was replaced in 1882–5 with a larger one by Dunn and Hansom, the glass was re-used, with the east and west windows being transposed. The (present) east window of five lights contains scenes from the life of St Cuthbert. Pugin was particularly delighted with the (present) seven-light west window which represents the Triumph of the Church, although problems were encountered in the cartooning stage when Pugin, severely plagued by eye problems early in 1847, entrusted some of the work to Oliphant with unfortunate results: 'Oliphant has been painting a lot of things & he sketched in while I was blind – *vile* they must all be torn up – I never saw anything like it. this is the 3rd time portions of the East window at Ushaw have been drawn.'[31] Later in the year, however, he was able to tell Hardman, 'The East window for Ushaw is nearly finished. The finest work of modern time & so you will say.'[32] The window was all in place by the end of September 1847, and Thomas Earley's letter to Hardman illustrates both the hazards and the delights of working in stained glass.

> 4 out of the 7 lights Ushaw East Window are 2 inches too long. Pugin has been here today, he has devised a remedy for the glass – I had the whole of the East Window in for him to see. it has a glorious effect he is much pleased with it . . . it came here without a single crack which is something extraordinary in so large a quantity of Glass.[33]

Somewhat different in character, but equally important for Hardman's, was the glass begun in December 1845 for the Anglican parish church of St Mary, Wymeswold (Leicestershire) which Pugin was restoring for its ecclesiologically-minded vicar, the Revd Henry Alford. Described as 'the first of the old parish churches to be restored upon Catholic lines with return-stalls and a chancel screen',[34] Wymeswold was one of Pugin's most significant Anglican commissions to which Hardman's contributed quantities of metalwork as well as stained glass.[35] The Wymeswold glass marks Pugin's transition from Wailes to Hardman. The east and west windows are by Wailes, the east window containing figures of apostles and evangelists under canopies. The first Hardman glass was installed towards the end of 1845 and consists of a three-light window on the south side of the baptistery, with patterned quarries, coloured ornament and and *agnus dei* in a roundel in the centre light. The east window of the north aisle, by Hardman (1848), has the Nativity in the centre.[36] The Ascension window in the south aisle was commissioned in 1853 as a tribute to Henry Alford when he left the parish, though possibly to an earlier design by Pugin, and completed by John Hardman Powell who appears to have been involved with the Wymeswold glass from the outset. Ornamented quarries and coloured

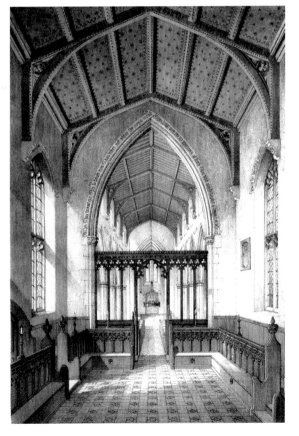

St Mary's, Wymeswold: print of c.1848 showing interior as restored by Pugin (History and Description of the Restored Parish Church of Saint Mary, Wymeswold)

St Mary's, Wymeswold: the Baptistery window 1845 (JHAL)

St Augustine's, Ramsgate: Lady chapel window (photo: Graham Miller)

traceries by Hardman appear in other windows. Some of the glass has recently (2004) been restored at the John Hardman Studio.

A characteristic of Pugin's glass as made by Hardman is the judicious use of white glass to give brilliance and sparkle to a window, rather than the unrelieved use of colour which tended to make some of Wailes's windows somewhat dark and subdued. Pugin was aware of this in 1841 when he was discussing glass with Lord Shrewsbury: '. . . I still maintain that some portion of *white* is *necessary* to *give value to the rest.* are not all pictures tested as regards tone & colour by a piece of white paper. there is no antient sample without some particles of white glass.'[37] Two years or so after setting up with Hardman, he was still not satisfied:

> . . . I am burning to produce something sparkling and brilliant, all our work is dead & heavy. We have not yet done a *brilliant* window. I am sure it can be done. I shall come back by Birmingham. I think of nothing else.[38]

Pugin and Hardman achieved the desired effect by working white glass into the canopy-work over figures of saints, thereby introducing brightness into the upper part of a window. White was also introduced into the borders of lights, and used to frame groups of figures in geometrical medallions. In the Lady chapel at St Augustine's, Ramsgate, the two south windows have geometrical panels set within white quarries patterned with yellow silver stain, two panels to each light, and with red fillet diamond shapes linking the panels. Within the panels are groups of figures depicting scenes from the Life of the Blessed Virgin Mary. Pugin was delighted with them and wrote to Hardman:

. . . These side windows look to me most brilliant . . . the effect is quite changed. I am sorry to say that our people don't feel it but I am sure they are far better than all images under canopies they increase the size of the window & are a splendid contribution to the church for which you deserve my humble recognition. Jane is delighted like me with them . . . the tone of the Lady chapel is 3 times as good.[39]

On a larger scale, a particularly fine example of the use of white glass by Pugin and Hardman is the west window of Hansom's church at Erdington: a five-light composition in which scenes from the Life of Christ are framed on twenty geometrical medallions formed by fillets of white glass which, above and below the medallions, become the stems for vine leaves and grapes. The borders are also edged with white, and contain white rosettes. Pugin was well aware of the effects produced by the setting sun on west-facing windows, including the reflection cast upon the church floor,[40] and the Erdington window, with its lines of white glass tracing a flickering light across the whole composition 'must surely have satisfied Pugin's longing for something sparkling and brilliant'.[41]

In praising Pugin's revival of the true principles of glasspainting, the High-Victorian architect George Edmund Street (1824–81) singled out the use of white as contributing to the brilliance of Hardman's windows, referring in particular to white edges to glass next to stone, the increased amount of white used towards the head of a window and in making canopies for figures, and the use of white foliage.[42] In the light of experience, some of Pugin's earlier windows were modified by the removal of coloured backgrounds and the insertion of white glass, for example at St Giles's, Cheadle.

Too much white glass, however, could spoil the intended effect. This was the case with a four-light window installed by Hardman's in 1850 in the south choir aisle of Chester cathedral. It was situated next to a rather dark Wailes window on the sunny side of the church, and although the pictorial parts were commended, the dominance of white glass in the upper part of the window was criticised because it 'gives a glaring effect to the whole which takes the attention off the pictorial representations & kills them as we say'.[43] Pugin's solution in such circumstances was to use grisaille rather than white. Grisaille consists of a monochrome patterned glass, the background being somewhat greyish, although the tones can vary according to the location of the window. Continental grisaille incorporated interlacing geometrical shapes in the form of fillets of coloured glass enclosing areas of patterned grisaille. Pugin acknowledged that 'the grisaille is miserable . . . we don't do it half strong enough'. His solution was, as ever, to refer back to medieval examples, and he proposed to send Powell 'to study the foliage &c from old thyings *real size* with the *real strength of line* that the old men used'.[44]

If the judicious use of white glass and grisaille to enhance – or to tone down – the brilliance of a window was a characteristic of Hardman's glass, another was their style of figure-painting. In Pugin's preferred period – the fourteenth century – human figures were depicted in their natural proportions, characteristically S-shaped rather than standing stiffly, and with the appropriate garments falling naturally into folds. In this respect Hardman's windows are different from those made by Wailes and the contrast is seen, for example, at Wymeswold where figures of saints in Wailes's east window stand almost to attention, whereas those in the Nativity window (by Hardman) in the south aisle are much more natural. In working with Hardman, Pugin was of course able to keep all of the design work and the cartooning under his personal control, which had not been possible with Wailes. The Nativity window also shows Pugin veering towards perspective in the way he thrusts the crib into the foreground. Elsewhere the depiction of vaulted interiors in canopy-work also contributes to a three-dimensional effect which was a feature of later fourteenth-century glass.

Much as Pugin preferred the Decorated style, in windows as in all other aspects of Gothic design, he had to design in the earlier and later styles both for his own buildings and for other architects. The early style, typified

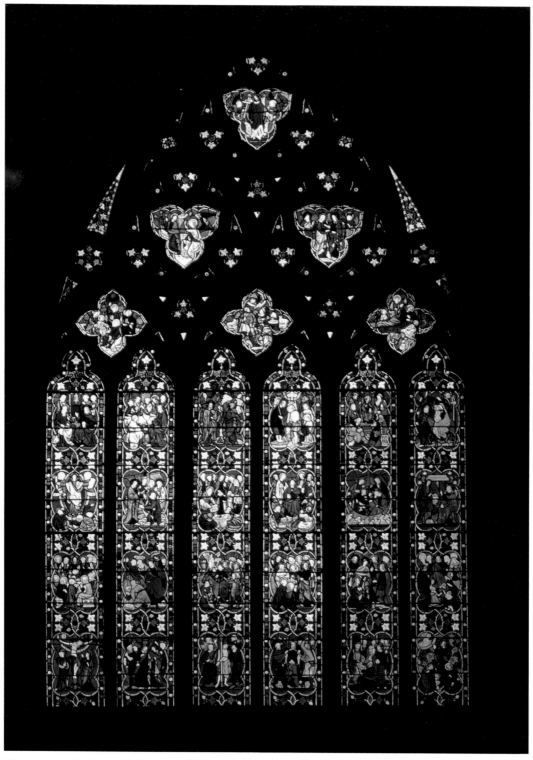

West window, Erdington Abbey; note the use of white glass to give the sparkle that is missing from the Ushaw glass (photo: Graham Miller)

by the glass at Chartres cathedral, is characterised by deep glowing colours and more austere figures than those of later glass. The later style was designed to go into the large rectangular spaces characteristic of the Perpendicular style, seen for example in the chapel of King's College, Cambridge. It is lighter in tone, with less ornament and colour but an increased use of white glass and yellow silver stain, and figure-work becomes more pictorial. Pugin, who in any case came to regard the Perpendicular style as debased, considered that the preponderance of white and yellow glass in late English windows made them pale and weak, and 'vastly inferior to the rich and brilliant colouring which preceded'.[45]

Pugin's and Hardman's essays into the field of early and late glass are well exemplified by work carried out in 1850 in the chapels of Jesus and Magdalene Colleges, Cambridge, including, in either case, glass for the east window. The difference in style of the two windows could not be greater. Jesus chapel has, for its east window, a triplet of lancets with a cinquefoil rose above, whereas the east window of Magdalene is five-light Perpendicular. Pugin and Hardman were therefore obliged to move out of their preferred *milieu* of fourteenth- and fifteenth-century styles to embrace early and late glass, and to do so simultaneously. The learning process is reflected in the correspondence about these windows, and it makes the Cambridge glass commissions particularly interesting and important in the history of the Pugin–Hardman partnership.

Jesus College Chapel was restored by Pugin in 1845–9. The commission came about through John Sutton, a graduate of Jesus College and a member of the Camden Society,[46] and it was he who instigated the glazing of the east window in the appropriate style. The challenge of working competently in the early style caused Pugin some anxiety, the more so since the Parisian brothers, Alfred and Henri Gérente, had already carried out some outstanding commissions in this style in England, including glass for Ely cathedral, only twelve miles from Cambridge. 'I am terribly anxious about Cambridge,' he told Hardman, 'for if that is not very good we shall have all the critics down on us.'[47] Pugin visited Paris, Chartres and Rouen in August 1849 to study early glass, and he reported to Sutton,

> I have just returned from Chartres where I have been for the express purpose of examining the early windows for your chapel & I have not only got most accurate details but actually a lot of the real glass from a glazier – & Mr. Hardman is going to match the tints exactly so I have every expectation of providing the *real thing*.[48]

As eventually executed, the lancets contained representations of the Passion of Christ contained in circular medallions– five per light – set into a background of foliage designs on a red ground. Though Pugin was pleased when he heard how well the windows had been received by the College, he was less happy after he had been to see them for himself: 'The windows are very disappointing . . . they don't look as if there was a powerful colour in them. Our ornament is too faintly painted.'[49] Even so, ten more lancets to Pugin's design were installed in the chapel – most of them posthumously – between 1852 and 1858.

Pugin's work in the chapel of Magdalene College was confined to the east window, and it was done in 1850–51. The design could not be more different from the windows at Jesus. It is in the true Late style, with figures, or scenes with figures, under tall canopies, and most are related to the life of St Mary Magdalene. As with early glass, it was necessary to seek the appropriate 'authorities' for colour and design, so Pugin suggested to Hardman that they should look at medieval examples, and especially those at St Mary's, Fairford, Gloucestershire, a fine late-medieval church with a complete set of original windows dating from c.1500:

> . . . I should like to go to Fairford with you for that is a fine specimen of Later glass just what we want for Magdalene College Cambridge. I want to make a fine window but I don't *see my way yet*. Our late glass is not either drawn or painted like the old work.[50]

Pugin entrusted the cartooning to Francis Oliphant. Since the figures in the Fairford windows are reminiscent of early Netherlandish painting, Pugin told him to work close to the Van Eyck School, and was pleased with the result: 'I have knocked on fine job out of Oliphant at last the St Mary Magdalene window for Cambridge.'[51] Following the installation of the window, the donor wrote to Hardman: 'I need hardly add that your window gives universal satisfaction to all who come to see, I only wish I could persuade the College to put painted glass into the other windows.'[52]

Pugin seems to have had doubts about taking the Late style further by following the 'painterly' tendencies of early-sixteenth-century glass as shown, for example in the west window at Fairford where the Last Judgement is painted right across the seven lights without any regard to the divisions created by the mullions and tracery. Not even the windows at King's College, Cambridge, convinced him that this was the right way to go, and he expressed his reservations to Hardman: '. . . don't talk about *beating* Kings yet. There is a long way to go but this late glass is in reallity [*sic*] a false system and the decline of the art.'[53]

The east window at St Andrew's church, Farnham (Surrey) represents one of the most ambitious Pugin/Hardman excursions into late-medieval glass. Each of the five lights contains two scenes, one above the other, from the life of Christ, all involving groups of figures set under very elaborate canopies. Oliphant was once again involved with the cartooning, and the correspondence about this commission highlights the problems created by different aspects of the work being carried out in three separate places: Ramsgate, London and Birmingham. Pugin was particularly annoyed at the failure of Hardman's painters to interpret correctly his detailed drawings and the cartoons:

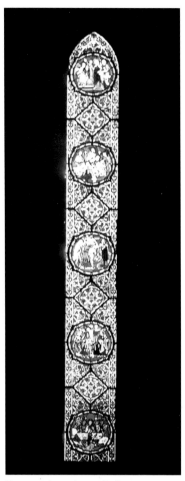

East window, Jesus College, Cambridge (photo: Graham Miller)

. . . The Farnham light is diabolical disgraceful . . . It is a most infamous careless *caricature* of the *cartoons* & all painted with *black* instead of *brown shadows* whish I have begged & prayed for but nobody in the place has the remotest idea of Late work . . . My dear Hardman if you dont turn over a new leaf about Late work the jobs may be given up at once . . . you ought to put down so much for me to come here once a week – where Late work is about for even you do not understand.[54]

When completed and installed, however, the Farnham window received especial praise from the Bishop of Winchester, Charles Sumner, who stated openly that 'he had seen no windows in England and very few on the Continent which he thought superior'.[55]

The windows at Farnham and the Cambridge colleges were, of course, Anglican commissions, and they are indicative of the progress of the Gothic Revival within the Church of England under the influence of the Cambridge Camden Society and the Oxford Society for Promoting the Study of Gothic Architecture. As early as 1847 Pugin commented, 'an Anglican job of course', when informing Hardman that he had just secured an order for over £4,000 worth of glass for a single church.[56] This comment serves as a reminder that although Hardman's earlier work in stained glass had been mainly for Catholic churches of which Pugin was the architect, Pugin received few new architectural commissions after the opening of St Giles's, Cheadle, in

East window, St Andrew's, Farnham, Surrey (photo: Graham Miller)

Sherborne Abbey, detail of the former west window (photo: Chris Singleton, Eyecatchers Photography)

1846. Other Catholic architects – Charles Hansom and William Wardell, for example – turned to Hardman's for glass, but the growing reputation of the firm, the spread of ecclesiology, and the fact that the Established Church had an abundance of wealthy patrons, stimulated the demand for Hardman windows among Anglican churchmen. That Hardman's were a Catholic firm working to the designs of a Catholic architect seems in itself to have been unimportant, but there were one or two instances of misunderstandings over subject-matter. Early in 1851 the anti-Tractarian Bishop of Manchester, James Prince Lee, objected to a new window in St John's church, Broughton, within his diocese, because it included a representation of the Blessed Virgin Mary wearing a crown. Such things, the Bishop believed, were symptomatic of a 'Romanising' tendency within the Church of England. Pugin refused to remove the crown, contending that his reasons were artistic rather than theological, and expressing regret that 'such very immaterial details (are) made the subject of grave and ever acrimonious dispute'.[57] The crown remained unaltered.

Hardman's were favoured by the vanguard of Anglo-Catholic clergy such as the Revd Arthur Wagner, and by Anglican architects such as Richard Carpenter (1812–55), the so-called 'Anglican Pugin'.[58] Hardman's made the seven-light east window for Carpenter's best-known London church, St Mary Magdalen, Munster Square, and a set of eighteen windows for St Paul's, Brighton, also by Carpenter, and of which Wagner was vicar. The set included a seven-light 'Jesse' window at the east end, other windows being filled with figures of apostles, evangelists and English saints.

Among Pugin's later windows were the south transept window and the west window at Sherborne Abbey (Dorset), where Carpenter was carrying out extensive restoration work. The theme of the eight-light transept window is the hymn *Te Deum Laudamus*, and it is made up of figures of kings, queens, bishop, abbots, saints and prophets arranged in pairs. The west window had been altered by Carpenter by the insertion of transoms which divided the former nine-light arrangement into one of twenty-seven lights arranged in three tiers. The Perpendicular character of the window demanded glass in the Late style, but the available space would not allow for both canopies and well-proportioned figures, so canopies were abandoned, and Pugin filled each of the lights with a single standing figure of an Old Testament patriarch or prophet. The omission of canopies also meant that Pugin could introduce more colour than would normally have been the case with a Late window. The window was installed in the summer of 1851, and both Pugin and Carpenter were pleased with the result.[59] It was removed from the abbey in 1995 to make way for new glass, the proponents of the change having displayed pitiful ignorance of Pugin's role in its creation, and of its significance in Pugin's adaptation of the Late style to a particular circumstance.

The restoration of the very large church of St Mary's, Beverley (Humberside), was a project upon which Pugin was engaged intermittently from 1841 to the end of his life, and this included the design of the big west window, consisting of fourteen lights and tracery. The subject-matter is Christ in glory and the Blessed Virgin Mary, surrounded by figures of apostles. Powell and Oliphant did the cartooning, and the window is entered into the daybook on 25 June 1850 at £300.[60] Another important restoration scheme was that of the former collegiate church of Ottery St Mary (Devon), undertaken in 1849–50 by William Butterfield, largely at the expense of John Duke Coleridge. Butterfield turned to Hardman for the glass, which included lancets in the Early style, a set of twelve clerestories, and an eight-light east window. Though Pugin was responsible for most of the design-work, the commission was not fully completed until after his death.[60]

The Catholic Church did, of course, have some wealthy patrons who were willing to pay for stained-glass windows from Hardman's. Among them was Charles Scott-Murray (1818–82), for whom a private chapel was built at Danesfield (Bucks.).[61] Close to Danesfield is the town of Marlow where Scott-Murray commissioned Pugin to build a small but important church, St Peter's, in 1847. It included a full set of nine windows, most of which contain figures of saints executed in the Decorated style with pronounced 'S' curves, although the small size of the windows did not allow for canopies.[62]

In addition to the ecclesiastical commissions, Pugin and Hardman designed and made glass for a number of secular buildings. Chief of these was the New Palace of Westminster where they began in 1846; also great houses such as Alton Towers (Staffordshire), Bilton Grange (Warwickshire) and Chirk Castle (Clwyd), where the work was mainly heraldic in character.[63] None of these was complete at the time of Pugin's death in 1852, and the work had then to be taken over by others such as John Hardman Powell and Edward Pugin. The same applied to Grace Dieu, the Leicestershire home of Ambrose Phillipps de Lisle, for whom Pugin had dreamt of creating a vast country mansion in the 'correct' Gothic mode. He had to be content with relatively modest additions to the existing house and chapel. In 1848–9 the chapel was given a north aisle by Pugin, and stained glass began to appear in the principal windows. Two windows on the north side of the chapel bear the dates 1848 and 1849, although the Glass Daybook shows that they were not completed until 1853. One of them is Eucharistic in character, with representations of the Last Supper and its Old Testament prefigurements. The inscription records that it was given in 1849 by the Hon. Edward Petre, another of the Phillipps' Catholic friends. The other, depicting St Elizabeth of Hungary, has an inscription asking prayers for the donor, Maria, countess of Shrewsbury. Though dated 1848, the inscription describes the countess as 'widow of John XVII Earl of Shrewsbury'. She did not become a widow until November 1852, and her husband was the sixteenth, not the seventeenth, earl. Such errors would surely not have passed unnoticed had Pugin still been alive at the time, and one wonders why Phillipps allowed them to remain uncorrected. A set of four two-light windows on the north side of the chapel were given by Phillipps in memory of Earl John, who was a close personal friend.[64] They are entered into the Daybook at 24 October 1853. The inscription below gives the date of Lord Shrewsbury's death correctly as 9 November 1852, and the order-book entry includes the instruction, 'These windows should be extremely dark Red and Blue'. They have, in fact, retained their colours rather better than

Grace Dieu Chapel, south aisle window

the St Elizabeth window on the south side, which is now badly faded in places, and the windows are almost the only survivors of a drastic 're-ordering' of the chapel in the 1960s when the rest of Pugin's furnishings, including the altar, reredos, pulpit, picture-frames and brass *coronae* were disposed of or destroyed.

Another late Leicestershire commission, and an important one, was a set of ten windows for the new parish church of St James, Great Dalby, near Melton Mowbray. The architect was Raphael Brandon (1817–77) a member of the Ecclesiological Society, although the correspondence about the windows was between Hardman's and the brothers E.H. and J.R. Hartopp, who were the principal benefactors. The documentation shows that Pugin was responsible for the designs, and made some alterations at the request of the clients, but the work was not completed until 1853, the year after his death.[65]

Towards the end of 1851, Pugin's health began to break down at an alarming rate. The years of stress and overwork were taking their toll, and members of the family were warned by his doctor, James Daniel, of the likely outcome.[66] Pugin's letters to Hardman at this time reflect his rapidly deteriorating condition, his desperate state of mind and feelings of worthlessness:

I have had a very bad day, the worst I have had for some time. so drowsy as to be falling asleep frequently during the day. all Daniels comfort is that I am an Example of a man who has lived 60 years in 40 & is now suffering for it[67]

. . . I am a wretched unhappy man I have no strength myself & everybody ill around me – & obliged to work. There is nothing worth doing.[68]

While in London in February 1852, Pugin a suffered a complete mental breakdown. John Hardman was among the close circle of friends who attended to him during his confinement at Kensington House, a private asylum. Meanwhile the cartoon room at Ramsgate closed, and Edward Pugin along with the Powells, Edwin Hendren and the other Hardman employees, returned to Birmingham to run the stained-glass operation from the studios, leaving Jane and the younger Pugin children at the Grange, to which Pugin was eventually able to return for the final weeks of his life.[69] During a rare lucid spell he made his last known architectural drawing: a perfectly executed design for a weathervane for the tower of St Mary's church, Beverley. He died on 14 September 1852, and was buried in the chantry which he had designed for himself in the south transept of St Augustine's, Ramsgate. John Hardman was among the cantors who sang the Offices for the Dead on the eve of the funeral.

Pugin's illness and death caused no abatement in the output or the demand for stained glass in the Pugin style. Throughout 1852 and for most of 1853 work designed personally by him was still in the various stages of production, with Powell in control of the cartooning. This included a very large east window for the chapel of Trinity College, Glenalmond, Scotland, begun in 1851 but not completed until January 1853. The architect, Alfred Barry, wrote to Pugin to express his concern at the lack of progress:

> I wrote to Hardman some months ago about a design for glass for an E. window which he was to finish. I have heard nothing of it & knowing unfortunately that you are far from well . . . I did not like to press for it . . . I should be loath to have the window which is very large & which will determine the effect of the whole Chapel spoilt by being in another hand.[70]

In the event, the window had to be finished 'in another hand', with Barry complaining about the 'grotesque stiffness of drawing . . . which if I am not mistaken I have heard poor Mr. Pugin treat with deserved contempt'.[71]

The final entries in the First Glass Daybook are for the completion of lancets for Jesus College, Cambridge, entered at 31 December 1853, and the east window for Staplefield, Crawley (West Sussex), completed in January 1854. Hardman's letter to the Revd Robert Wilson concerning an error in the costing of the window tells its own sad story:

> . . . I can only suppose that when Mr Pugin wrote the letter which you quote of January 11(1852) he made a mistake & put £80 instead of £100. At the time he was very far from well in fact the fatal malady which carried him off was growing rapidly upon him.[72]

Notwithstanding Pugin's periodic fits of self-criticism and self-doubt, the fact remains that from humble beginnings in the summer of 1845 he and Hardman, within the space of six years, built up a successful stained-glass business, the products of which were admired and sought by architects and private clients all over Britain and beyond. The First Glass Daybook catalogues the early success of the enterprise, with its entries for major churches and cathedrals both Catholic and Anglican, for private houses and for public buildings such as the New Palace of Westminster. The Great Exhibition of 1851 was another *coup*, Hardman being the only glasspainter to exhibit in the Medieval Court, where his glass was seen in the broadest context of the Gothic Revival, and he was the only Englishman to receive a prize medal for stained glass.[73] Pugin's mastery of design and colour were undoubtedly the key factors in the success of Hardman's revival of medieval glass, and also his close study of old glass and glassmaking techniques, experiment and sheer perseverance. The close relationship between the two families, and Pugin's thorough tutoring of John Hardman Powell, ensured the future success of the firm as the Gothic Revival continued to expand.

4. AFTER PUGIN –
PERSONALITIES AND PROJECTS

After the death of Pugin the continued success of the metalworking and stained glass enterprises rested largely with two young men: Edward Welby Pugin, then aged eighteen, and John Hardman Powell, aged twenty-five. Edward Pugin had, of course, to pick up his father's unfinished architectural work and establish his own architectural practice, using Hardman's just as Augustus Pugin had done, to supply any structural and ornamental metalwork, stained glass and other furnishings. Powell, now married and with a young family of his own, had earned his Master's complete confidence and trust. As Pugin had told Hardman in 1848,

> . . . you now have an artist of your own who possesses accurate copies & tracings of every document from which I have been accustomed to work & you will be able to carry on the work independently of me.[1]

From 1851 Powell had himself been taking on pupils and assistants, training them no doubt in the same rigorous fashion as he had been tutored by Pugin. Thus he wrote to his uncle in Birmingham:

> . . . Frank Wyse is going on very well, he will never be much of an artist but will fill in and be useful. he is a nice fellow and very willing to do his best at times . . . he is capitally rigged out for the winter for £2.5.0 (I think) and was very thankful when I told him . . .[2]

Powell had witnessed Pugin's will, but he was counted as the only witness since Edward Pugin had signed his name on the envelope rather than on the document itself, and so Pugin was deemed to have died intestate. His books, pictures and collection of antiques were sold at auction, some of them being bought by John Hardman. Edward had already gone to Birmingham, and he was soon followed by Jane Pugin and the younger children. Hardman had advised her to go and live near her uncle, John Knill, in London, but she suspected that he had an ulterior motive, namely that of having more influence over Edward and marrying him off to one of his daughters.[3] Eventually all of them moved into no. 44 Frederick Street, Birmingham, and The Grange was let to Pugin's friend, Alfred Luck. By October 1856, however, Edward was living in London, and a month later Anne Pugin left Birmingham to join him at no. 5 Gordon Square.[4] Finally the family returned to Ramsgate – Edward in 1858 and Jane and the other unmarried children three years later – and The Grange remained in the family until after the death of Cuthbert Pugin in 1928.

The initial move to Birmingham not only enabled Jane to keep her family together; it also achieved what had not been possible in Pugin's lifetime, namely the bringing together of the different aspects of the Hardman operation into one place, although Powell continued to divide his time between Birmingham and Ramsgate where he and Anne had first set up home. Eventually they moved to Hunter's Road, Birmingham, but there were times when they had to be apart, and the letters which Powell wrote to 'Annie' during his absences show that behind the bewhiskered and solemn-looking face that is seen in family photographs there was a

Hand-drawn Christmas card sent by
J.H. Powell, 1873 (private collection)

Sketch by John Hardman Powell of himself and friends at 3 Southwood Terrace, St Lawrence, Ramsgate (private collection)

delightfully jovial and lively character who gently teased his wife, often poking fun at himself, and who was
also something of a *bon viveur.* Powell's letters are frequently animated with humorous drawings. One of
these, sent to Anne in Birmingham on 27 February 1854, shows Powell at home, sitting round a table with
four companions, all of them smoking and drinking. 'This is being urged on me daily now you are away,' he
writes. 'Am I to do it? They say that the smoke will be clean off before you return.' In another letter, the lolling figure of Powell with a cigar in his hand is captioned, 'Your own dearest at 9 o'clock in Mr Walmsley's
queer house', Richard Walmsley being one of Powell's Ramsgate friends. This is contrasted with a pair of
sketches, one with Powell drawing at his easel and the other showing him vested in cassock and surplice for
service at the altar, with the caption, 'the dearest at home, *of course* in real character – as you know him'. Yet
another sketch shows him fishing from a small boat, with the habitual cigar in his mouth.[5] None of this would
have amused Pugin had he still been alive, for Pugin disapproved of strong drink and prohibited smoking at
The Grange; and of fishing he famously said, 'Fishing, my dear Sir! life is not made for that sort of thing.'[6]
Powell also used his drawing skills to design Christmas cards, mostly of a non-religious and humorous kind,
to send to family and friends.

A letter to Anne in the spring of 1854, written from The Grange, and addressed to Hunter's Lane, Birmingham, suggests that by this time the Powell house at St Lawrence had been sold and that John was lodging
temporarily with Alfred Luck. It is also clear that by this time he looked upon Birmingham as 'home':

St. Augustine's Ramsgate

My dearest Annie

If the weather is as fine at Birmingham as here it is time the gardener dug in the manure and set some radishes, mustard & cress &c but nothing else as the ground is so cold, please see him soon. Mr Luck has everything of this kind grown this year even lettuce but the sun has much more power here than at Birming–. also if the men are gone he should rake up the gravel and put all straight. I hope to be home about the middle of the week but it depends a little upon the day Mr Hardman comes to London. I have written to him to say not to start if he can before Wednesday . . . I am getting very sick of this sort of life, there is nothing but drawing worth doing, this gentlemanly life is detestable (sketch of Powell tweaking moustache, and captioned, 'what you may expect').

. . . I shall be home soon. it was a great mistake not bringing you with me – especially now the weather is fine.

Some of the Baltic fleet are expected on Monday

Your affectionate husband

John H. Powell[7]

It would seem that by the end of the year Powell was permanently back in Birmingham, at Hunter's Lane.[8] Their three-year-old daughter, Mildred – Pugin's first grandchild – was soon to gain a sister, Agatha, born in 1855, and there followed a succession of ten other children. Their firstborn son, Bernard John, born in 1856, died in infancy, but there were two other sons, Dunstan (1861–1932) and Sebastian Pugin Powell (1866–1949), both of whom were to continue their father's – and grandfather's – principles of design well into the twentieth century. John Powell's two elder brothers were also working for Hardman's: William (1820–95), who looked after the brasswork, and James (1825–65), who handled much of the correspondence.

The Hardman Index of Stained Glass give an indication as to how this part of the firm's operations developed in the 1850s and 60s. In 1848 eighty-one stained-glass jobs are recorded. In 1851 – the last full year of Pugin's active involvement with the firm – there were only forty-nine, but this number includes the supply of very large quantities of glass to the New Palace of Westminster valued at £3,123.[9] In 1854 there were 101 stained-glass jobs, followed by 128 in 1857, 138 in 1860, 144 in 1863 and 160 in 1866. Some of these ranged from small jobs such as single lights and tracery pieces costing just a few pounds, to large five- and six-light windows costing several hundreds. Exhibitions played their part in bringing the firm to the attention of a wider public. Hardman's had stands at the international exhibitions in London in 1862, and in Paris in 1855 and 1867. The steady increase in orders was a major factor in the relocation of the firm at 43 Newhall Hill, where glass production continued until 1970. Looking back in 1866 over precisely this period of expansion and growth, Powell wrote,

For the last few years as many as from 80 to 100 hands have been employed, and in nearly every instance Birmingham youths have been taken as apprentices. One was a bricklayer's lad, another cleaned an engine, another made his first outlines in chalk – caricatures of his friends, of course, on the soles of the shoes he had to brush – a circumstance which first drew Mr. Hardman's attention to his talent.[10]

Just as Edward Pugin developed his own architectural style that was based on his father's but not merely imitative of it, so Powell's designs in metalwork and stained glass became gradually more his own, though remaining true to Pugin's principles of Gothic design. This is observable particularly in his glass, where figures become more elongated, and his groupings of figures are not always made to fit neatly into bordered quatrefoil panels as Pugin's had done. Powell's compositions also became much more dramatic and expressive. A set of windows made to Powell's design for William Butterfield's new church at Langley (Kent) in 1855 received particular praise:

> The whole reflect the greatest credit upon the artist, Mr Hardman of Birmingham. The tints are good, and the drawing free from those grotesque archaisms which some glass-stainers appear to think a point of conscience to imitate from the medieval examples. Another point which deserves great praise is the judicious admixture of white glass we have rarely seen better than those under review.[11]

Powell's metalwork drawings and studies, of which there are many volumes, are finely executed and very detailed, much more so than Pugin's, but then Pugin had, of necessity, to make drawings very quickly, giving only enough detail as was needed to inform those – such as Hardman – who executed his designs. Many of Powell's metalwork drawings are works of art in their own right, for example the exquisite designs for medals, seals, and bookplates crisply done in ink, and full of fine detail. When it came to guiding principles, however, Powell followed Pugin to the letter. In his lectures on to students at the Birmingham School of Art, he stressed that 'all Art-Craft should be honest, never pretending to be what it is not, fitted for its purpose, and showing that it is so', and that each craftsman should study thoroughly the nature and capabilities of the material in which he works.[12] Powell's analysis of an English parish church of the 1450s, and what students of art could learn from it, echoes Pugin's belief in the need to study 'the Real Thing': everything to the smallest detail is in *harmony*, all true, all honest and worthy of a Xtian Church, where the most captious critic could not find a peg without its purpose, or ornament without its moral; all integrity from top to base, and strong as if to last forever . . .'[13]

John Hardman, junior, whose sound business sense had combined so successfully with Pugin's design skills as the key elements in the success of Hardman and Co., was plagued with ill health when he was only in his forties, and in 1857 he ceased to have an active role in the firm. In 1863 he and his wife moved to Clifton Court, near Bristol. The metalwork daybook for 1864 contains several entries for items for this house. John died in May 1867 aged only 55, and was buried in the Hardman chantry in St Chad's cathedral. In the address given at his funeral Mass, Canon Edgar Estcourt paid particular tribute to Hardman's devotion to the Church which – as in the case of Pugin – had been the driving force of his life.

John Hardman's commitment to the Church and to St Chad's cathedral was shared by his son, John Bernard Hardman (1843–1903), who at the age of twenty had to leave off his education at the University of Dublin in order to join the family firm when his father moved to Bristol. John Bernard was much involved with St Chad's choir as choirmaster, and he augmented his father's original endowment by £500. In 1868 he married Mary Margaret Tarleton, by whom he had six children including two

J.H. Powell: window at St Mary's, Langley, 1855 (photo: Anne Clinch)

81

sons, John Tarleton (1873–1953) and Gerald James (1875–1953), the last two members of the Hardman family to be directly involved with the firm.

For thirty years following Pugin's death, the dominant force in the field of design was undoubtedly John Hardman Powell, who handed on the Pugin tradition to rising generations of artists and craftsmen. Amongst these was George Bernard Maycock (1827–1908) who had worked as a glass-designer in Preston for the architect Joseph A. Hansom, and married Hansom's daugher, Sophia Lousia, in 1853. For a time they lived in the Hansom house at Clifton, near Bristol, where John Hardman junior was then living in retirement. Joseph Hansom's brother, Charles, for whom Hardman's made a significant number of windows, also lived in Bristol, and one of his sons, George, was employed at Hardman's in the 1860s, so it may well have been through these connections that Maycock joined the firm in the early 1860s, remaining there as an artist for some forty years. John and Anne Powell were godparents to the Maycocks' son, Bernard Joseph, and John Bernard Hardman stood as godfather to one of their daughters.[14] The Maycocks came to live in proximity to the Powells and to John Bernard Hardman, for all of them had, by the 1880s, taken up residence on the Hagley Road, the Hardmans at 150, the Maycocks at 229, and the Powells at 252.

Powell's other protégés included Joseph Aloysius Pippet (1841–1903), who became a prolific artist, carrying out many decorative schemes for the company, and also designing metalwork, stained glass and textile items. He appears to have joined the firm as a young apprentice in about 1853. During Powell's lifetime Pippet's role seems to have been that of 'reliable designer and co-ordinator of design practice to an exacting master and keeper of the Pugin flame'.[15] Both Powell and John Bernard Hardman had occasion to reprimand him for suggesting deviations from the Pugin tradition. When some decorative work was being carried out

at Oscott in 1882, Pippet's suggestion that an alternative scheme might be tried was swiftly rebuffed by Hardman: '. . . A difficult thing is it not to improve on old Pugin in matters of decoration? Nothing must be done at Oscott in the way of alteration until Mr. Powell has approved them.'[16] Powell also wrote to Pippet, 'I fear that you will think that I am your unjust persecutor',[17] but by maintaining strict overall control he upheld the high standards of design that had been instilled into him, sometimes painfully, by Pugin himself. Under Powell's supervision, Pippet decorated the interior of one of E.W. Pugin's most lavish churches, All Saints', Barton-upon-Irwell, Manchester (1865–8), the wall-paintings including figures of the architect himself, and of members of the de Trafford family who financed the building.

The most complete example of the collaboration between Powell and Pippet may be seen at St Peter's church, Hascombe (Surrey), where Hardman's carried out decorative work for the architect Henry Woodyer (1816–96). The church had been built in 1864, but the decorative work was not started

J.A. Pippet: decorative scheme for St Peter's, Lancaster, 1894, ink and watercolour (JHAL)

until 1883, and it was paid for by the rector, the Revd Vernon Musgrave. The decoration of the chancel and the chancel arch was complemented by altar frontals and banners worked by Pippet's wife, Juliet, and by some outstanding Hardman metalwork including a jewelled chalice and processional cross.[18]

Pippet's three sons, Elphege, Oswald and Gabriel, followed their father into the Hardman firm, Elphege eventually becoming a director. Each one developed a special skill: Elphege specialised in decorative schemes, Oswald had a talent for calligraphy and illuminated addresses, while Gabriel became a renowned designer of mosaic and also of *opus sectile* in which slabs of coloured opaque glass are cut and assembled together in panels as with stained glass, but without any leadwork. Stations of the Cross, for example, and other devotional pictures for wall-mounting, were produced in this way.

The Hardman Index of stained glass shows that between 1866 and the turn of the century the firm supplied glass to over 1,800 different buildings in Britain and overseas. At one end of the scale there were multiple commissions for large and important churches, for example the twenty windows installed in Gloucester cathedral between 1866 and 1888 to complement the fifteen already in place. Buildings with which Hardman's had been involved from Pugin's time account for some notable Catholic work. Fifty glass jobs are entered to Oscott College alone, and forty-eight for St Chad's cathedral, although some of these relate to minor alterations and repairs. An individual window could cost as much as £1,000 as in the case of the great west window of Beverley Minster, or as little as £30 for a single figure in a lancet such as the one made in 1871 to an earlier Pugin design for the Masfen memorial window in St Mary's, Stafford.[19] It has been pointed out that although church-building and (amongst Anglicans) ecclesiology may have provided the initial impetus for the revival of stained glass, the continued expansion of the market through to the end of the century was the result of other influences. A fall in the price of glass, coupled with a growth in prosperity amongst the middle classes, made stained glass more affordable, and donating a window or subscribing towards one became a fashionable thing to do.[20] Domestic commissions also grew in number, and the Hardman records show that not all of these were for the homes of aristocrats and country gentlemen.

In the 1880s some significant developments took place in the management of the Hardman company, notably the division which occurred in 1883 whereby the glassworks and the production of memorial brasses remained at Newhall Hill, trading as John Hardman & Co., while the metalworking operations were transferred to King Edward's Road under the name of Hardman, Powell & Co., with John Hardman Powell's brother William (1820–95) in control. In the same year John and Anne Powell and their family moved to Blackheath, London, so that John could supervise the firm's London office which was situated in King William Street, off the Strand. Dunstan Powell then succeeded his father as a partner in the firm and as chief designer. His younger brother, Sebastian Pugin Powell, joined his uncles, Peter Paul Pugin and Cuthbert Welby Pugin, in the firm of Pugin & Pugin which undertook a great deal of work in Scotland and the north-east, with Hardman's being commissioned to provide glass, metalwork and decorative schemes for their churches. It was through S.P. Powell that the firm was able to continue for a further forty-five years after Peter Paul's death in 1904.[21]

John Hardman Powell died at Blackheath on 2 September 1895. He was buried in the Pugin vault at St Augustine's, Ramsgate, close to the master whose 'true principles' he had followed devotedly for fifty years, and in the church which he had helped to complete after Pugin's death in 1852. The principal lights of many of the windows at St Augustine's had been filled with plain quarries as a temporary measure, and it was left to Powell to fulfil Pugin's intention of replacing them with coloured glass. They are mainly on the south and west sides of the church, and include the large four-light window over Pugin's tomb-effigy in the south transept. Nearby, in the entrance to the Lady chapel, is Powell's own memorial to his master: a pair of tall metalwork gates incorporating the fleur-de-lis, and made by Hardman's in 1862.

Although Edward Welby Pugin's career was considerably shorter than Powell's – he died in 1875 at the age of forty-one – he designed 150 churches and conventual buildings and undertook a number of secular commissions including the gargantuan Granville Hotel in Ramsgate which was a major cause of his eventual

John Hardman Powell in old age (oil painting in private collection)

St Augustine's, Ramsgate: tomb of A.W.N. Pugin, and memorial window by J.H. Powell (photo: George Garbutt)

bankruptcy. Edward also made significant contributions to the development of Hardman's, notably in the fields of metalwork and stained glass. He was of course living in Birmingham between 1852 and 1856, and therefore working in close collaboration with his brother-in-law. While noting the individuality which marked Edward's mature architectural style, his obituary records that, like his father, he was deeply involved in the furnishing and decoration of his interiors:

> . . . not only were buildings . . . created but decorations of all description were being designed: metalwork, carpets, wall decorations, vestments, tiles and in fact, wherever it was necessary to call in the decorative art, his busy pencil was called into requisition.[22]

One of Edward Pugin's early churches was Shrews-bury cathedral, a project that had been close to the heart of the sixteenth Earl of Shrewsbury and for which A.W. Pugin had produced at least one rough sketch, on the back of one of his drawings for the Palace of West-minster. As eventually built, however, the cathedral was a more modest affair than Edward had envisaged, lacking, amongst other things, the tall spire which would have rivalled those of Shrewsbury's medieval churches. Hardman's contribution to the building at the time of its opening in 1856 included the seven-light east window containing figures of Our Lady Help of Christians and St Peter of Alcantara to whom the cathe-dral is dedicated. Among the metalwork items supplied

Mortuary card for John Hardman Powell, 1895 (JHAL)

in October 1856 were the font-cover, tabernacle, cross and six brass candlesticks for the high altar.[23] Further additions of glass were made between 1877 and 1892, and in 1885 J.A. Pippet undertook the decoration of the Sacred Heart chapel. The details entered on the cost-sheet for the east window give an insight into Hardman's business practices in the mid-1850s, showing the charges made for the glass per square foot and for the various processes of production and installation. As might be expected, the making of cartoons and the actual painting of the glass were the most costly parts of the operation.

Shrewsbury cathedral: Sacred Heart altar with decoration by J.A. Pippet

Glass – 276 feet at 5/–	£69	0	0
Cutting	6	0	5
Painting	56	12	7
Leading	21	16	2
Burning	5	3	6
(i.e. firing in kiln)			
Cementing	2	6	6
Expenses	8	0	10
Cartoons	22	4	5
Total	191	3	11

The raw figure was then subject to Hardman's mark-up which in this case was 82 per cent, bringing the total cost of the window to £350. Added to this were the costs of the men's time in fixing the window, and the provision of wire guards, amounting to a further £31.[24]

Contemporary with Shrewsbury Cathedral is Oulton Abbey near Stone (Staffs.), another commission which E.W. Pugin inherited from his father and completed in 1854. Like Shrewsbury, it is in the Decorated style favoured by A.W.N. Pugin, but with some original touches too. What is remarkable about Oulton is that it has suffered less from later 're-ordering' than most other Pugin churches. Though comparison with old photographs reveals certain subsequent modifications to the reredos and to J.H. Powell's fine metalwork screen, the decorative work by A.J. Pippet over the chancel arch remains intact.

By the 1860s Edward Pugin was developing his own Gothic church-style characterised by an apsidal east end, short chancel, and cross-gabling, with the interior being treated as unified space with the altar visible from all parts of the nave – just as the Anglican Tractarians had believed it should be. The church of Our Lady and St Hubert, Great Harwood, near Blackburn (Lancs.), is an interesting early example of this type. Built in 1859, it has a broad nave all under one roof, an apse with windows set under separate gables, and a tower with a broach-spire set midway along the north side of the nave. Hardman's provided all the metalwork and stained glass, all of which was in place by mid-1865. The driving forces behind the building were the parish priest, the Revd William Dunderdale, and Mr James Lomax of Clayton Hall, Accrington, head of a noted Catholic family whose descendant, Michael Trappes Lomax, was to write a biography of A.W.N. Pugin.[25]

The Hardman daybooks record many items of metalwork ordered in time for the opening of the church, the most expensive of which was 'a gilt monstrance, richly beaten sexfoil star on round foot; hexagon engraved stem, beaten knop set with 6 amethysts; rich pierced and beaten foot set with 12 carbuncles, rays & engraved cross set with 1 amethyst. £35'.[26] Other entries for Great Harwood are 17 March, 25 May (1858) and 18 February (1859). A full set of stained-glass windows was complete by August 1865. The first windows to be glazed were those of the apse, done in time for the consecration. They are of three lights, and include scenes from the lives of the Blessed Virgin Mary and St Hubert.[27] The other windows were quickly filled, with figures of saints or with coloured ornament, the last one to be completed being the five-light west window depicting the Fall of Adam, with groups of figures set in oblong geometrical shapes against a blue background. The Glass daybook enters this to Fr Dunderdale at £200. The total expenditure on glass was in excess of £1,500 in little more than six years, and it remains one of the most important collections of Hardman stained glass of this period.[28] Hardman's also made the brass inscription plate intended, eventually, as a memorial to James and Frances Lomax as the founders of the church.[29] It shows the kneeling figures of Mr & Mrs Lomax holding a model of the church, beneath a canopied figure of the Blessed Virgin Mary.

Edward Pugin's larger churches include Belmont Abbey, Herefordshire, which began with a small school-chapel built on the estate of Francis Wegg-Prosser of Belmont House, with Hardman supplying the metalwork.[30] Between 1857 and 1867 a considerable amount of rebuilding took place, with Hardman's again supplying metalwork and stained glass, including the east and west windows.[31] From 1859 to 1916 Belmont served as the pro-Cathedral for Wales, and it contains the tomb of Bishop Thomas Brown who was successively Vicar Apostolic of Wales (1840–50) and – following the restoration of the Hierarchy – first Bishop of Newport and Menevia. Stanbrook Abbey, Worcestershire, is another of Edward Pugin's monastic churches (1869–71) to which, as at Belmont, his half-brother, Peter Paul (1851–1904) made important additions. Born on 29 June 1851, Peter Paul was little more than a year old at the time of his father's death, and his training as an architect was undertaken by Edward, who eventually made him a partner in what became the firm of Pugin & Pugin.

Next to Peter Paul, the most significant architect to have received training from E.W. Pugin was Edmund Kirby (1838–1920). Born in Liverpool and educated at Sedgley Park School and Oscott, Kirby's artistic skills drew him to the attention of A.W. Pugin, who may have been responsible for introducing him to his son and to Hardman's.[32] Kirby subsequently worked in Edward Pugin's Liverpool Office, and eventually set up his own architectural practice in 1867. The Hardman archives show that he used the firm quite extensively for the supply of metalwork and stained glass for the large number of ecclesiastical and secular commissions that he undertook in the Liverpool area and in Wales. These range from the spectacular reredos at Abergavenny priory, complemented by an equally spectacular east window by Hardman, to the Liverpool Liberal Club (1879) for which Hardman's supplied large quantities of gas-fittings, pendants and stained-glass panels.[33]

A particularly fine example of Edward Pugin's mature style, and a church to which Peter Paul Pugin made significant additions, was St Gregory's, Longton (Stoke-on-Trent). Though sadly demolished in 1970 on account of mining subsidence, St Gregory's is particularly well documented in the Hardman archive at Lightwoods House, where some fine coloured drawings and photographs of the interiors constitute a most valuable record of what has been described as one of the most important churches in the Birmingham archdiocese.[34] Begun in 1868 under the supervision of Edward Ilsley – a future Bishop, and Archbishop, of Birmingham – St Gregory's consisted of a tall aisled nave with clerestories, and a high vaulted chancel terminating in a polygonal apse roofed in a series of small gables with – externally – statues in between. Peter Paul designed a new altar and reredos in time for the consecration in 1887, and these show his development of Edward Pugin's Benediction altar in which the reredos becomes taller and more dominant, incorporating as its central feature, above the tabernacle, a niche for the exposition of the Blessed Sacrament surmounted by a stone spirelet. He was responsible for the design of over four hundred such altars, for churches in Britain and overseas, using the Cheltenham firm of R.L. Boulton to undertake the carving and sculptures.

Hardman's contributions to St Gregory's were considerable. The installation of stained glass began in 1870, first in the central window of the apse. More glass was installed in 1903, i.e. the remaining windows of the

St Gregory's, Longton: decoration scheme by Elphege Pippet for P.P. Pugin's altar (ink and watercolour, JHAL)

Design by Elphege Pippet for wall-decoration, St Gregory's, Longton (ink and watercolour, JHAL)

apse, and those of the Lady chapel and Sacred Heart chapel.[35] At the same time some new oak benches and wrought iron screens were purchased to standard catalogue patterns, and the altar and sanctuary were completely redecorated. Two superb drawings by Elphege Pippet show the treatment of P.P. Pugin's altar, and the decorative scheme for the sanctuary walls which is described as 'an adaptation of the curtain of the Holy of Holies'[36] with the six-winged seraphim guarding the Sacred Presence.

Peter Paul Pugin carried out some of his most significant work in the Glasgow area, principally for Charles Eyre, a former priest at A.W.N. Pugin's St Mary's, Newcastle upon Tyne, and Archbishop of Glasgow from 1869 to 1893. His decorative schemes were undertaken by the Pippets, and there is a significant number of these in the drawings collection at Lightwoods House. Several churches in South Wales, for example St Mary's, Llanelli, and Our Lady and St Patrick, Maesteg, were decorated in similar fashion with rich diapering and gilding. It had been the firm belief of A.W.N. Pugin that coloured and gilded decoration was a most necessary accompaniment to stained glass in order to achieve harmony throughout the building; otherwise 'the effect of stained glass . . . is too spotty; the contrast between plain walls and the most vivid colours is too violent'.[37]

One of the most spectacular collaborations between Peter Paul Pugin and John Hardman & Co. was the furnishing and decoration of the very large red-brick church of Our Lady and the Angels at Princethorpe, Warwickshire. Built in a rural setting about ten miles south-west of Rugby, Princethorpe was begun in 1832 as a convent for French Benedictine nuns who had escaped from the Revolution in 1792. The first church, dating from 1835–7, was by a Mr Craven, allegedly experienced in building religious houses, but it did not impress A.W.N. Pugin who, in September 1841 wrote to his Oxford friend, John Rouse Bloxam, 'I was sorry

Church of Our Lady and the Angels, Princethorpe (photo of c.1904, courtesy Princethorpe College)

to percive [*sic*] that you were going to visit Princethorpe. it is a miserable specimen of the tawdry trashy taste of the *Modern* religious, it is not even a ghost of an ancient nunnery'.[38] It was left to Peter Paul to re-cast it in a more appropriate mould, which he did in 1898–1901, financed by Hilda de Trafford, a daughter of Sir Humphrey and Lady Annette de Trafford who had contributed generously to E.W. Pugin's churches in Manchester in the 1860s. The extensive correspondence between Pugin and the Mother Superior at Princethorpe reveal a somewhat gentler and more patient handling of exacting clients than that of Augustus Pugin, but Peter Paul could be equally persuasive in communicating his ideas of what was 'appropriate' for such a church and its furnishings.[39] Having been spared the ravages which denuded so many splendid interiors in the mid-twentieth century, the furnishings and fittings are almost as Pugin left them, one notable exception being a reliquary cabinet made to contain a fragment of the True Cross. Made of oak, it has plated metal fittings including cresting, and door-plates finely engraved with the *agnus dei* and pelican. It now forms part of the Hardman metalwork collection at Lightwoods House. Still *in situ* in the chapel is the metal rood-screen. The light and transparent quality of E.W. and P.P. Pugin's metalwork screens meant they fared slightly better in the post-Vatican II 're-orderings' than did the more solid ones of the carved wooden variety. Of delicate ironwork, gilded and painted, the Princethorpe screen has dominant fleur-de-lis motifs, and is complemented by screens in the ambulatory arches of the apse. The altar is of white marble supported on pillars of polished granite. It has a prominent tabernacle with a gilt-brass door by Hardman, and above this an exposition throne in the form of a plinth flanked by a pair of kneeling angels. The altar stands under a soaring baldachino of wood and metal, arrayed with carved figures. The decoration of this, and of the reliquary under the altar, was designed by Joseph Aloysius Pippet, who also designed the wall-paintings in the Sacred Heart Chapel and in the Library. As one might expect, there is Hardman glass in the windows.[40]

Anglican commissions accounted for a large proportion of Hardman's stained-glass work as the spate of restorations and new building continued, much of it paid for by private patrons. An Anglican counterpart to the Trappes Lomax family of Great Harwood were the Rowleys of St Neots, Huntingdonshire, much involved from the 1840s with the restoration of the large medieval parish church of St Mary's. Charles Percival Rowley, of Wintringham Hall, was the driving force behind the provision of stained-glass windows to replace the medieval glass which, with the exception of a few fragments, had been lost or destroyed.[41] In devising the scheme for the windows, twelve of which were made by Hardman's between 1859 and 1880, Rowley worked in close collaboration with the Revd Charles Lyndhurst Vaughan, vicar of St Neots from 1854 to 1865. Significantly, perhaps, Vaughan was a member of the Ecclesiological Society, and he is known to have been a Tractarian.[42] The subject-matter of the windows is, however, firmly Bible-based, unlike the Great Harwood ones with their array of medieval saints, and they follow the life of Christ from the Annunciation through to the Ascension. The windows are almost entirely 'Perpendicular' in architectural style, of three or more lights each, and with panel tracery. The east window (1864) is divided horizontally by a transom, creating ten lights. In the lower section is the crucifixion, while the upper lights show Christ in majesty flanked by angels, saints and the symbols of the evangelists. The groups of figures are characteristic of John Hardman Powell: expressive and full of movement. Strong colours are used, particularly the reds and blues, relieved by white borders which clearly define each of the lights. To give proper emphasis to the principal subject, the figure of the crucified Christ is painted disproportionately larger than the figures in the groups, and the arms extend into the adjacent panels. Canopies, which one might have expected to see at the head of each light, have been dispensed with – as earlier in the Pugin window at Sherborne – to allow the maximum use of space in a transomed window.

Two of the St Neots windows were of particular importance to Hardman's on account of their being displayed at international exhibitions: the east window of the Lady chapel (the Adoration of the Magi) at the Paris Exhibition of 1867, and a north aisle window (the washing of Jesus' feet in the house at Bethany) at the Centennial Exhibition, Philadelphia, USA, in 1876.[43] The 'Bethany' window is interesting also from a stylistic viewpoint. It differs markedly from the other four-light windows in that there are no canopies over the figures, although there would have been room for them; neither are there any borders to the lights. Instead, the composition is set out in the 'painterly' fashion in which the whole expanse of glass is treated as if it were a single space, regarding the vertical mullions as mere intrusions into the scene. This fashion of glasspainting was popular in the United States at this time, a fact of which Hardman & Co. were undoubtedly aware, although it goes completely against the Puginian principle of respecting the architectural integrity of a window.

As the restoration of churches like St Neots proliferated, so the demand for stained glass increased, and it was readily accepted in Anglican churches that were not necessarily Tractarian or liturgically 'advanced'. Among the Anglican architects of the Gothic Revival none was more famous – and some might even say notorious – than George Gilbert Scott (1811–78). Out of the twenty-six cathedrals of the old and monastic foundations, only three were untouched by Scott, and at least eight hundred parish churches were either restored or built anew from his office. Among these was Worcester cathedral, on which he worked from 1864 to 1874, with Hardman's undertaking some important commissions in metalwork, stained glass and decoration, a good deal of which was paid for by the Earl of Dudley. Hardman's supplied what Pevsner unkindly described as 'the many corny statues' on the facade of the north porch.[44] In 1873–4 they undertook the complete decoration of the vaults of the whole of the eastern limb of the cathedral: choir, transepts and Lady chapel. The Lady-chapel roof is entered into the metalwork daybook at 31 October 1873 charging £400 to the Restoration Committee. The scheme included thirty-two half-figures of angels playing musical instruments. The treatment of the transept roofs, which included half-figures of saints, was charged at £760, and Lord Dudley paid £405 for 'enriching' the mouldings of the ribs in the choir aisles.[45] Hardman glass, designed by Powell, filled the ten lancet lights which make up the east window, and windows in the choir aisles. Powell's most spectacular

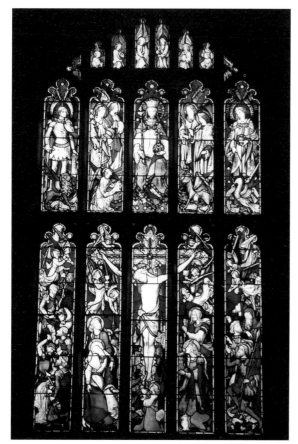

Above: St Neots: the 'Bethany' window exhibited in Philadelphia in 1876 (photo: Simon Huguet)

Left: St Neots, Huntingdonshire, east window (photo: Simon Huguet)

achievement was undoubtedly the great west window done in 1874. This window, of eight lights and tracery, including a large rose at the top, depicts the Creation. The figures and scenes are set in roundels and octofoils, some of which extend behind the mullions. The combination of rich colours and white borders makes the whole composition sparkle. In 1876 the Earl of Dudley received the final bill for £1,800, of which £877 was Hardman's mark-up.[46]

One of the three cathedrals with which Scott had nothing to do was Carlisle. Here Hardman's installed a large nine-light east window in 1861, re-setting some fourteenth-century glass including a seated figure of Christ. In 1912 the design was re-used for the east window of the Church of the Immaculate Conception, Farm Street, London, which may account for the surprisingly modest estimate for that window of £850 'including all expenses'.[47] Large east and west windows seem to have become something of a Hardman speciality, based no doubt on their earlier successes in Pugin's time. Tewkesbury Abbey, Gloucestershire, gained a transomed west window of twenty-one lights in 1886. Smaller churches purchased what they could afford, or received a gift from an individual or family wishing to commemorate themselves by way of a window. Thus the little village church at Llanenddwyn, on the road between Harlech and Barmouth (Gwynedd), was able, in 1884, to have its east window glazed with representations of the Nativity, Crucifixion and Ascension – the whole of Christ's life encompassed economically in just three lights – through the generosity of the Williams family of Pentrebach who commissioned it, for £90, as an *in memoriam* gift.[48] No doubt the congregation at Llanenddwyn were as delighted with their small window as the people of Tewkesbury Abbey were with their huge one, which also came by way of a gift, the donor being the Revd. Charles Grove who gave it in memory of his wife.[49] Grove also paid for ten large aisle windows, of three and four lights each, between 1888 and 1892,

Worcester cathedral: detail of west window by J.H. Powell.

Worcester cathedral: decoration of vaulting by Hardman & Co.

and was himself commemorated by a Hardman window following his death in 1896. The Grove windows were complemented by gifts of Hardman glass from other benefactors, thus making Tewkesbury Abbey a particularly important place for the study and appreciation of Hardman's work towards the end of the nineteenth century, which compares very favourably with windows elsewhere in the church by James Powell of London and by Heaton, Butler and Bayne. Hardman's last addition was a three-light window in St. Margaret's chapel, designed by Dunstan Powell (1908) and depicting the life of St. Margaret of Scotland.

Next to A.W.N. Pugin himself, the most colourful figure of the Gothic Revival was undoubtedly William Burges (1827–81), the leading exponent of the High Victorian dream,[50] but whereas Pugin's vision was of a restored Catholic England cast in the mould of the fourteenth century, Burges's attachment to the Middle Ages was aesthetic rather than theological, and for him the noblest Gothic style was Early French. His ecclesiastical commissions were overwhelmingly Anglican. Like Pugin, he embraced the whole spectrum of ecclesiastical art, but his taste for the exotic drove him beyond the boundaries of Gothic Europe to the arts of Turkey, Persia and the Far East, and into a world of fantasy. This is reflected above all in Burges's metalwork designs.

An admirer of Pugin though he undoubtedly was, Burges did not turn to John Hardman for any of his glass, while for most of his metalwork he used either Charles Hart (d.1880) or the partnership of Jess Barkentin (?1800–1881) and Carl Krall (1844–1923). In the 1860s, however, some significant pieces were made by Hardman to Burges's designs, with Burges often supplying semi-precious stones for setting. The earliest commission

Tewkesbury Abbey: west window, 1886

Tewkesbury Abbey: The Entry into Jerusalem; one of a set of six windows in the north aisle by Hardman & Co., 1892

(1860) was for a parcel-gilt silver chalice set with stones and with a crystal knop (a favourite device of Burges's), a matching paten, and a glass flagon with silver parcel-gilt mounts and embellished with stones.[51]

In 1862 Burges was called upon to supply furnishings for St Michael's church, Brighton, designed by G.F. Bodley for the *avant-garde* Ecclesiologist, the Revd Charles Beanlands. Some of the metalwork was made by Hart and Barkentin, but it was Hardman who made the so-called 'Beanlands chalice'. Entered into the Hardman metalwork daybook for 30 June 1863, it is described as:

> Silver gilt chalice and paten. Chalice 7" high, cup 4½" diameter, foot 6¼" diameter; foot covered with engravings of emblematical figures, inscriptions etc. Crystal knop with pierced mountings, set with stones, leaf set with lapis lazuli and malachite. Paten 7⅛" diameter engraved in centre with cross. £34.

The 'emblematical figures' are allegories of the Four Rivers of Paradise, the Tree of Life, the Tree of Knowledge, and the Heavenly Jerusalem. A year later an even richer chalice was made for St Michael's by Hardman to Burges's design, set with amethysts and other stones supplied by Burges, and with four large enamels on the foot.[52]

Burges may or may not have been the designer of the Purchas chalice, given in 1874 to St James's, Brighton, in memory of the Revd John Purchas (d.1872), but it carries the Hardman maker's mark. Purchas was another

William Burges: the elephant inkstand made by Hardman (pencil drawing by Jamal E. Mustaphe, 2007, from original photograph and working drawing)

William Burges: the Beanlands chalice (photo in JHAL)

of the celebrated 'martyrs of ritualism'. The metalwork daybook for 1874 is, unfortunately, no longer extant, but the chalice is unmistakably in the 'Burgesian' style.

Burges commissioned some secular work from Hardman, some of it for his own use. The commissions include a silver-gilt cup engraved on the inside and with a band of foliage set with intaglios, and a coral knop[53] and the mounting of a jade cup with a gilt metal foot set with stones provided by Burges.[54] The letters relating to these pieces show Burges to have been a very exacting client, and James Powell, who handled most of the correspondence, had to bear the brunt of his displeasure when the job was not done satisfactorily:

15 Buckingham Street

Strand

April 29 1863

My dear Sir,

I am very sorry that I cannot congratulate you on the mounting of the jade cup, it is the worst and most careless work that I have ever seen turned out from Hardman & Co. First of all many of the bezils of the stones are split, the fact of the matter being that a jeweller was not employed to put the jewellery in as he ought to have been. The mounting of jewels is certainly not a difficult art for one sees innumerable instances of it in the shop windows . . . two of the stones are broken, one being placed upside down to hide the defect . . .

. . . the addition to the handle of the jade cup should have been fixed on to the mounting by pins or rivets – instead of which it has been done by shellac – to apply which heat has been used and thus opened the joint where the cup has been mended.

. . . I am exceedingly sorry to have to say so much for I have never had a work executed so badly before – In fact in its present state I shall be ashamed to show it as having come from Birmingham.

I sincerely hope that you will look a little better after the Elephant for if that is spoiled I really do not know how I shall be consoled.

I remain

Yours very truly

W. Burges[55]

Burges was even more angry when he received the bill for the work, which was five months late in completion and for which he was charged £3 more than the original estimate.[56]

The 'Elephant' mentioned in the letter refers to the most extraordinary and exotic of all Burges's metalwork objects: an elephant inkstand which stood on his drawing-room table at Tower House, Kensington, and which has been described as the very epitome of Burges's special genius.[57] The elephant itself was a Chinese bronze incense-burner, and the entry in the metalwork daybook for 9 July 1863 reveals how it was adapted to its new function:

W. Burges. Mounting a bronze elephant as an inkstand, with castle on his back, with 2 places for ink, and a spirit lamp at the top, the mounts taking the form of a castle & being gilt metal, the case for the lamp, the elephant & sundry ornaments being supplied by Mr. Burges, the whole standing on a piece of marble supplied by Mr Burges, let into an ebony stand or tray for pens, wax etc. £27.

It is unlikely that Burges would have entrusted Hardman's with this prestigious piece had he not been confident in their ability to construct it to his satisfaction, although the troubles with the jade cup clearly shook him. Burges supplied a detailed diagrammatic drawing showing where all the different stones, beads and ivories were to be set, and further correspondence about the elephant covered details of the gilding, the inscription which was to be engraved in Lombardic letters around the base of the tower, the silver inlays of the ebony pen-tray, and the choice of ornaments including an agate bead which 'formed part of a rosary which a relative of mine brought from Jerusalem'.[58] Delays in completing the inkstand proved irksome; on 5 May he urged John Hardman Powell 'as a friend' to do what he could to speed things up:

> . . . There is the London Season & I want to show the said inkstand to lots of people & give them an idea of the executive power of Hardman & co. but I can't & if your people do not look sharp the season will be over before I have it.

As it turned out, it was not until July that the job was completed, and Burges wrote on the 13th that it had 'arrived quite safely & works well'.[59]

The elephant was indeed a rare thing, and quite outside Hardman's normal range of metalwork, but the significance of it, as typifying Burges's broad eclecticism, was commented upon by his friend, the architect E.W. Godwin:

> Observe the power of adaptation. The things he is dealing with are Chinese and Japanese, but the whole in thirteenth-century – Burgesque. A few pieces of metal in his favourite style to unite them, and lo! This strange group of Eastern things fall into their places as if they had originally been designed for the purpose.[60]

It is clear also that, in spite of the difficulties, Burges regarded John Hardman Powell as a friend. He may have quarrelled with James over the price of the jade cup, and vowed that 'this is a battle that I intend to fight out with him . . . and by 'St. Eloy' I intend to hold him to it' – St Eloy being the French rendering of Eligius, the patron saint of metalworkers.[61] At the same time, however, he told John,

> You and I only quarrel on the mutual ground of art – & a very good thing for all it is tha
> do not all think alike. I read an epitome (a very short one) of your lecture. it was cap
> where could I find it at large.[62]

There is evidence too in some of Powell's metalwork drawings that he was influenced by the same eclectic spirit which was characteristic of Burges, if not actually by Burges himself. Some studies of hemispherical covered bowls, for example, and globe-shaped thuribles sitting in tripod stands, reveal an odd mixture of Gothic and oriental motifs.

Several of Powell's drawings in the Lightwoods collection are of metalwork items intended for the new catalogue that Hardman's issued in the 1860s and they are numbered accordingly. The catalogue underwent several revisions, running eventually to over 150 pages. It reveals the huge range of metalwork items that the firm produced in the later part of the nineteenth century, from the well-established patterns of altar-plate to elaborate wrought-iron screens and railings of the kind that Edward Pugin introduced into many of his churches. Gas-fittings became something of a speciality, showing how Gothic was capable of being adapted to new forms of lighting, while candlesticks, branches and coronae were still produced in infinite variety. Secular plate

Thurible and stand: drawing by J.H. Powell (JHAL)

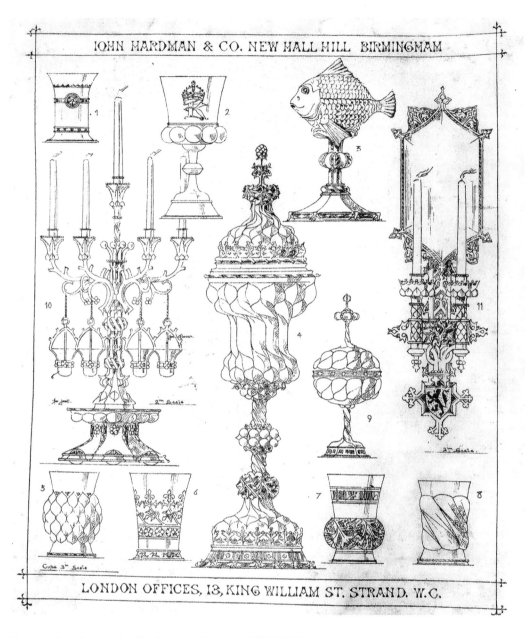

JOHN HARDMAN & CO. NEW HALL HILL BIRMINGHAM

LONDON OFFICES, 13, KING WILLIAM ST. STRAND. W.C.

Secular plate illustrated in Hardman catalogue, c.1885 (JHAL)

was also included in the catalogue: grace cups with ornate covers, beaker-shaped drinking cups and commemorative pieces. Catalogue items were ordered in bulk by firms of church furnishers for stock, one such firm being Burns & Lambert of Portman Street, London. Goods could also be sent on approval to established customers. Among these was the Revd William Bennett, one of the controversial figures of the Anglo-Catholic movement who, having been ousted in 1850 from St Barnabas', Pimlico, for alleged 'illegal' ritual practices, became vicar of Frome, Somerset. In October 1863 Bennett sent back to Hardman's a cross and candlesticks which had been sent on approval but which he 'did not quite like in all respects', and enclosed a rough drawing with detailed instructions about the modifications he required, adding, 'Please to let your artist make a drawing in proper proportions & send it to me, & then we can finally decide'. The alterations were duly made

Design by J.H. Powell for chalice for the Revd
Robert Liddell, 1870 (pencil/ink, JHAL)

Cartoon for window in north-west chapel, St
Paul's cathedral, London, 1879 (photo in JHAL)

and on 28 December Bennett wrote, 'The Altar Cross arrived safely and is in all respects just the thing that I desired. I now wish to give you the order for another.'[63]

Amongst the other Anglican ritualists for whom Hardman's produced specially designed items was the Revd Robert Liddell, of St Paul's church, Knightsbridge. Alternative chalice-designs were drawn for him by J.H. Powell in 1870, and the one which was actually made was particularly elaborate, with a richly beaten foot and knop, and set with a large number of gemstones supplied by Liddell himself.[64] It is entered at £60 with the addition of £5 for 'setting 60 stones extra to number estimated'.

As well as items made specially to order, catalogue goods could always be embellished by the addition of gemstones, enamels, or additional engraving, to make them distinctive and individual. Conversely, catalogue

Above: J.H. Powell: design
for seal for King Edward VI
School, Birmingham, 1858
(pencil/ink JHAL)

Right: J.H. Powell: design
for drinking cup for Francis
Warre Cornish, 1862 (pencil/
ink, JHAL)

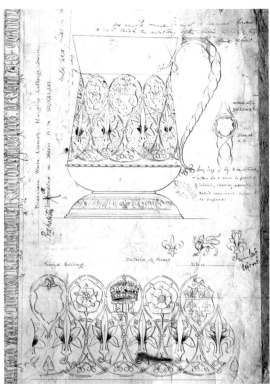

Cup presented by Stuart
Knill to the City of London,
1893 (photo: Andrew Ford)

Drawing for mayoral chain to design by C.A. Buckler,
1897 (ink and watercolour, JHAL)

items could be simplified to suit the budgets of less wealthy donors or parishes. For example, 'monstrance no. 4', as illustrated in the catalogue, could be supplied in plated metal with a pierced and beaten centre but without rays at £8, at £9 with rays, and at £9 and £14 respectively in gilt metal. It was this ability to work to budget without compromising the quality of the finished item, however small, that made Hardman's products so popular.

Although the prevalent nineteenth-century building style amongst Catholics and Anglicans was Gothic, Hardman's designed in other styles to suit different locations. One of the most-admired objects in the Medieval Court at the Great Exhibition was a large Byzantine-style corona commissioned by the Rt Hon. Sidney Herbert for his church at Wilton, and when goods were ordered for J.A. Hansom's church at Ulshaw Bridge, North Yorkshire, the covering letter noted that 'The church is a sort of Byzantine but as the vestments are to be Gothic I think the things ordered may be so, though not too loudly proclaimed'.[65] Baroque chalices were included in the metalwork catalogue, and in 1878 Powell designed a magnificent pastoral staff in the Celtic style for the Rt Revd Angus MacDonald for presentation to him as the new bishop of Argyll and the Isles.[66] In the same year Hardman's made a window for the north chapel of St. Paul's cathedral, London, in memory of the late Dean Henry Mansel. (1820-1871). Round-headed, and entirely in the Classical style as it had to be in such a setting, it depicted the appearance of the Risen Christ to St. Thomas.[67]

Hardman's received many commissions from civic and educational institutions, and from individuals within them. In 1858 the Governors of King Edward's Grammar School in Birmingham commissioned a new seal, for which Powell produced alternative drawings. They are finely detailed, showing the young king crowned and seated in front of the Tudor Gothic entrance to the school, flanked by two kneeling pupils. The entry in the metalwork daybook for the executed design charges £25 to the Governors for the engraving of the seal, directing that two wax impressions are to be sent to Sir Charles Barry and Mr Edward Barry.[68] Charles Barry was the architect of the school (1833–7) and A.W. Pugin had designed many of the interior fittings. Hardman's made several windows for Eton College in 1881–2, the finest of which was a six-light west window in the hall. Powell's detailed design depicts King Henry VI as the founder and principal benefactor, and incidents in the later history of the college.[69] In 1862 a very handsome cup, engraved with the arms of Eton College and King's College, Cambridge, was made for Francis Warre Cornish (1839–1916), assistant master at Eton, also to Powell's design.[70]

Among the civic items made by Hardman's are two very fine silver-gilt standing cups presented to the City of London by Stuart Knill and his son John, both of whom became Lord Mayor of London; Stuart in 1893 and John in 1909.[71] The cups are identical in form, with pointed quatrefoil bases, enamelled shields, and slender stems with intertwining rope-work. Engraved bands of Gothic lettering around the bowls record the donor. The repoussé covers are crowned with figures: St George for Sir Stuart, and St Michael for Sir John. A particularly splendid *fin de siècle* piece is the mayoral chain of office made in 1897 for the town of Arundel, Sussex, and presented by the Duke of Norfolk to mark Queen Victoria's diamond jubilee. Made of 18 carat gold, the chain is ornamented with enamels including red and white roses, and the arms of England, Scotland, Wales and Ireland. It was designed by Charles Alban Buckler (1824–1905), the architect responsible for the virtual rebuilding of Arundel Castle between 1879 and 1890 and who, as well as being an architect, was also Herald of Arms.[72]

The Arundel chain and the Knill cups are fine examples of special commissions which show that Hardman's gold – and silversmithing work was still highly prized at the beginning of the twentieth century. The order books also reveal a sustained demand for more modest items in plated metal, for decorative work, and for stained glass windows. Though most of it was for the domestic market, Hardman's were well-placed to take advantage of some late flowerings of the Gothic Revival that were occuring overseas, and particularly in the United States from whence the firm received some of its largest early-twentieth-century commissions.

5. DOMESTIC WORK: VILLAS, PALACES AND 'BRASS CASTLES'

Although Hardman's metalworking and stained-glass enterprises were directed, initially, towards the furnishing of churches and convents, they also supplied a growing domestic market with items such as door-furniture, grates, candlesticks, coronae and gasoliers, tableware, and heraldic and decorative glass. The principal customers were, to begin with, members of Catholic families who were also involved with church-building programmes; aristocrats and landowners such as the Earl of Shrewsbury, or city businessmen such as Jane Pugin's cousin, Stuart Knill. Hardman's also made metalwork fittings for the furniture manufactured – principally from Pugin's designs – by J.G. Crace. As Gothic became increasingly the fashion of the Victorian age, partly as a consequence of Pugin's and Hardman's efforts at the Great Exhibition, so the market expanded to embrace many of the nouveaux riches who had made their fortunes in the textile mills and warehouses of Manchester, Leeds and Liverpool, and who caught the spirit of the Gothic Revival. Pugin's work at the House of Lords placed him in an unrivalled position as a designer; it was there for all to see. 'The Palace of Westminster style came to be in vogue . . . Private customers, clerical and lay, could buy Pugin's metalwork, wallpapers and fabrics from Hardman in Birmingham and Crace in Wigmore Street, or order them from Minton at Stoke'.[1] Pugin's own home, The Grange, established a new concept for middle-class dwellings: the detached suburban house set in its own grounds, as distinct from the symmetrical Georgian terrace built on the street-front.[2] It was widely imitated, and many architects and builders naturally turned to Hardman's to provide architectural metalwork and internal fittings.

All of the structural metalwork for The Grange, and other furnishings too, came from Hardman's. Several bedsteads, in brass and iron, are referred to in the correspondence, also pole-screens and table-candlesticks. As one would have expected, Hardman's supplied all the metalwork for the chapel at The Grange, to Pugin's designs. [3] An entry in the metalwork daybook for 10 September 1844 lists, amongst other things, shields for the fireplaces, cornice-poles, a prie-dieu, a corona and chain, a tea-table and three caddies. An intriguing entry to Pugin on 10 April 1848 is for '12 best percussion muskets with steel bayonets . . . 12 bayonet scabbards, cartridges and caps': a reminder that 1848 was the year of revolutions in Europe, and of Chartist agitation in England. Pugin was deeply afraid of radicalism and civil unrest, to say nothing of periodic anti-Catholic demonstrations, and among the other defensive measures he took at The Grange was the installation of heavy shutters which would pull up from beneath the cills on the inside of the house to barricade the windows. When John Hardman Powell married Anne Pugin in 1850, Hardman and Pugin undertook the decoration and furnishing of the young couple's new home at 3 Southwood Terrace. Hardman supplied all the metalwork, Lucy Powell the linen, and Pugin designed the furniture and soft furnishings to be made by Crace.[4]

The designing of domestic metalwork and tableware seems to have been a speciality of John Hardman Powell. His many drawings of teapots, coffee-pots, sugar-bowls and dessert-dishes are matched by entries in the Hardman daybooks for these and other items of secular plate. Among the regular customers were members of the Somers Cocks family, related to Earl Somers of Eastnor Castle, Herefordshire, where Pugin had undertaken decoration and furnishing of the Drawing Room. One of the most interesting items is a silver toast-rack entered to Miss H.M. Cocks of 47 Harley Street, London, on 23 December 1856 at a cost of £15. Not only is Powell's drawing for it preserved in the Hardman (Lightwoods) archive, but the toast-rack itself was bought in 2005 for the Hardman collection, having turned up in a sale-room in Australia. A beautifully made piece of tableware, it has twisted and plain pillars, scrolls, and 'Puginesque' trefoils; delicate in appearance yet robust for its purpose. The initials JSC on the shield below the handle indicate that it was intended as a gift to John Somers Cocks. A similar toast-rack was made for Lt Col Charles Lygon Cocks, of Treverbyn Vean, Cornwall, whose other orders included a silver salver, teapot and sugar-basin.[5]

Pugin's vision of what a country gentleman's residence ought to be is set out in *The True Principles* (1841), in which he condemns the neo-Palladian style as foreign and the 'Gothick' castellated style as a mere sham. His ambition to build a 'true principles' house at Garendon (Leicestershire) for his friend, Ambrose Phillipps, never materialised, but the drawings show what might have been: ranges of asymmetrical buildings grouped around a quadrangle.[6] Two buildings predominate: the chapel and the great hall, and although in practice Pugin had to be content with altering and extending Gothic houses which other architects had built, chapels and great halls generally entered into the scheme of things. The great hall was for Pugin a part of the social dimension of his Gothic vision, countering the post-Reformation development of the country house from which the great hall – and the social cohesion which it represented – had disappeared. But Catholic England, as Pugin reminded his readers, was 'merry England', where 'under the rafters of their capacious halls the lords of the manor used to assemble all their friends and tenants at those successive periods when the church bids all her children rejoice'.[7] Thus Pugin's work at Bilton Grange (Lancashire), Chirk Castle (Clwyd), Scarisbrick Hall (Lancashire) and Lismore Castle (Ireland) included furnishing

Design for teapot by J.H. Powell, c.1860 (pencil/ink, JHAL)

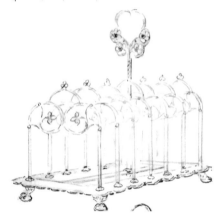

J.H. Powell: design for toast rack, 1856 (pencil/ink, JHAL)

Silver toast rack made by Hardman's to Powell's design, 1856 (Hardman collection)

and decoration – sometimes within existing structures – of a hall complete with screens passage, minstrels' gallery and great chimneypiece. Hardman's, along with Crace and Minton, were invariably involved in the provision of metalwork, glass, furniture and ceramics.

The most ambitious of Pugin's great halls was undoubtedly the new dining room at Alton Towers (Staffordshire) where Pugin worked for the sixteenth earl of Shrewsbury from 1837 to 1852.[8] Hardman's supplied the metalwork for Pugin's structural and decorative additions to the house. These included a set of eight large *coronae* for the new Talbot Gallery which Pugin added to the southern range in 1839, and various items for the chapel.[9] Among the somewhat bizarre objects which Pugin had to construct for Lord Shrewsbury was a life-size equestrian figure of John Talbot, first Earl of Shrewsbury (d.1453) in full armour, for which Hardman's made a jewelled coronet and an enamelled and engraved sword.[10]

The basic structure of the great hall at Alton was already in place. What was originally the entrance hall on the north front of the house had been converted into a state dining room in the mid-1830's before Pugin's arrival, but, since it rose from basement level, the room was inconveniently placed in relation to the first-floor state rooms. Proposals to correct this simply by raising the floor level were seized upon by Pugin as an opportunity to build something entirely new, and this led to his issue of an ultimatum to Lord Shrewsbury: 'I have nailed my colours to the mast: a bay window, high open roof, lantern, 2 grand fireplaces, a great sideboard, screen, minstrel gallery; all or none.'[11] Pugin got his way with all of these things, and rather more. The sideboard was made specifically for the display of a set of fourteen plated-metal dishes, some parcel-gilt, and all by Hardman. The largest, thirty inches in diameter, is entered into the daybook at £45. The others ranged in diameter from sixteen to twenty-four inches. All of them were quite distinctive, having rich borders and beaten work including Talbot shields, crests and mantling, mottoes and other inscriptions. It was without doubt the most impressive array of domestic plate made by Hardman's. Several of the larger dishes were finished in time to be displayed on the sideboard at the Great Exhibition, but the set was not completed until after the death of the sixteenth earl.[12] The catalogue of the sale of the contents of Alton Towers which followed the death of the seventeenth earl in 1856 lists the fourteen dishes, with brief descriptions, under the heading 'sideboard dishes, by Hardman', and they were, presumably, sold. The sideboard itself – for which Hardman supplied metalwork fittings including branched candelabra – presents another mystery. Though displayed at the Great Exhibition, it is not listed in the 1857 Alton Towers sale catalogue, or in subsequent inventories of the contents of the house. Given the unfinished state of the great hall in the early 1850s, and the dynastic changes that took place within the Talbot family at this time, it is possible that the sideboard may have gone elsewhere.[13]

The Shrewsbury sideboard and dishes displayed at the Great Exhibition (Illustrated London News, 20 September 1851)

A.W.N. Pugin: design for chandelier for dining room, Alton Towers, c.1850, pencil/ink (BMAG Loans Collection)

Chandelier made by Hardman's for Alton Towers (Palace of Westminster)

Hardman's other metalwork for the Alton dining room comprised door-furniture, grates and fire-irons for the two huge fireplaces, and a massive gilt-brass chandelier of forty-two lights. The chandelier was one of two – the other for the drawing room at Eastnor Castle – designed by Pugin and based on the originals he had seen in Nuremberg. The body is octagonal in section, with a twisted stem and scrolled branches ornamented with crystals and, originally, enamelled shields. It was put on show in the Medieval Court, but the huge chain for it was not sent to Alton Towers until July 1855, and only in 1859 was it finally hung: further indications that, for many years after the death of Pugin and Lord Shrewsbury, the dining room remained in an unfinished state.[14] Having failed – probably on account of its size – to attract a buyer at either of the Alton Towers sales (1857 and 1924) it remained in the house until the interiors were stripped in 1951, and was later discovered in sections in a dealer's shop, from where it was taken to the V&A Museum, restored, and hung in the Pugin Room at the Palace of Westminster.[15]

Pugin's all-or-nothing ultimatum to Lord Shrewsbury had included a bay window. Two windows were made for the dining room: the five-light south window containing Talbot

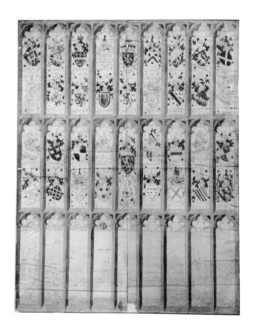

John Hardman Powell: projected arrangement of heraldic glass in north window, Alton Towers dining room, c.1851 (ink/watercolour, JHAL)

heraldic devices flanking the central figure of the first Earl of Shrewsbury – 'The Great Talbot' – and the huge oriel of twenty-seven lights at the north end. The 'Great Talbot' was shown at the Great Exhibition, but Powell lost the scheme for the heraldry in the side-lights, and got the labelling wrong. '. . . the ridicule to which it has exposed me is abominable,' wrote an angry Pugin. 'Willement was there making fun & others. . .'[16] Though still intact in 1951, the Talbot was subsequently removed, and the remaining glass rearranged. The bay window at the north end of the hall was made up of eighteen transomed lights filled with heraldic glass, the devices being taken from the shields of arms of the Talbots and related families. The nine lower lights were, apart from ornament in the tracery heads, deliberately left plain to illuminate the room and (eventually) the plate collection on the sideboard. Powell made the coloured drawing showing the arrangement of the shields, although the window as finally executed shows an altered arrangement. Pugin himself complained to Hardman, '. . . even what I design is spoilt by others. my great window of dining hall which would have been a grand thing is now totally ruined by recent alterations'.[17] Only a small part of the window had been finished by the time of the sixteenth earl's death in November 1852, and the final account was made out to his cousin and heir in February 1856.[18]

Important items of Hardman metalwork at Alton Towers included a number of heating stoves, clad in Minton tiles and provided on all four sides with elaborate guards of brass and iron. Inspired by north German examples, such stoves were both an efficient method of heating large spaces, since heat was radiated from all four sides, and also highly decorative. An inventory of 1869 lists four such stoves, situated in the Great Drawing Room and Long Gallery.[19] One of them was shown in the Medieval Court, and the metal screenwork, which included brass pillars at each corner and vanes with enamelled Talbot lions, is entered into the Hardman daybook at £70.[20] 'An iron stove for tiles part wrought part cast ironwork with doors, cresting on top' is charged to Herbert Minton at £24.17s.6d. on 5 December 1851, and referred to as 'No.3'. New rooms on the top levels

of the house, begun by A.W. Pugin and continued after his death by E.W. Pugin, were still being furnished in the 1860s. Grates, fender guards, fire-irons and other metalwork, to the value of £715, were charged to the twentieth earl of Shrewsbury in November 1869 for rooms variously named as the Pugin bedroom, Pugin dressing room, Fountain room and Bachelor's room.[21]

Pugin's early decorative work at Alton Towers – specifically in the chapel and the Talbot Gallery – was cited before a Parliamentary Committee in 1841 as being 'quite applicable to the style of architecture of the new Houses of Parliament'.[22] That was the opinion of the architect Charles Barry (1795–1860), whom Pugin had already assisted in the design of the Gothic interiors of the King Edward Grammar School in Birmingham (1833–5).[23] Following the destruction by fire of the old Houses of Parliament in October 1834, the Lords and Commons committees for rebuilding agreed that the architect of the New Palace should be selected by open competition. By stipulating that the new buildings must be either Gothic or Elizabethan in style, the committees ensured

The Great Stove (M. Digby Wyatt, *The Industrial Arts of the XIX Century*, 1851–3)

104

architectural continuity with what had gone before, and also set the seal on the late-Gothic style as uniquely expressive of Britain's social and political order: 'the stylistic language of government in Britain'.[24] In view of their earlier association, it was hardly surprising that Barry called upon Pugin to assist in preparing his competition designs. Having won the competition, Barry turned to Pugin for help with the Estimate Drawings used by the quantity surveyors to calculate the building costs. In 1844 Barry once again approached Pugin – whose reputation as an architect and writer was now firmly established – to provide drawings for the internal fittings and decorations for the House of Lords, which he was anxious to complete as soon as possible. Barry admitted to Pugin that he was 'in a regular fix', and that he was prepared to 'enter into some permanent arrangement'.[25] Pugin was able to set out his own terms and conditions, which resulted in his official appointment under government contract as superintendent of woodcarving, but responsible also for metalwork, tiles and glass.

It seems incredible, therefore, that the earliest printed accounts of the New Palace of Westminster should have made not a single reference to Pugin's huge contribution to its design and furnishing. An illustrated booklet produced in 1857 by Warrington & Co. of London describes the House of Lords as 'without doubt the finest specimen of Gothic Civil architecture in Europe; its proportions, arrangements and decorations may be said to be perfect'. Hardman is named for the 'intricate and masterly workmanship' of the brass doors at the entrance to the Peers' Chamber, and Minton for the richly tiled pavement of the Lobby. Some individual artists and sculptors such as William Dyce and John Gibson are listed too, but the name of Pugin – who was recalled by Barry specifically to make the working drawings for the House of Lords – appears nowhere. Charles Barry is, of course, identified as the architect, and a concluding tribute to 'the able author of the whole' implies that Barry was responsible for everything.

Whether or not this astonishing omission reflects a deliberate suppression of the facts or a genuine ignorance of the nature and extent of Pugin's involvement is a matter of opinion. What is certain is that after the death of both Pugin and Barry a bitter dispute broke out between their sons, Edward Pugin and Alfred Barry, over the roles of their respective fathers.[26] For his part, Edward Pugin claimed that Barry had designed only the ground plan, and that all the elevations and details were Pugin's. Alfred Barry, on the other hand, repeatedly minimised Pugin's role. Though both sides marshalled their protagonists, John Hardman Powell, who had been closer than anyone to the actual situation, remained curiously silent. This was explained many years later by Powell's son, Sebastian Pugin Powell, in a letter which may better reflect the truth than either of the extremes:

> The public know so little of the process by which a building of this kind must necessarily be designed, and they are not sufficiently interested to learn. My dear father knew more about the matter than any other man, and he kept out of that controversy because he saw just this very thing. What you see in the main is Pugin – pure Pugin, but behind it all there is Barry in the plan and framework of the building – pure Barry. After all, what you see of a man is mostly his clothes; yet they would not be up to much if hung on a peg instead of on his shoulders. It is hard to express this, but an architect understands . . .[27]

The establishment of the contract for Pugin's services at Westminster enabled him to bring in Crace, Hardman and Minton, who were already accustomed to working from his drawings. As regards metalwork, Barry believed that Hardman's workshop was 'the only one in the kingdom where such work is properly executed'.[28] Hardman's had by this time been in the business of metalwork manufacture for only six years, and the bulk of its output was ecclesiastical. The New Palace of Westminster needed not just large quantities of rich metalwork, but a wide variety of mainly secular items. Although some of these – gas-pendants for example – were later removed, the palace still contains more examples of brass and ironwork designed by Pugin and made by Hardman than any other building, and not merely items for which there was clear medieval 'authority' such as locks, handles and candelabra. Pugin had to stretch his imagination and apply his 'true principles' of Gothic design to such un-medieval objects as calendar-stands and ink-stands, bracket-clocks and mantel-clocks, gas-fittings and bell-pulls. Having pilloried 'those inexhaustible mines of bad taste, Birmingham and Sheffield' for their misuse of Gothic forms and features in the design and manufacture of metalwork, Pugin could hardly allow himself or Hardman to fall into the same trap by producing 'staircase turrets for inkstands, monumental crosses for lightshades . . . and four doorways and a cluster of pillars to support a French lamp'.[29] So, when designing a table clock for Westminster, Pugin considered first of all its function as a timepiece. The dominant features needed to be the dial and the chiming bell, so what he produced was essentially a cube with the dial occupying as large an area as possible in the front face, and surmounted by a dome-like bell. These essential features were then ornamented with diminutive flying buttresses at the angles, brattishing around the top, and an openwork crown above the bell, but there was no attempt to make it resemble 'the whole front of a cathedral church reduced to a few inches in height'.[30]

Table-clock designed by Pugin and made by Hardman's (Palace of Westminster)

The care which Pugin took over even the smallest items is reflected in a design for an inkstand and paper rack. Inscribed 'Inkstand for Westminster No.3', the drawing gives not only the plan and elevation, but is covered in minute annotations including details of how the components should fit together, the nuts and bolts, and the gauge of the metal to be used.[31] Pugin was, of course, working from his home in Ramsgate for most of the time. The metalwork drawings and letters were sent by post to Hardman in Birmingham, and Hardman had the job of ensuring that the items were executed according to Pugin's precise directions. Then there was Barry, based in London, who had to approve designs before Hardman could proceed with them. 'He is such a man for alterations', wrote Pugin to Hardman, 'that one is never safe till the final order is given.'[32]

It is difficult to say exactly how many metalwork drawings for the New Palace of Westminster passed between Pugin and Hardman. The metalwork daybooks for 1845 to 1851 – when work for Westminster predominated – contain over 1,500 entries for objects produced in the Hardman workshops to Pugin's designs. Metalwork drawings in a private collection on loan to the Birmingham Museum and Art Gallery are inscribed with four-figure numbers, some in excess of 3,000, but not all of these relate to Westminster. These, and the scores of letters to Hardman, bear testimony to a huge volume of work which took its toll on Pugin's health. In addition to inflammation of the eyes, he suffered periodically from tremors of the hands. A design for an umbrella stand for Westminster which he sent to Hardman includes a note written over a perfectly drawn curve, 'Pugin's compass hand firm again. alleluia'.[33]

The strain of overwork was compounded by deep personal unhappiness following the sudden death of Pugin's second wife, Louisa, in 1844, and the breakdown of his relationship with Mary Amherst, whom he had subsequently courted with a view to marriage. There were times when he felt desperately lonely. Even the house at Ramsgate in which he had taken such delight in designing and building, lost its charm. 'I can assure you', he told Hardman in 1847, 'that if it were not for the creation of the church at Ramsgate . . . I would never return or do anything for anybody. I would sooner go before the mast than live in this dismal solitude & now there are no fires the rooms are melancholy beyond description when everybody is gone to bed & I am obliged to work late. no sleep.'[34] From December 1844 onwards John Hardman Powell was at Ramsgate to

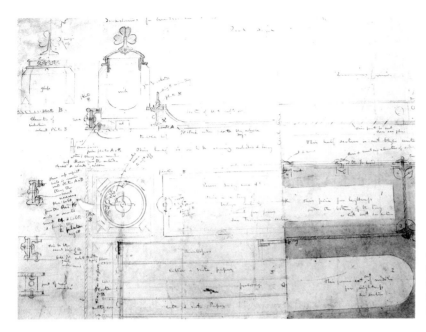

A.W.N. Pugin: drawing for ink-stand, pencil/ink (BMAG Loans Collection)

assist Pugin, but to begin with he was *in statu pupillari* until Pugin had educated him in his own methods and corrected the bad drawing habits he had brought with him. Young Powell also seems to have suffered from the kind of mood-swings that dogged Pugin. In explaining to Hardman why certain drawings were being sent to him in pencil rather than inked-in, Pugin wrote, 'Powell is in the dumps & we cannot get on at present. he gets miserable fits like me.'[35]

Hardman's first commissions were for metal crowns, cresting and vanes for the roofs of the palace. There are some ninety-nine entries for gilded vanes of various sizes in the metalwork daybooks for July to December 1845. Internally the most pressing task was to complete the metalwork for the House of Lords, which was due to open in 1847. The most difficult item was the brass railing running around the gallery. Pugin made his first design in February 1845, and a trial piece was made. After Charles Barry had seen it *in situ*, he insisted on several significant alterations to the original design, much to Pugin's displeasure.[36] The final entries were made in the daybook on 12 July 1847, the total cost of the railing being £2,006.13.6d.

Hardman's, alas, lost the order for the gas-branches for the House of Lords, following the failure of a lighting trial, and James Faraday eventually supplied the apparatus, but Pugin and Hardman came into their own with the lighting of the floor of the chamber, which Barry insisted would be by candles only. Two huge candelabra were made for the throne end of the chamber. Made of brass, they stand seventeen feet tall, and have branches for twenty-nine lights each. At the bar end of the chamber were four smaller standards, eleven feet tall, and carrying thirteen lights each.[37] Only those at the throne end are still *in situ*; the whereabouts of the other four are unknown.

The remaining brasswork carried out by Hardman's for the Lords' Chamber included an outer railing running between the candelabra at the throne end, and somewhat more elaborate railings and gates in front of the throne itself. John Webb of Old Bond Street, a noted antiquary and furnisher, made the throne, the design of which was based on the fourteenth-century Coronation Chair in Westminster Abbey. The metalwork fittings were supplied by Hardman: twenty-two gilt enamels, and a matching number of oval crystals set in gilt mountings.[38] 'The throne is very handsome,' remarked Queen Victoria following her first visit to the Chamber in April 1847. 'Perhaps there is a little too much brass and gold in the decorations, but the whole effect is very dignified and fine.'[39]

Palace of Westminster: The Peers' Lobby
(Palace of Westminster)

Palace of Westminster: The Lords' Chamber
(Palace of Westminster)

Above: A.W.N. Pugin/J.H. Powell: design for metal panel, Victoria Tower, Palace of Westminster, pencil/ink (JHAL)

Left: Brass door-grille made by Hardman's for Palace of Westminster (Hardman Collection)

J.H. Powell: design for railings, Palace of Westminster, ink/watercolour (JHAL)

Palace of Westminster: font in the chapel of St Mary Undercroft (Palace of Westminster)

The Peers' Lobby, immediately to the east of the Lords' Chamber, was furnished with several outstanding pieces of metalwork designed by Pugin and made by Hardman. First of all there are the gates of pierced brass leading from the lobby into the chamber. Weighing one and a half tons, their design was inspired by the gates and railing of Henry VII's chapel in Westminster Abbey.[40] In the centre of the Peers' Lobby a large eight-pointed star made out of deeply engraved and enamelled brass plates serves as a frame for the centrepiece of the Minton pavement.[41] Four gasoliers were made to stand in the corners of the Lobby. The design was based on the standing candelabra in the House of Lords: a single shaft of gilded cast iron some twelve feet high surrounded by four detached columns, and supporting a coronal for the gas jets.[42]

Large quantities of door furniture – hinges, knobs, escutcheons, saw-pierced finger-plates – were supplied by Hardman's as work on the Palace progressed and continued beyond the deaths of Pugin and Charles Barry. Many of the doors were fitted with brass grilles in a variety of patterns, hinged to facilitate the cleaning of the glass panels behind. Most of these appear to date from the 1860s, when Edward Barry secured a new contract with Hardman's for the completion of outstanding metalwork and stained glass.[43] Fireplaces in the principal rooms were equipped with grates, andirons and firebacks in the typical Pugin–Hardman style. Hinges, handles and other metal fittings were also made for furniture such as cupboards, desks and chairs. Most of the brass light-fittings – principally gas-pendants – have long since been taken away, and the great chandelier planned for the Central Lobby never materialised, possibly because after Pugin's death, Hardman felt unable to proceed with it alone, and in 1855 a corona was substituted.

Although Pugin designed metalwork for St Stephen's Hall and the Commons area, much of it was unfinished at the time of his death. The most spectacular items were the gasoliers for the Commons' lobby; more costly than those in the Peers' lobby, for Pugin was able this time to insist on brass.[44] Metalwork drawings by John Hardman Powell in the Lightwoods Collection include an unexecuted design for the Commons' mace, and some superb designs for metal panels in the gates under the Victoria Tower based on Pugin's original sketches. One is of a lion, and another of the chained hind, a symbol of King Richard II which appears frequently in decorative schemes elsewhere in the palace. There is also a coloured drawing for the railings in New Palace Yard, annotated '£11 per foot. Lamp & pedestal £21'. Work continued throughout the 1860s, for example the brasswork for the Speaker's House, while door furniture and brass panels for the Committee Rooms, Tea Rooms and Waiting Rooms is entered as late as 1871.[45]

The Crypt Chapel, properly called the Chapel of St Mary Undercroft, is one of the most important survivals from the old Palace, having been the undercroft of St Stephen's chapel, but it was severely fire-damaged. From the mid-1850s onwards it was thoroughly restored by Edward Barry in the High Victorian manner, glowing with wall-paintings, coloured decorative work and much gilding. Hardman's supplied the metalwork which included a domed brass font-cover set with large glass bullseyes around the base, and crowned with a figure of St John the Baptist.[46] J.H. Powell designed seven windows of four lights each, which depict the life of St Stephen.[47] Poor external light accounts for a lack of sparkle, but the Crypt Chapel windows are the only set to have survived intact at the Palace following the extensive bomb-damage in 1885 and in the 1940s, and the deliberate removal of coloured glass which began as early as the 1860s in order to admit more light.[48]

When Hardman's began work at the Palace, their stained-glass operation was little more than an idea in the mind of Pugin, and their first glass was not produced until the end of 1845. Glass, however, formed an important element in Barry's furnishing scheme, and he drew upon Pugin's extensive knowledge in working out his scheme, which was principally for heraldic glass. Initially the Edinburgh firm of Ballantine and Allen were recommended by the Royal Fine Arts Commission. The glass for the House of Lords was to contain figures of English and Scottish sovereigns from William I to William IV and Queen Adelaide, but Ballantine's poor figure-work – still in the 'painterly' style of the 1820s – led Barry to turn to Pugin for new cartoons for the twelve windows, each of eight transomed lights. None of them has survived, and the cartoons have also

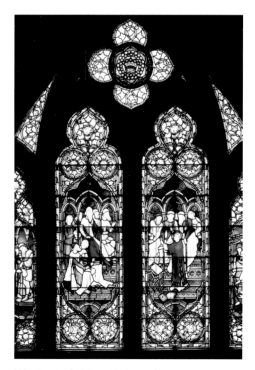

Window in St Mary Undercroft
(Palace of Westminster)

New Palace of Westminster: glass on Committee Stairs (Palace of Westminster)

disappeared, but the sketches and studies of individual figures by Pugin and Powell reveal a very different approach, based on close studies of what Pugin called 'the Real Thing'. Though designed by Pugin, the windows were actually made by Ballantine, but not before Hardman had made a specimen window to make sure that they got it right.

Hardman's were entirely responsible for four other major glazing schemes carried out during Pugin's lifetime: the Peers' Lobby, the Victoria Hall, the Commons' Chamber, and the great window in the south end of Westminster Hall which was filled with the arms of various sovereigns from William I. Pugin's schemes for St Stephen's Hall and the Central Lobby were not carried out until later, under John Hardman Powell. St Stephen's Hall was furnished with entirely heraldic glass instead of the combination of figure-work and heraldry envisaged by Pugin. In both the Central Lobby and St Stephen's Hall, glass from the House of Commons was re-used as a consequence of the lowering – for acoustic reasons – of the Commons' ceiling, this reducing the size of the windows by a half. Pugin was placed under great pressure. In 1849 he wrote to Hardman concerning the original scheme, 'The house of commons cartoons go off tonight, they have to drawn [sic] again, there is no end of trouble with them . . . this is the 3rd time they have been drawn'.[49] Then came the alterations which Barry wanted to complete quickly. In January 1851 he wrote to Hardman, 'I had hoped long ere this I should have received from you some of the painted glass for the House of Commons', and in August 1852 he was still waiting for a trial light to be made.[50]

Glass was lost from the Palace through deliberate removal following complaints by members that the windows admitted neither light nor air. Then, in January 1885, a bomb planted by the Irish Fenians exploded in Westminster Hall, destroying the south window and causing extensive damage to glass in the Commons' Chamber, the Division Lobbies, St Stephen's Hall and the Crypt Chapel. Hardman's were able to undertake repairs and reinstatements using the original cartoons. The biggest loss of all occurred during the German air raids of 1940–44 in which the House of Commons was completely destroyed. Hardman's were not the only firm involved in the post-war re-glazing, and their records of the original schemes were not, apparently, as complete as they had been in 1885.[51] Even after the loss of so much original glass and metalwork, however, the Palace still exhibits on an unparalleled scale the skills and achievements of Hardman & Co. from the days of Pugin through to the 1950s.

In February 1846 Pugin wrote to the sixteenth Earl of Shrewsbury, 'I am going to decorate the interior of a very curious house called Chirk Castle on the Welsh border.'[52] This would appear to be the earliest reference to the extensive work which Pugin carried out at Chirk for Colonel Robert Myddelton Biddulph. The family were not Catholic, but Robert's wife, Fanny, was related to the Mostyns of Talacre who most certainly were, and who also knew Pugin. This may account for Pugin's involvement. Chirk Castle is substantially medieval, but with large east-wing additions made in the Gothic style by the Chester-based architect, Thomas Harrison, in the 1820s. Pugin attempted to create something resembling a Great Hall by inserting a screens passage, massive chimneypiece, heraldic glass, and a Hardman gasolier into what was known as 'Cromwell Hall'. Hardman's provided new brass fittings for Harrison's Gothic doors in the east wing, elegant gasoliers and more heraldic glass in what is now known as the Pugin corridor, grates and andirons to complement Pugin's fireplaces, and a good deal of exterior metalwork.[53] You will always find me ready', Pugin wrote to Myddelton Biddulph, 'for a moderate consideration to provide you with anything from a coal scuttle of the time designed on the real principles of the old men'.[54] E.W. Pugin continued the work after 1852, with the provision of more Hardman gasoliers, and alterations to the chapel. An iron stove-guard with fleur-de-lis finials at the corners, though smaller and less ornate than the ones made for Alton Towers, remained at Chirk until the 2004 sale when it was bought for the Hardman collection. Though smaller and less ornate than the ones made for Alton Towers, it is the only known example of a Pugin–Hardman stove-guard to have survived. Much of Pugin's extensive decorative work was, regrettably, obliterated in the 1950s. It was one of his most expensive domestic commissions.[55]

If Pugin found Chirk something of a challenge – 'enough to drive a man mad . . . it is worse than the House of Lords'[56] – then his work at Bilton Grange was equally so, this time on account of an uneasy relationship with the client, Captain John Hubert Washington Hibbert. In 1847 he told Hardman, 'I had a letter yesterday from Capt. Hibbert that really took all the life I had left out of me. I will never have anything to do with house building again.'[57] Although Pugin was adding to an existing house, and with Hibbert constantly altering the plans, he was able to develop it considerably. One of the new additions was a large dining room with minstrels' gallery, and big windows with heraldic glass by Hardman, i.e. a 'great hall'. Lord Shrewsbury thought that something similar would suffice for Alton, but Pugin had other ideas: 'Your lordship cannot seriously mean to have so plain as job as Bilton . . . Everyone would condemn it and me too.'[58] Hardman made more than twenty windows, mainly heraldic, in 1847–8, for various rooms at Bilton.[59] As at Alton Towers. work continued long after Pugin's death, with Edward in charge, and Hardman supplying large quantities of metalwork in 1854–5.

Chirk Castle

Chirk Castle: Hardman gasolier (now converted to electricity) and stained glass in Pugin Corridor

Scarisbrick Hall, near Ormskirk (Lancashire), was the first great house with which Pugin was involved, starting in 1837 to carry out alterations to the Gothic residence built by Thomas Rickman (1776–1841) for Thomas Scarisbrick whose brother, Charles, inherited the property in 1833.[60] Externally, he added cresting and vanes to the roofs, and Rickman's great hall was given the characteristic Pugin treatments, including screens and gallery, a large stone fireplace and a high open roof with wind-braces.

Pugin appears not to have visited Scarisbrick again after 1845, but another phase of work began in the 1860s after the death of Charles Scarisbrick and the succession to the estate of his sister, Lady Anne Hunloke, at the age of seventy-two. Edward Pugin was in charge, and his high-Victorian development of his father's style is particularly evident in the east-wing rooms and the huge tower. Large quantities of metalwork are signed off to E.W. Pugin in the Hardman daybooks: vanes, finials, cresting, window-casements, door furniture, grates, fire-irons and light-fittings. The latter included two gas *coronae* of twenty-four lights each.[61] A cross, candelabra and cruets were among the

Iron stove-guard from Chirk Castle (Hardman Collection)

Scarisbrick Hall: Edward Pugin and Anne Scarisbrick portrayed in stained glass (photo: Lancashire County Museums)

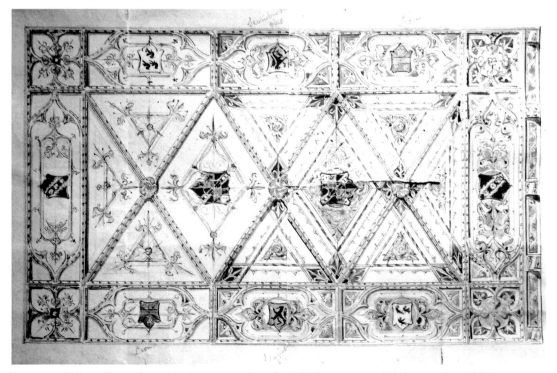

Design by Elphege Pippet for ceiling decoration, Scarisbrick Hall dining room (ink/watercolour, JHAL)

new items supplied for the new oratory next to the Blue Drawing Room.[62] A very fine pair of copper-gilt candlesticks is entered at £90 in the daybook on 18 December 1862. They have gadrooned pans, bases set with jewels and enamelled inscriptions, and stems inset with roundels and lozenges enamelled with Scarisbrick heraldry.

Metalwork additions were also made to the older parts of the house. New grates and andirons were ordered for the old library, study and dining room, the andirons having brass finials and shields with arms. Those for the great hall were particularly fine: 'rich cast dogs with brass dove on top, rich large rose, £85.[63] The landings to the grand stairs were given brass rails and panels incorporating large and delicately pierced letters A and S.[64]

Amongst the pieces of furniture made by Hardman's for Lady Scarisbrick was a large brass four-poster bed, possibly designed by J.H. Powell, and signed off to Edward Pugin at £150.[65] It had scrolled panels and Scarisbrick heraldic devices, and was originally furnished with an ornamental wooden canopy and silk brocade drapes. The bed was sold in 1923 along with many other furnishings from the hall. Much later it was acquired by the American singer, Cher, who amassed a large quantity of Gothic Revival furniture and art in her Malibu mansion. As her tastes changed to Moroccan–Tibetan, she put the Gothic items under the hammer at Sotheby's, Beverley Hills, on 3 and 4 October 2006, when the bed was sold for $84,000.[66]

Armorial glass to Powell's design was made for the window over the minstrels' gallery, Edward Pugin specifying that 'what colour there is should be of a deep sparkling character'.[67] In the Blue Drawing Room Powell designed glass depicting the Arts and Sciences, and he was also involved in the design of the coffered and painted ceiling, the cornice of which incorporates her ladyship's initials and the Scarisbrick dove emblem.[68] The richly coloured glass was originally reflected by large mirrors in gilt frames on the opposite wall. One of these mirrors is now in the Hardman collection at Lightwoods House. Lady Anne's bedroom above was furnished with glass containing allegorical figures of the four seasons, and on the east staircase which connects the drawing room with the bedroom a two-light window shows Lady Anne in conversation with Edward Pugin, who is holding a plan of the house.[69] This, along with the appearance elsewhere in the decorations in the east wing of the associated letters A and P, led one commentator to speculate that perhaps 'the widow in her seventies had become a bit sweet on her young architect, for it was unusual for a Victorian architect to be commemorated in this way'.[70] Be that as it may, Anne Scarisbrick died in 1872, Edward Pugin went bankrupt a year later, and it was the firm of Pugin & Pugin who installed the last of the Hardman glass at Scarisbrick, in the south porch, in 1889.[71]

Other Catholic families in the north-west for whom Edward Pugin worked extensively were the de Traffords of Croston Hall, near Preston (Lancashire), built and furnished by Pugin in 1869. Every room and corridor was systematically equipped with Hardman light-fittings, gas brackets and pendants.[72] The Manchester architect, J.S. Crowther, also used Hardman's extensively, for example at Redclyffe Grange, Alderley Edge (Cheshire), where large consignments of metalwork furnishings were sent in 1855.[73]

Among the Catholic aristocracy who commissioned work directly from Hardman's was John Patrick Crichton Stuart (1847–1900), third Marquess of Bute, and one of the most extraordinary figures of the Victorian age. His large estates and properties in Scotland and South Wales, his enormous wealth, his passion for antiquarianism and languages, and his conversion to Catholicism in 1868, provoked curiosity and controversy, and his subsequent marriage to Gwendolen Fitzalan Howard, a granddaughter of the Duke of Norfolk, related him to England's most senior Catholic family. Bute was well known for his employment of William Burges to build Cardiff Castle and the even more fantastic Castell Coch (Glamorgan).

Burges had his own preferred glasspainters, decorators and metalworkers based in Bute's workshops off North Road in Cardiff, but some work for Cardiff Castle was placed with Hardman's. This included some metalwork fittings for various rooms, and a set of soup-plates engraved with the Bute coat of arms.[74]

Paxbrede made by Hardman's for Marquess of Bute, to a design by William Burges (private collection)

Following his conversion to Catholicism, the Marquess visited Rome, and was confirmed by Pope Pius IX on 11 February 1869. The pope also presented him with an oval miniature of the Sacred Heart which Hardman's subsequently incorporated into a silver-gilt pax-brede, but in a very different style from the Gothic ones they had made in the 1840s. The frame has a semicircular top, the front is set with twenty stones cut *en cabochon* and has claw-feet, while the handle is in the form of a salamander. A finely engraved inscription on the back records Bute's confirmation and the Pope's gift, and over it are set enamelled shields with the Papal and Bute arms. The design has more than a hint of Burges about it, although no letter from Burges in this connection has come to light.[75]

In February 1870, Hardman's carried out what was for them a most unusual decorative commission, namely the painting, decorating and gilding of the cabins, saloons and other apartments on Lord Bute's private yacht, *Ladybird*. The panels of the Music Room were covered with gold diaper, and metalwork fittings included eleven zinc shields painted with heraldic devices, and a set of sixteen parcel-gilt candle-sconces equipped with Gimball movements to keep them upright in rough seas. When the yacht was sold, the sconces were removed, and they are currently kept at Mount Stuart (Rothesay, Isle of Bute).[76]

Hardman silverware ordered by Lord Bute for his private chapel at Mount Stuart in 1871 included a set of six silver candlesticks entered at £210, and the mounting of four carved pearl shells on silver bodies to serve as flower vases.[77] Among the items of domestic plate was a pair of five-light brass candelabra four feet high, and two very handsome silver-gilt candlesticks, one with a horse supporter and the other with a stag supporter, costing £63 each. A pair of identical candlesticks was made with matching lion supporters.[78]

Pugin's family home – The Grange – at Ramsgate was the epitome of the 'smaller detached houses' which he considered to be a product of 'the present state of society', and objectionable only if they were made to appear simply as 'diminutive representations of larger structures'.[79] As with any other type of building in Pugin's *oeuvre*, purpose and function governed the design, and the plan determined the elevations.[80] The purpose was to house a family, with space for children, guests and servants, and Pugin's arrangement of rooms around a

Left: Candle-sconce with gimbal movement, made by Hardman's for the Marquess of Bute's yacht, Ladybird. (private collection)

Silver-gilt candlesticks with stag and horse supporters made by Hardman's for Lord Bute (private collection)

E.W. Pugin: Burton Manor, Stafford

central double-height staircase hall reflects, on a smaller scale, the social cohesion of the medieval Great Hall and goes against the Victorian 'norm' in which family, servants and children were confined to separate areas.[81] The early impact of The Grange on domestic architecture is seen dramatically in Edward Pugin's first major domestic commission, Burton Manor (1854–5) on the southern outskirts of Stafford. Clearly visible from the M6 motorway near to junction 13, Burton Manor was commissioned by a local Catholic barrister, Francis Whitgreave, who, as a friend of A.W. Pugin, was a regular visitor to The Grange and wanted something similar for himself. The plan, the elevations and the dispositions of the principal rooms bear an uncanny resemblance to the Pugin home, down to details such as chimneypieces, ceilings and balustrades. Hardman's – naturally – supplied the local builder, Woollams of Stafford, with all of the metalwork fittings: crestings, finials, vanes and a wrought-iron cross for the roofs; and for the insides they provided everything from engraved brass door-furniture to fire-grates and kitchen equipment.[82] Modified or extended to meet the needs of individual clients, the model was widely adopted in other places and by other architects and builders, with furnishings and fittings from the Hardman metalwork catalogue available from stock in an increasing variety.

Others who caught the 'passion for Gothic' sought to transform existing houses through structural alterations and new furnishings. Among these was Miss Hales of Hales Place, Canterbury, who engaged E.W. Pugin, through whom huge metalwork orders were placed with Hardman's in 1864–5. The house also included a chapel for which Hardman supplied windows to Pugin's design.[83] In Cheshire, Lord Crewe employed Edward Barry to create a 'ferocious Victorian interior' within his 'Jacobean prodigy house'[84] following a fire at Crewe Hall in 1866. Crace did the decorating, and Barry went to Hardman for the metalwork.

'Brass castles' is an expression used to describe large houses built and furnished in grand style by industrialists who made large fortunes out of the textile mills and ironworks in the north of England. or through trade.[86] One of these was Abney Hall (Greater Manchester), built in 1847 by the cotton manufacturer Alfred Orrell, and extended, decorated and furnished from 1849 onwards by James Watts (1804–78), a wholesale draper and one-time mayor of Manchester. Watts almost certainly visited the Great Exhibition, and towards the end of 1851 he engaged John Gregory Crace to undertake the furnishing and decorating of the new rooms at Abney. To draw up the designs Crace called on Pugin for what was to be his last major commission, and he brought in the tried and tested team of Hardman, Minton and Myers to do the metalwork, ceramics and carving, the architects being Travis & Mangall of Manchester. Hardman's supplied all the door-furniture – lock-plates, handles, fingerplates and hinges – which is all of exceptional quality. Gasoliers – one of which was described as 'experimental' – were installed in the principal rooms and staircases, some with elaborate scroll-work, beaten leaves and heraldic shields.[86]

Metal furnishings supplied to Abney Hall by Hardman's included a pair of brass candelabra for ten lights, with twisted stems and set with crystals and enamels.[87] The great sideboard for the dining room – which may or may not be one and the same as the one meant for Alton Towers – was fitted with brass candelabra of seven lights each.[88] An eight-light transomed window on the staircase was filled with Hardman glass: patterned quarries, geometrical shapes and coloured borders. The Crace decoration of the ceilings, walls and doors of the principal rooms is as rich as that in any of the homes of the Catholic gentry, yet James Watts was neither Catholic nor Anglican, but a Protestant Dissenter who consciously renamed his house (originally called The Grove) after a seventeenth-century Presbyterian mayor of London, Thomas Abney. For Watts at any rate, Puginian Gothic was a matter of taste, rather than of principle. What also makes Abney exceptional is that when, in the twentieth century, Victorian Gothic became unfashionable, the family simply locked up the rooms in

Abney Hall, Greater Manchester, Hardman door-furniture

Abney Hall: gasolier by Hardman's, ceiling decoration by Crace question and lived in other parts of the house, instead of destroying the Crace decorations and furnishings as others might have done, thus allowing them to survive into a more appreciative age.[89]

Of all the 'brass castles' with which Hardman's were involved, the most remarkable is undoubtedly Meanwood Towers, at Headingley on the outskirts of Leeds (West Yorkshire). It is remarkable on account of the sheer volume of expensive silverware supplied to its owner, Thomas Kennedy, and also because of the extraordinary character of Kennedy himself, who spared no expense in the creation and furnishing of his new family home.

Though born in Lancashire, and son of a Zurich-based businessman, Thomas Stuart Kennedy (1842–94) was of Scottish descent, and related to the Kennedys of Knockgray, an aristocratic family whose shield of arms – *Argent, a chevron gules between three cross-crosslets fitchée sable* – was engraved on several items of silverware he commissioned from Hardman's. One of his cousins was Sir Andrew Fairbairns, who made him a partner in the firm of Fairbairns, one of the most successful manufacturers of textile machinery in Leeds. His first dealings with Hardman's appear to have been over a pair of candlesticks:

12 Grove Terrace

(Leeds)

15 Feb. 1865

Gentlemen,

I am in search of Gothic candlesticks for a drawing room. I have seen some very good ones like the sketch [rough drawing of candlestick with circle in centre of stem] with arms at the centre of the circle. I think they were of brass. Could you make them? Also I want various other medieval things such as firegrate, bedstead & other ironwork which I believe you produce.

Yrs. truly,
J S. Kennedy[90]

Even in his early twenties, Kennedy appears to have been a wealthy man, and he married into a wealthy family, the Thorntons of Sturry, near Canterbury. Like the Kennedys, the Thorntons were industrialists and one of their mills was close to The Grange at Ramsgate. Powell later recalled that the Thorntons were amongst A.W. Pugin's earliest friends in Ramsgate, and that their children played together.[91] Edward Pugin would therefore have known Clara Thornton from childhood, and it was almost certainly through her that Thomas Kennedy was introduced to the Pugins in the 1860s. It is possible that Edward was present in Canterbury cathedral when Thomas and Clara were married in 1865.

Correspondence between Kennedy and Hardman in March 1865 was about jewellery for his fiancée, including a gold ring and a locket, and Hardman was eventually asked to make the wedding ring. On 3 March Kennedy wrote a letter of thanks 'for having taken so much trouble about the jewelry', and adding, '. . . I hope to be able to pay a visit to Birmingham in the course of a week or two that I may speak with you personally about many little matters necessary in furnishing a house'.[92]

The house was, clearly, the new marital home. Two pairs of candlesticks of the kind mentioned in Kennedy's letter were completed in August 1865, and a little later Hardman's supplied two iron bedsteads with brass pillars diapered with the crosslets from the Kennedy arms, and a quantity of picture-frames, fenders and fire-irons.[93] A gold bracelet ornamented with medallions, pearls and enamels, entered at £18 on 20 December, was very probably a Christmas present for Clara.

In August 1865 Edward Pugin sent Kennedy a drawing of a proposed wooden garden building to be known as Orchard House, for which iron finials were requested from Hardman,[94] and in September Kennedy sent Hardman a tracing of a sideboard 'for which Mr. Powell promised me a drawing . . . I should like heraldry in the sideboard more than anything, but do not wish to overdo it'.[95]

Thomas Kennedy was a well-known mountaineer, a friend of the celebrated Edward Whymper (1840–1911) and the Revd Charles Hudson (1828–65), and he took part in the first successful ascent of Switzerland's Dent Blanche. If he had not been preoccupied with his marriage to Clara Thornton and furnishing a house, he might well have been in Whymper's party which made the first successful – and fateful – attempt to reach the summit of the Matterhorn in July 1865, having tried unsuccessfully in 1862. Tragically, four of the climbers, including Hudson, fell to their deaths on their way down, leaving only Whymper and two of the guides. In collaboration with Whymper, Mrs Hudson and others, Kennedy planned a memorial window to be placed in St James's church, Skillington, near Grantham (Lincolnshire), where Charles Hudson had been vicar, and was determined that Hardman's should carry out the work. He provided Powell with coloured sketches of alpine scenes and views of the Matterhorn, including 'the route by which Mr Hudson ascended . . . and the little rock on which Mr Knyvet Wilson was killed'.[96] The two-light window was eventually made by Hardman's according to Kennedy's instructions, and installed in the south side of the nave. A large brass plaque fixed to the cill records the names of the twenty-four subscribers, among whom was William Hardman. The two lights show the figures of two Old Testament 'mountain' figures, Noah and Moses, set against an Alpine background. An over-arching rainbow is set with angel-faces. The base-panels have symbols appropriate to Charles Hudson: on the left-hand side a chalice and paten, Bible and prayer-book, and on the right an alpenstock, pick and climbing-rope. A smaller single-light window with a view of the Matterhorn was made for the chancel, and charged to the Revd Andrew Wood, Hudson's successor at Skillington.[97]

Meanwood Towers, Leeds: the front entrance (photo: Jane Hedley)

Thomas Kennedy's mechanical interests extended to the design of clocks. A number of letters to Hardman refer to the making of an ingenious electric clock. Battery-powered electric clocks had been in existence since the 1840s, but instead of using electricity to power the clock mechanism directly, Kennedy designed a pendulum clock 'with an electrical contrivance destined to wind up the main-spring; this motion will be continually at work, winding up as fast as necessary to drive the clock'. There was also to be a chiming mechanism designed to play a variety of tunes including 'at 6 or 6–30 p.m. "The Roast Beef of old England"'.[98] Two designs by J.H. Powell for clock-cases may possibly relate to this commission, and they illustrate the extent to which Hardman & Co. were extending their range of

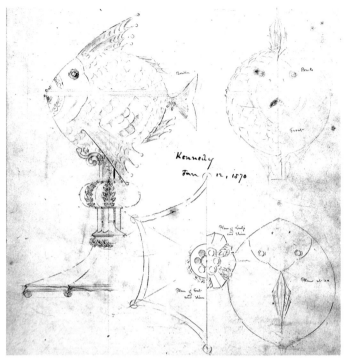

Memorial window to Charles Hudson
at Skillington church, Lincs.

Design for 'fish' trophy; John Hardman Powell, 1870
(ink/colour, JHAL)

domestic metalwork and furniture at this time. 'Don't you think the clock will be the finest thing ever made?' Kennedy wrote to Powell. 'I think that the inside of it will be a curiosity: it will certainly go 20 or 40 years without being touched, excepting perhaps, to have the works cleaned and oiled.'[99]

In 1865 Kennedy ordered a large quantity of domestic silverware from Hardman's, making him one of their most important clients. There was a silver-gilt punch bowl, with an inscription and an enamelled shield. As Christmas drew nearer, Kennedy wrote anxiously to Hardman, '. . . I hope you will be able to complete the silver before long, more especially the <u>Punch Bowl</u>; this is just the season for using it'.[100] Other items included a scrolled toast-rack similar to the one made in 1856 for John Somers Cocks,[101], complete tea- and coffee-services, salt-cellars, spoons, egg cups, richly beaten dessert-dishes, and a parcel-gilt card-tray with the Kennedy arms enamelled on a shield. Thirteen items, or sets of items, are entered to Kennedy in the metalwork daybook on 22 December 1865, at a total cost of £295.15s. and he also commissioned Edward Pugin to design a sideboard on which to display his silver collection.[102] Further pieces were commissioned in 1869–70, among them two silver-gilt seals, a glass claret jug with pierced gilt metal mounts, and another toast-rack.[103] Powell designed a hanging lamp in the shape of a ship complete with mast and rigging, and the most curious piece of all was a standing cup in parcel gilt, the body of which was in the form of a fish.[104] The daybook entry shows that the cup was for presentation to a swimming club. As with other commissions, the 'fish cup' design later appeared amongst the grace cups, goblets and drinking-cups that could be ordered from the Hardman metal-work catalogue. Another cup ordered by Kennedy had a distinctly mountaineering flavour, ornamented with allegorical figures representing various alpine peaks, and it was displayed by Hardman's at the Paris Exhibition of 1867.[105] It is evident that the Kennedys and the Powells had become friends. In a letter dated 30 January Kennedy wrote, 'When shall you & Mrs. Powell visit us; we have our blue room always at your service.'

The 'brass castle' which Kennedy adorned with Hardman metalwork, and to which the Powells were invited, was yet another house, built for him at Headingley in 1867 by Edward Pugin. Meanwood House – or Mean-

Meanwood Towers: detail of dining-room window (photo: Jane Hedley)

wood Towers as it later became known – was built of rock-faced gritstone with ashlar details such as mullioned windows and a moulded pointed archway into the front entrance-tower. High Victorian, and different in many ways from Burton Manor of twelve years earlier, it is nevertheless constructed around a double-height inner hall with a marble staircase, carved balustrade and a galleried landing. The entrance tower originally had a timber-framed top storey with a pitched roof, but, like the tall ornamental chimney-stacks, this has disappeared. Hardman's supplied the architectural metalwork and fittings for the house, and a quantity of stained glass which was added in the early 1870s. The upper lights of the dining-room windows have patterned quarries and borders, and at the centres there are roundels depicting various blood-sports: trout-fishing, coursing, salmon-spearing, grouse-shooting, hawking and wild-boar hunting.[106] Five panels with singing birds at the centres were completed in December 1873 for the drawing room. At the same time ornamental coloured glass was inserted over and on either side of the front door. Yellow silver stain predominates, and the side-panels have inscriptions in Gothic letters.[107] Most of the Hardman glass survives in the building, but it has not been possible to trace any of the fine tableware or other items of metalwork which Kennedy bought in such abundance.[108]

In the grounds of Meanwood Towers Kennedy built an organ-house with seating for 800 people. The centrepiece of this building was a three-manual organ commissioned from the celebrated German organ-builder, Edmund Schulze, who came in person to superintend the installation of the instrument, which was another of Kennedy's expensive gifts to his wife.[109]

The windows of the organ-house had seventeen panels of Hardman glass depicting musical subjects.[110] Sadly, within a few years of the completion of the house, Clara became ill and could no longer play the organ. It was therefore sold, and it was eventually installed in St Bartholomew's church, Armley, Leeds, where is still is. Nor did the Kennedys live for very long at Meanwood. In 1883 the house was sold, by which time Thomas and Clara – who had no children – had moved to Askham Richard, near York. Meanwood Towers, now divided into apartments, still stands as a monument to an industrialist's *folie de bâtir* that was in its way as spectacular and short-lived as that of the sixteenth earl of Shrewsbury.

6. MEMORIALS AND FUNERAL FURNISHINGS

From the very early days of the firm until well into the twentieth century, Hardmans were involved in various branches of what may be described as funerary art, from the printing of obituary notices to the manufacture of memorials; from the making of coffin-handles to the furnishing of chantry chapels. The inspiration for it came, as one might expect, from Pugin, whose vision of a revived Catholic England encompassed the burial and commemoration of the dead as well as the spiritual and physical welfare of the living. Early nineteenth-century funeral practice was, in Pugin's view, characterised by purely secular pomp in the case of the wealthy, by the widespread use of pagan art-forms such as inverted torches, obelisks and broken columns in the design of memorials, and, as far as the treatment of the poor was concerned, a complete lack of reverence and decency. All of this was lampooned in the first and second editions of Pugin's *Contrasts* (1836 and 1841), where Francis Chantrey's lolling figure of the Earl of Malmesbury (1823) in Salisbury cathedral is contrasted with that of Admiral Gervase Alard whose fourteenth-century effigy in St Thomas's church, Winchelsea, rests in prayerful attitude on a canopied tomb-chest with figures of saints in niches. In the 1841 edition a neo-Classical and almost wholly secular memorial to the fictitious Bishop John Clutterbuck is contrasted with a medieval-style memorial brass showing a bishop in full pontifical vestments and flanked by figures of saints and angels. Another additional plate, entitled 'Contrasted Residences for the Poor', shows a body being carted off for dissection from a nineteenth-century workhouse, while in the contrasting plate of the medieval poorhouse, a pauper is being decently buried with full Catholic rites.

The instructional value of a properly ordered Catholic churchyard containing nothing but Christian symbolism was set out in Pugin's first *Dublin Review* article, *On the Present State of Ecclesiastical Architecture*, written in 1840–1.[1]

> . . . nothing can be more calculated to awaken solemn and devout feelings, than passing through the resting-place of the faithful departed. How often is the pious Christian moved to pray for his deceased brother, when he sees graven on his tomb, – 'Of your charity pray for my soul' . . .

Nor was it just a matter of theory and wishful thinking. Pugin saw to it that each of his churches had a churchyard with a large cross or crucifix to act as the common memorial and mark the ground hallowed for burial, 'and from which all modern funeral monstrosities will be rigidly excluded'.[2] When it came to the building of St Chad's, Birmingham, there was no space for a burial ground, but the crypt was large enough

Contrasted episcopal monuments from Pugin's *Contrasts*, 1836

The Hardman chantry, St Chad's cathedral, Birmingham

to accommodate a number of burial vaults including those of the Hardman family and those of cathedral clergy. The crypt chapels above the vaults were equipped with altars for the offering of Mass for the deceased, and strict rules were applied at the outset concerning the nature of memorials and the type of commemorative inscription:

> . . . none but Catholic memorials for the dead will be allowed. Urns inverted torches hourglasses and all *pagan* emblems of mortality will be rigidly excluded, pompous inscriptions of modern presumption will here give place to the humble petition of a Christian.[3]

The Hardman chantry, dedicated to St John the Baptist, has a stone altar above which is a stained-glass window depicting the Crucifixion, and a brass plaque on the south wall contains no more than the 'humble petition' to pray for the soul of John Hardman, 'A benefactor of this Church'.[4] Similar brass plaques record other members of the Hardman family in the same simple manner: a conscious avoiding of the lengthy and often unctuous eulogies seen on

123

many Protestant memorials of the eighteenth and nineteenth centuries. The standard set by the Hardman chantry was followed elsewhere, for example the Knill and Petre chantries in St George's, Southwark, the Drummond chantry at Albury (Surrey), and of course the Pugin chantry at St Augustine's, Ramsgate. Some Anglican families also took up the idea, notably the Rolles at Bicton (Devon) and the Suttons at West Tofts (Norfolk), while Henry Drummond, who commissioned a mortuary chapel attached to the parish church at Albury (Surrey), was a prominent member of the Catholic Apostolic Church. Hardman's provided metalwork and stained glass for all of these chapels, in collaboration with George Myers (stonecarving) and Herbert Minton (ceramics). Pugin's views on the care of churchyards, and of what was appropriate by way of memorials, were shared by the Anglican Ecclesiologists, and this helped to bring about a considerable change in Anglican attitudes towards memorial design and the treatment of burial grounds.

From the 1840s onwards entries appear in the Hardman daybooks for badges, shields and banners for various gilds attached to Catholic churches. Many of these gilds had as one of their objects the assurance of a proper Catholic funeral for its members, and were a more spiritual equivalent of the 'Assurance Collecting Societies' or Burial Clubs that became popular amongst Protestants in the industrial north. A pair of Gild funeral lamps and other funeral furniture was supplied to St Patrick's church, Leeds, in January 1844; and gild shields and a funeral pall were made by Lucy Powell for the Holy Gild of St Wilfrid in Preston.[5]

When Pugin's second wife, Louisa, died on 22 August 1844 after a short illness, John Hardman Jnr offered a burial space in his chantry at St Chad's, so the funeral took place at the cathedral eight days later. Preparations for the obsequies included the construction of a catafalque in the cathedral, standing under a *chapelle ardente*, or illuminated canopy, consisting of four strong pillars fourteen feet high supporting a pitched roof covered with black cloth and ornamented with heraldic devices. Attached to the structure were candelabra carrying many clusters of candles.[6] There seems little doubt that John Hardman would have undertaken the whole of this work, with the textile items being made at least in part by Lucy Powell and the Misses Brown. These included the special mourning dress which drew comment from *The Tablet* where it was noted that 'The clerical mourners wore, according to ancient usage, birettas and priest's cloaks, while the laity were habited in the solemn mourning robe and hood of the middle ages'[7] After Louisa's interment the *chapelle ardente* and its furnishings were given to St Chad's by Pugin for use at future funerals.

It was also in 1844 that Pugin published his *Glossary of Ecclesiastical Ornament*, the final page of which consists of a chromolithograph showing a funeral Mass being celebrated with all the 'proper' accountrements: the coffin covered by a herse and full-length fitted pall, six herse-lights with shields attached, and the altar vested with frontal, dossal and curtains in the appropriate liturgical colours. All of these furnishings were, of course, available from Hardman's.

It was Pugin, apparently, who goaded Hardman into becoming more deeply involved with the supply of funeral furnishings and stone memorials, initially in connection with burials in the churchyard of St Augustine's, Ramsgate. In a letter written in December 1851, he mentions that 'a solemn funeral of a child' in St Augustine's had been ruined by the 'vilest' metalwork fittings – 'intended to be Gothic' – of the coffin, and he continues,

> . . . Where is my remedy? It is no use sending a drawing of any thing to you or to Myers. I am obliged to go to *Staffordshire* for Head Stones & where am I to go for coffin furniture unless I can find out some ingenious man. I don't know where he is to be found . . .[8]

The reference to Staffordshire as the source of Pugin's headstones is interesting. St John's churchyard at Alton, opened in 1843, was very much a model for others, and not least in the design of its memorials, which include small floriated crosses, coped slabs and simple inscriptions, all executed to Pugin's design by John

A. W. Pugin, *Glossary of Ecclesiastical Ornament*, 1844: chromolithograph of funeral Mass in progress

Funeral of John Talbot, XVI Earl of Shrewsbury, *Illustrated London News*, 25 December 1852

Bailey, a member of a family of stonemasons employed at Alton Towers,[9] and it would seem that Pugin was using Bailey to make headstones for St Augustine's. Memorials and coffin furniture were soon to appear as stock items in the Hardman trade catalogues.

Hardman supplied the coffin furniture and some other metalwork items for Pugin's funeral at Ramsgate in September 1852,[10] but his most comprehensive undertaking was the funeral of John Talbot, sixteenth Earl of Shrewsbury, in November of the same year. The entries in the metalwork daybook (9 December 1852) run to four full pages and they show that Hardman's, in conjunction with Edward Pugin, were the complete funeral furnishers, with J.H. Powell taking a prominent role. They also give an insight into what was now considered, in the manner of Pugin, to be appropriate for the funeral of an earl who was also England's leading Catholic layman.[11] It was, additionally, a major test for eighteen-year-old Edward, barely two months on from his father's death, and for Powell in his new role as chief designer. The daybook reveals that the design-work for the earl's funeral was a joint undertaking, with Pugin and Powell receiving £40 for their drawings and designs. The total expenditure – some £1,400 – was equivalent to the building cost of one of A.W. Pugin's smaller churches.

Lord Shrewsbury died in Rome on 9 November 1852. His body was sealed in a copper coffin before being brought to England, where it lay for a time in St George's church, Southwark, and then in the Talbot Gallery at Alton Towers pending the redecoration and furnishing of the Towers chapel in readiness for the funeral which took place on 14 December. The preparations were extensive. The drapes made to cover the walls of the huge chapel consumed 1,340 yards of black cloth, serge, fringe and lace. St John's church in Alton village, where the interment took place, was similarly draped. A *chapelle ardente*, even more elaborate than the one at St Chad's cathedral, was constructed in the centre of the Towers chapel. Designed by Pugin and Powell and built by George Myers, it was cross-gabled and was supported on twelve carved and painted pillars. A total of 72 brass standards and branches were attached to the roof and pillars, and the triangular gables were painted with Talbot heraldry at a cost of £43. The *chapelle ardente* must have lived up to its name, for 375lbs of wax candles were supplied for the candlesticks and branches which stood on and around it.

Framed hatchments in two sizes were painted with the Shrewsbury coat of arms and Talbot-dog supporters, and one of these was eventually hung above the earl's grave at St John's, where it remained until the 1960s.[12] The Misses Brown were paid the considerable sum of £540 – the largest single expediture out of the total funeral bill – for needlework. The coffin pall of black velvet, richly embroidered with the Talbot motto *prest d'accomplir* and heraldic devices in heavy gold thread, is entered at £192.10s. There were four black velvet copes for the officiating clergy, and a richer one for Bishop Ullathorne, who presided. Frontals, dossals and curtains were made for the altars, and hangings and drapes for the funeral 'car' which conveyed the coffin to its place of burial.

Coffin-pall made by Lucy Powell and associates for Lord Shrewsbury's funeral

J.H. Powell: bracket and coronet placed over Lord Shrewsbury's grave in St John's church, Alton, 1853 (pencil/ink, JHAL)

Mortuary card for Agnes Penistone, daughter of A.W. Pugin (JHAL)

The earl's outer coffin, made of Spanish mahogany and covered with crimson velvet, was fitted with gilt metal handles, a cross supported by Talbot dogs, and an inscription plate. Items loaned by Hardman's for the occasion and subsequently returned to Birmingham included the six 'Exhibition' candlesticks (i.e. those displayed in the Medieval Court in 1851) for the altar, and various other standard candlesticks and branches. Hardman's undertook the printing of 1,500 cards for admission to the lying-in-state, 150 for admission to the funeral itself, and 350 'dole' cards which entitled the bearer to a dole of bread after the funeral: another medieval revival. They also made the travel arrangements for forty choristers from St Chad's cathedral to sing at the funeral, and provided them with black cloth caps.

After the funeral Mass a long procession went ahead of the coffin to St John's church, and it is recorded that as the head of the procession reached the door of the church, the coffin could just be seen emerging from the gatehouse, a mile away in the valley below.[13] Lord Shrewsbury was buried on the north side of the altar. A wrought-iron bracket to hold the earl's coronet was designed by Powell and fixed to the wall above the grave,[14] and in 1856 a memorial brass, engraved with a full-length figure of the earl, was supplied and fixed by Hardman's under Edward Pugin's directions.[15] A similar one was made for Bertram, the seventeenth earl, who died in 1856 aged only twenty-three, but Earl John's widow, who also died in 1856, was commemorated by a modest brass plate fixed to the wall. The *chapelle ardente*, the funeral pall and the black copes were presented to St Chad's cathedral and were listed in the cathedral records as 'designed by Edward Welby Pugin and made by Hardman & Co. and the Misses Brown of Great Charles Street, Birmingham'.[16] They were subsequently used at the requiems of bishops and archbishops. The pall and one of the copes still exist, along with some pieces of metalwork from the *chapelle ardente* which must surely have been the most elaborate piece of funeral furniture ever supplied by Hardman's.

By comparison with the four-page entry for Lord Shrewsbury's obsequies, other entries in the daybooks for funeral furnishings seem slight. An entry for 20 February 1856 charges John Hardman Powell £11.7s.6d. for a triple coffin as was usual for vault burials – an inner coffin sealed inside a lead one, with an outer coffin of oak – and metal furnishings, for his infant son, John Bernard, who died at the age of nine months and was buried in the Hardman vault at St Chad's. When it came to the funeral of Mary Margaret, wife of John Bernard Hardman, in 1879, the firm supplied only the brass handles, cross and inscription plate for the coffin, and a quantity of 'mortuaries', i.e. printed notices and cards inviting prayers for the deceased.[17] The designing and printing of mortuaries became something of a Hardman speciality, with particularly elaborate ones being designed for family members such as Lucy Powell (1863), John Hardman Powell (1895), for successive bishops and archbishops of Birmingham, and for members of the Pugin family including Cuthbert, the last of A.W.N. Pugin's sons, who died in 1928.

Memorials and coffin furniture were included in the Hardman metalwork catalogues for supply to undertakers and private clients, but Hardman's also continued to provide a complete service when required. In 1879, for example, they constructed a new vault in Yardley Wood churchyard for the Wilkes family, and erected a memorial of which Pugin would certainly not have approved, namely a 'pagan' obelisk of polished Aberdeen granite.[18] It was, however, the design and making of monumental brasses in the 'true' style established by Pugin which earned Hardman's an almost unrivalled reputation as memorial artists.

Pugin's study of medieval monumental brasses was based on the published works of those who had already carried out extensive surveys, such as Edward Blore and Richard Gough,[19] upon his own studies and observations which included the making of drawings and rubbings, and it is known that his collection of antiquities included a fragment of a fifteenth-century Flemish brass showing the head of a bishop with figures of saints in niches above.[20] His writings extolled the virtues of memorial brasses in the revival of Christian art. In an article in the *Orthodox Journal* written in 1838 he contrasts the elegance of fifteenth-century brasses set into the pavements of churches with the latter-day 'blisters' of white marble which disfigure the walls. The article concludes with a plea for the revival of memorial brasses with appropriate inscriptions:

> . . . Such was the style of the monumental inscriptions during the ages of faith, and most fervently it is to be hoped that the brass effigy and the orate pro anima ['pray for the soul of . . .'] will again distinguish the graves of the faithful, while hideous tablets and heathen emblems be left to Protestants, from whose ignorance and ideas such frightful and incongruous monuments could alone have originated.[21]

Pugin was able to show that memorial brasses need not be expensive. Those who could afford a full-length engraved effigy under a canopy might well spend in excess of £100, but a quarter-size figure might cost as little as £10, and a plain inscription with a simple emblem such as a chalice for a priest's memorial could be done for between £3 and £5.[22] Elsewhere he comments on the poor quality of a memorial brass to a priest which had recently been installed in one of his own churches:

> . . . the inscription on the brass plate on the floor is miserable. it is precisely what a protestant might have stuck up to commemorate a murder. it does not possess a particle of Catholic spirit either in matter or appearance. I would undertake for £5 to have a small brass of a preist [sic] engraved with a suitable inscription in antient Letters . . .[23]

The materials and the engraving skills needed to execute Pugin's designs already existed in Birmingham, and of course everything was done through Hardman's. The engraving of figure-work and lettering on brass plates was a specialist skill, as was the indenting of the stone slabs into which the finished brasses were generally inlaid. For the former, Hardman routinely used John Joseph Heath, an engraver and copper-plate printer based at 68 Great Charles Street, until he had recruited and trained his own engravers, although the Brass daybooks show that even then some of the work continued to be subcontracted to Heath. A local stonemason, William Cook, supplied the stone slabs and inlaid the brasses.

In May 1841 Pugin wrote excitedly to Daniel Rock, former domestic chaplain to the Earl of Shrewsbury, '. . . we are now reviving the monumental brasses at Birmingham. they will not come very expensive, we are now going in with Dr. Milners which will be a strict revival of an old one'.[24] Bishop John Milner (1752–1826) had been Vicar Apostolic of the Catholic Western District, founder of St Mary's College, Oscott, and an early pioneer of the Gothic Revival whose writings Pugin greatly admired. Pugin planned an elaborate chantry chapel for him at Oscott, but had to rest content with a memorial brass set into the floor of the chapel. Entered into the metalwork daybook on 25 May 1842 at a cost of £100, the brass consists of a full-length figure of the bishop vested in full pontificals, and standing under an ogee canopy. The inscription is set within an outer border. The design of the figure was modelled very closely on the brass to the fourteenth-century Bishop John Trilleck in Hereford cathedral, and shows how carefully Pugin sought medieval 'authorities' for memorials as with every other aspect of his revivals. For the correct bishops, priests, members of the nobility and academics there were actual examples on which to draw. When it came to those who had no distinctive vesture, Pugin produced designs of his own, adapted

Brass to Thomas Roddis, St Giles's church, Cheadle (photo: David Meara)

from nineteenth-century day-dress. 'The present female costume is by no means ill-adapted for sepulchral brasses,' he commented, while 'for the humbler classes, a cross, with the instruments of their trades and crafts, with marks and devices, would be sufficient and appropriate'.[25] A good example of the latter is the memorial designed by Pugin for Thomas Roddis of Sutton Coldfield (Warwickshire), who died in 1845. Roddis was a talented sculptor who carved much of Pugin's alabaster work, and he was commemorated with a floriated cross at the centre of which were the tools of his trade: square, compasses, mallet and chisels.[26]

As well as life-size figures, memorial brasses could be made to show smaller figures of the deceased, sometimes kneeling under elaborate tabernacle work surmounted by a cross. An early example of this is the brass commemorating Lady Gertrude Fitzpatrick (1842) at Grafton Underwood (Northamptonshire), which Pugin illustrated in his *Apology* (1843). Her hands are joined in prayer, as Pugin believed that 'the devout position of the hands contributes greatly to the solemn effect',[27] and because the figure is in semi-profile, Pugin asked the widower, Richard Fitzpatrick, that if the memorial were to be fixed in an upright position, he would 'see that the image kneels towards *the East* this is indispensable'.[28] It was eventually fixed – as Pugin preferred – horizontally on a table-tomb.

As well as pictorial brasses there were those consisting simply of a large floriated cross within a border containing an inscription. Examples of this type include the one to Dame Margaretta Sarah Morris (d.1842) illustrated in Pugin's *Apology* (p. 36), and three brasses to members of the Drummond family in their chantry at Albury church which is one of the richest of its kind, with intense decorations by Hardman's painter, Thomas Earley. A large floriated cross is set into the altar-tomb of Sir Charles Throckmorton (1757–1840) at St Peter's church, Coughton (Warwickshire) who, loyal Catholic though he was, had no regard for Pugin and the Gothic Revival. The irony of the situation was not lost on Pugin, who wrote to Lord Shrewsbury:

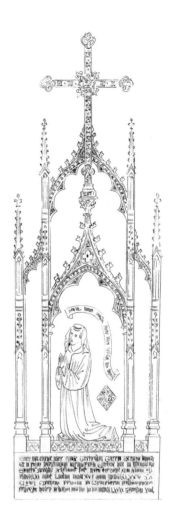

Brass to Gertrude Fitzpatrick, ink/watercolour drawing by John Hardman Powell after original by A.W. Pugin (JHAL)

> . . . I am going to make a brass for the late Sir C. Throckmorton who declared while living that nothing I make should ever enter his house and said the only subscription he would make for St. Chad's would be a barrel full of powder to blow it up . . .29

The most elaborate brass made by Hardman's to Pugin's design was the one created especially for the Great Exhibition. To begin with there was a suggestion that the Exhibition brass should commemorate Sir Robert Peel, who had died suddenly in June 1850, but then there were the questions of design and of what might happen to the brass afterwards. There were no medieval precedents to turn to, and no suitable likeness from which to work. 'I really don't see my way at all about it,' Pugin told Hardman, 'and it will never look like anything for Sir Robert it will be so different to the man – nobody will understand it and it will be a dead loss.'[30] His solution was to design a canopy brass with figures of saints in niches and a priest in full vestments underneath. There would be no inscription, so that once the Exhibition was over the memorial could be used for some suitable ecclesiastic. 'If no one else had it I will keep it for Father Costigan,' wrote Pugin,[31] Costigan (1788–1860) being the priest from Margate who officiated from time to time at Ramsgate. It was not until 1865, however, that the brass was finally put to use, as a memorial to Bishop John Milner in the church in which he was buried: SS Peter & Paul, Wolverhampton.

The Exhibition brass served as the model for others, including that of the Revd Alfred Luck of Ramsgate, who died in 1864. Luck had been a close friend of Pugin, had rented the Grange for a time after Pugin's death, and had been a benefactor to St Augustine's and to the associated Benedictine monastery. It fell to John Hardman Powell to design Luck's memorial, and to begin with he did no more than repeat the Exhibition design. Several modifications were then carried out. The canopy was simplified by the removal of the figures in niches, the inscription was given in English below the figure of the priest and in Latin in the border, while some details of the vestments were altered, and the anonymous face in the Exhibition brass was replaced by that of Alfred Luck himself. The finished brass was fixed in St Augustine's. In 1888 a similar brass was made by Hardman's to commemorate Wilfrid Alcock (1831–82), a former abbot of St Augustine's who died and was buried in Auckland, New Zealand. As appropriate to his status as the first mitred Benedictine abbot in England since the Reformation, he is depicted wearing a cope and mitre, and carrying a pastoral staff.[32]

The designing of brasses was, of course, something that Powell had to take on following Pugin's death. His early brasses were closely modelled on Pugin's, and there are many fine examples in the Hardman archives of

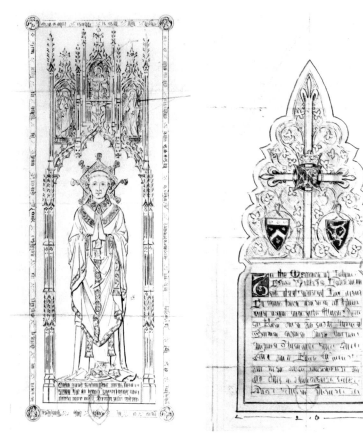

John Hardman Powell: adaptation of Great Exhibition brass as preliminary drawing for brass to Alfred Luck (JHAL)

J.H. Powell design for brass to Sir W. Cradock Hartopp, Sutton Coldfield, 1865 (ink/colour, JHAL)

his studies of Pugin brasses as well as his own designs. One of his first efforts, carried out under Pugin's immediate supervision, was a memorial to the Ryland family in All Saints' church, Sherbourne (Warwickshire). It is
a large brass, covered entirely with elaborate ornament, heraldry and lettering, but devoid of any figure-work.
It was in connection with this brass that Pugin told Hardman that Powell was 'naturally a scamp at drawing',
and doubted if he would ever have the perseverance to succeed in this very disciplined area of work, but at the
same time he acknowledged that Powell had a great talent for figure-drawing.[33] In Powell's later brasses his
figure-work becomes much more detailed and refined than Pugin's, with closer attempts at portraiture. It was
Powell who designed the brass to his uncle, John Hardman Jnr, which was placed in St Mary's convent, Handsworth, in 1868: a kneeling figure with an inscription below in a mixture of Gothic and Lombardic letters.

The ordering of a memorial brass from Hardman's was a process not unlike that of commissioning a window, involving the preparation of drawings and sometimes lengthy consultations with the client. Having perhaps
seen an example of their work *in situ*, the potential client would either write or pay a visit to the Birmingham
showroom. A preliminary design would be worked out by Pugin – later by Powell and others – using the basic
design features such as canopies, borders, a floriated cross or a figure of the deceased, the amount of detail and
the size of the brass governing the price. A quantity of numbered drawings exist in the archive, done in ink and
watercolour, of different types of brasses, with their prices, and the folds in some of these suggests that they
were sent to clients through the post as examples of the kind of thing that could be done. Illustrations of 'stock'
brasses eventually appeared in the metalwork catalogues, ranging in price from £5 to £45, with a note that special
designs and estimates could be sent on application. Once a design had been agreed, the brass would be engraved,
and then a rubbing would be taken and sent to the client. Alterations could still be made at this stage. Finally hot
wax in various colours could be run into the engraved lines to enhance the contrast; the
brass was then polished, set into its stone slab and dispatched in a packing-case to
the client. Additional rubbings of the finished brass could be supplied on request,
and rubbings of every specially commissioned brass were kept at Hardman's as a
record and for future reference.

Rubbings are taken by placing a large sheet of paper over the brass and rubbing it all over with a cake of black wax, which adheres only to the flat areas and
makes all the engraved lines stand out clearly in white, creating an exact full-size
copy. Rubbings were often sent to potential clients to show what was possible and
to assist in the selection of a design. Sixteen rubbings of various brasses were sent
to the Revd T. Luck before the memorial to Alfred Luck at Ramsgate was decided
upon.[34] Rubbings and designs were also sent much further afield. In July 1863 rubbings of twelve brasses were sent to Thomas Kemp of Sydney, and a little later
several designs were sent to the Revd D.P Williams, described as 'Chaplain, Delhi,
India'.[35]

The largest array of Hardman brasses to be seen in one place is at Oscott
College, where fifty-five, dating from 1842 to 1907, are to be found in the
side chapels. Forty-four of these are grouped together on the wall of the
Weedall chantry in the form of a Mortuary Tree. Dating from 1867, the tree
itself consisted of diagonal bands of stencilling and scroll-work designed
by William Powell, and the brasses hung, as it were, from these stylised
'branches'. The stencilling has since been painted out, but the array of miniature brasses, in various shapes, survives. Some include figure-work, and
all commemorate past members of the Oscotian Society including Henry
Weedall (d.1859), the first president of the re-founded college, and Cardinal
Wiseman (d.1865).

Westminster Abbey has two important Hardman brasses, one to the

Memorial brass to John Hardman
Jnr., St Mary's convent, Handsworth. The scroll above his head
contains a verse of Psalm 26 set
to plainchant: 'Lord, I have loved
the habitation of thy house: and
the place where thine honour
dwelleth'; allusions to Hardman's
close links with the cathedral and
choir of St Chad's, Birmingham.
(photo: David Meara)

engineer Robert Stephenson (d.1859) and the other to the architect Charles Barry (d.1860). The Stephenson brass was commissioned by George Gilbert Scott, and was selected from a set of four designs which reveal the efforts that were made to portray a modern railway engineer on a medieval-style brass. The first design was a cross brass with a demi-bust in the head and a locomotive in a pointed trefoil at the base. Another showed Stephenson as a full-length figure dressed in an Inverness cloak – 'for which Mrs Powell says the long lines of the cloak are a great advantage' – and set under a medieval-style canopy. The most complex design combined the full-length cloaked figure with a locomotive under the feet, set under rich tabernacle work, with border inscriptions, mottoes and heraldic devices. The executed design was the simplest of those offered. The locomotive and canopy were omitted, and Stephenson was represented in modern dress with a large fringed scarf over his shoulder, and framed in a lettered border[36] Devoid of any background or canopy work, the figure appears to be floating in a void. Set into a slab of red Aberdeen granite, the brass was fixed in the Abbey in 1862 at a cost of £250.

In terms of elaboration and expense, the memorial to Sir Charles Barry moved in exactly the opposite direction, so that Hardman's original estimate of £150 given in 1860 rose to £700 by the time the memorial was finished four years later. Even when the design had been agreed, there were delays in completing the work. Though failure to deliver on time was not entirely uncharacteristic of Hardman's, it provoked an anxious letter from Charles Barry Jnr in July 1863:

> Will you let me know *for certain* when we may expect to see the Monumental Brass to my Father in its place at the Abbey. When you began the work in the early part of the year you promised in a fortnight afterwards to write me this information about which all the family feel anxious but you have not done so.
>
> I suppose the work must now be far advanced. An early reply will oblige.[37]

Brass to Robert Stephenson, Westminster Abbey (photo: David Meara)

Barry's supposition was wide of the mark, for it was several months before the brass was fixed in the Abbey. It consists of a full-length floriated cross set with the *agnus dei* and the symbols of the Evangelists, set between a finely detailed elevation of the Victoria Tower of the Palace of Westminster and Barry's ground plan of the Palace.

The brass daybooks in the Hardman archive show that in addition to large and prestigious memorials there were very many small inscription plates consisting of lettering only, or with only a little ornament or heraldry. Some were associated with memorial windows made by Hardman's, or fixed to other pieces of church furniture. In 1846 a set of twenty-two inscribed door-plates and pew-plates was supplied to Manchester Corporation for fixing to their private seats in the Collegiate Church (now the cathedral) – a thought that would have annoyed both Pugin and the Ecclesiologists for whom the whole notion of private pews was anathema.

Surprisingly, perhaps, the commission for a memorial brass to Sir George Gilbert Scott (d.1878) in Westminster Abbey was given not to Hardman's but to the London metalworking firm of Barkentin & Krall, established as recently as 1870; a reminder that Hardman's did not have the monopoly on monumental brasses. Building on their antiquarian interests which included publications on medieval brasses, the Waller brothers of London had been in business almost as long as Hardman,

Brass to Sir Charles Barry,
Westminster Abbey
(photo: David Meara)

Design by Dunstan Powell for memorial to Eliza Jenkins, Corpus Christi Church, Baltimore, USA (ink/colour, JHAL)

while the Coventry firm of Francis Skidmore & Son had been making brasses since the mid-1850s.[38] With their long-established reputation, however, Hardman's nevertheless held their own in the face of growing competition. The firm's records show a total of 68 jobs in 1880, 93 in 1898, rising to 125 in 1900. For the first few years of the twentieth century the level remained at around the 100 mark, before a sharp decline set in just before the outbreak of the First World War. In 1912 the number of jobs dropped to 49, and from the middle of that year brass sales were recorded in the Glass Daybooks rather than in separate ledgers. The value of brass orders declined from a peak of £1,396 in 1902–3 to £559 in 1911–12.

Many of the later orders were for smaller items such as inscription plates, and there were fewer full-size figures. An exception was the brass made in 1908 for Duke John Vincent Gandolfi who was buried in the church of Our Lady and St Alphonsus, Blackmore Park (Worcestershire), a church built by Charles Hansom in 1846 and furnished by Hardman's to Pugin's designs. The Gandolfis were of Genoese origin, and had made their fortune in the silk trade. Designed by Mrs Swinnerton Hughes, the memorial shows the duke kneeling at the foot of a crucifix, and there is a border of roses and the Plantagenet badge.[39] Other large brasses commissioned at this time include those commemorating members of the Jenkins family in Corpus Christi Church, Baltimore, USA (see below pp.P.150).

The Boer War stimulated a demand for monumental brasses of a rather different kind: war memorials to contain lists of those killed in action. In 1904 a Hardman brass of this kind was made for the Anglican church in Pietermarizburg (Natal) in memory of Natal Carbiners, including a list of battles, and with a soldier under a canopy. A set of six bronze plaques was made for Beverley Minster to commemorate soldiers of the East Yorkshire Regiment killed in the Boer War.[40]

The First World War also generated a demand for memorial brasses containing a roll of honour, but the number of memorials for individuals continued to decline. They had become expensive, and they were no longer fashionable. Following medieval precedent, Pugin had intended that memorials should be set into the floors of churches or on a tomb-chest. Increasingly, however, they came to be fixed on walls, especially the smaller memorial tablets. With their reflective surfaces enhanced in many cases by over-zealous polishing, they were later judged to be every bit as intrusive as the marble 'blisters' which Pugin had roundly condemned back in the 1840s. The production of memorial brasses at Hardman's ceased in 1939.

7. HARDMAN'S ABROAD

In his oration at Pugin's funeral on 21 September 1852, Thomas Grant, Bishop of Southwark, predicted that Pugin's unparalleled artistic influence would eventually be found in 'a church recalling his name on the banks of the Mississippi, or a chalice designed by him in India'.[1] It was to prove no exaggeration, built as it was on the earlier planting of Pugin's designs and Hardman's products in Australian soil, and as early as 1842 Pugin himself had predicted that 'the right thing will find its way at the antipodes'. This gleeful remark was made to Robert Willson after his appointment as Bishop of Hobart had been confirmed.[2] By 1852 Hardman's metalwork and glass was well established at the Antipodes; by the mid-1860s they were exporting to India, and the American market began to open up in the 1880s.

Closest to home was Ireland, where Hardman's established a considerable interest in the wake of Pugin, who began to build churches there from 1838. By 1841 Hardman's had a travelling representative in Ireland, for in a letter dated 13 December in that year a Mr Dowling of Dublin enquires about three brass altar bells 'ordered from your traveller' and asks for a large quantity of Miraculous Medals and Sacred Heart medals to be added to the order.[3] In July 1850 the Revd Roger Power of St John's church, Waterford, visited Hardman's Birmingham showroom to see some specimens of altar furniture, and followed this up by an enquiry about the prices of lamps, coronae, thuribles, crosses and candlesticks. A subsequent letter offered the following piece of advice:

> Would you allow me to say that I think you would get many orders in Ireland if you established a repository in Dublin. There are many who would gladly order such altar furniture as you supply if they had the opportunity of seeing it.[4]

In 1853 a branch of Hardman's was set up in Dublin by Thomas Earley and Henry Powell. It became an independent firm in 1864, and continued in business until the 1970s.

The establishment of Pugin and Hardman in Ireland owed a great deal to Lord Shrewsbury, who was also Earl of Waterford and Wexford, and to John Hyacinth Talbot, MP, of Talbot Hall and Ballytrent, County Wexford, who was Lady Shrewsbury's uncle. Pugin's early Irish churches included the neo-Norman St Michael's, Gorey (1839–42), the chapel of St Peter's College, Wexford (1838–51), and St Alphonsus's, Barntown (1844–51), to which Talbot donated the east window, by Hardman of course. There followed two cathedrals: St Mary's, Killarney (begun in 1842) and St Aidan's, Enniscorthy (begun in 1843). Work continued on many of these buildings after Pugin's death. In 1878–9 Hardman's supplied large quantities of door-furnishings and gas-fittings for the college buildings at Wexford,[5] which were being completed by J.J. McCarthy (1817–82) – 'The Irish Pugin' – who also added the chapel to Pugin's seminary buildings at Maynooth. Meanwhile Edward Pugin set up in partnership with his brother-in-law, George Coppinger Ashlin (1836–1921), the fruits of this partnership including the church of SS Peter and Paul at Cork (1859–66) and St Colman's cathedral, Cobh.

St Mary's cathedral, Killarney, has a fascinating history which illustrates both the scale of Pugin's vision for large Irish churches, and the insensibility of those who unpicked significant parts of that vision in the

135

St Mary's cathedral, Killarney: woodcut from appeal leaflet of 1854 (courtesy Maurice O'Keeffe)

Hardman electrolier from Killarney cathedral, restored 2007 (Hardman collection)

1970s. The building of the cathedral spans seventy years, from 1842 to 1912. Cruciform in plan, and with a central tower and spire, Killarney is truly of cathedral scale, in the early-thirteenth-century lancet style. The inspiration for it was Irish, namely the ruined cathedral of St Brendan at Ardfert. John Hardman Powell later commented on the appropriateness of the building to its Irish setting:

> The Cathedral, Killarney, is perhaps most characteristic of the Master. He found granite to be the native material
> to build in, so it is granite in design, perfect in architectural line and proportion, no carving, with the simplest of
> straight mouldings for the masons to hammer out with a sound like smiths on anvils.[6]

Pugin sent out drawings for Killarney in April 1842, and he was there in person in June. More drawings were sent in December, and the foundations were finished by January 1843. Then came the Great Famine, which halted many Irish church-building projects until well into the 1850s.

In March 1850 Pugin wrote to the editor of the *Tablet* expressing delight that attention had been drawn to the incomplete state of the cathedral: 'All essentials of the edifice are already finished.' Pugin claimed that only £1,000 was needed to open it. In August 1850 the *Tablet* reported that 'although long since roofed in', Killarney was still unoccupied, with all but one of the windows blocked up with boards, and deemed fit only for paupers from the workhouse to worship in.

Work restarted in 1853, the year after Pugin's death, with J.J. McCarthy as architect. McCarthy was described as a 'friend and fellow labourer' of Pugin, 'his great master'.[7] Though McCarthy was in charge at Killarney, E.W. Pugin supplied designs for the high altar, reredos and tabernacle. The cathedral was consecrated in August 1855. It was the first such ceremony to have been held in Ireland for three centuries, and the *Tralee Chonicle* described it as 'more like a dream of the middle ages than a thing of modern reality'.[8] The Hardman metalwork daybooks for 1854–5 enter a quantity of goods for St Mary's, including the cross, tabernacle and candlesticks for the high altar, benediction candlesticks, thurible, processional cross and a brass corona. A large and very elaborate monumental brass set into a black marble slab was also commissioned to commemorate Valentine Browne, third Earl of Kenmare, the cathedral's principal benefactor, who had died in October 1853.[9] A second brass, commemorating the countess, was installed in 1857, and two years later a metalwork screen was added to St Joseph's chapel.[10] Stained glass was introduced in the 1860s, beginning with the east window of the Blessed Sacrament chapel (1863), the south window of St Brendan's chapel (1867), then into the south transept with a window of three tall lancet lights and rose above (1874).[11]

Until 1908, St Mary's still lacked its central tower and spire. These were added by Ashlin & Coleman. The nave was lengthened at the same time, and new furnishings and fittings added between 1908 and 1913. Hardman metalwork items included electric lighting equipment in the form of twelve polished brass 'electroliers', made on similar principles to earlier *coronae* powered by candles or gas, with twisted stems and branches, ornamental rosettes and 'Puginian' trefoils. Each one is over a metre tall, and they were made to hang in the aisles. A timber rood-screen was also designed by Hardman's, with intricate tracery in the heads of the divisions, but it was never executed.

The rood-screen, had it ever been made and installed at Killarney, would undoubtedly have suffered the same fate as other furnishings – including the altar and reredos – which were ejected from the cathedral during a radical 're-ordering' of 1972–3 when even the walls and arches were stripped of their plaster and decoration, revealing rough masonry that the architect never intended to be seen. One commentator at the time tried to justify it by stating that Pugin's philosophy of church architecture was probably bad for the church of his time in that he gave the stamp of his genius to that mood of 'other worldliness which had already arisen in the emerging church of the early 19th century', and that 'Pugin's work has been enhanced' by the removal of the post-1852 furnishings and decorations'.[12] Pugin might have expressed his feeling rather differently: '. . . It could hardly have been treated worse if it had fallen into the hands of the Hottentots . . . It is quite useless to attempt to build true churches, for the clergy have not the least idea of using them properly',[13] which is what Pugin actually wrote about the unfinished state of Enniscorthy cathedral which, as it turned out, survived post-Vatican II liturgical minimalism rather better than its sister at Killarney. The collection of Hardman metalwork from Killarney was sold, put into storage, and later unearthed by a local historian[14] through whose good offices it was taken in 2006 to the Hardman Studios where one of the electroliers has been completely restored to reveal the superb quality of the brasswork. The collection also includes an altar cross, a tenebrae herse and two gasoliers.

St Patrick's cathedral, Armagh, suffered a similar fate to Killarney. The original architect, Thomas Duff (c.1792–1848), began in the Perpendicular

Sebastian Pugin Powell: unexecuted design for rood-screen for Killarney cathedral (ink/colour, JHAL)

style, but his successor, J.J. McCarthy, changed it to Decorated, and it was consecrated in 1904. Ashlin and Coleman carried out an elaborate decorative scheme, designed by Hardman's, in 1900–5, but much of it was removed in the 1970s, along with the high altar, pulpit and screens, fortunately however, the fine mosaics by Gabriel Pippet are still *in situ*. Ireland was not, of course, unique in this respect, but these examples serve to illustrate how extreme interpretations of *The Constitution on the Sacred Liturgy* of the Second Vatican Council have had a destructive effect upon the integrity of many buildings in which the visual arts and crafts were seen as complementary to the architecture and expressive of the Catholic Faith. They also underline the importance of the Hardman collection with its examples of metalwork, stained glass and other furnishings which have been removed from churches during 're-orderings'. An exceedingly fine pen and watercolour drawing in the collection shows a stone screen designed, almost certainly by Sebastian Pugin Powell, for St Cronan's church, Roscrea, Co. Tipperary. The screen is of the jube type, i.e. as well as carrying the Rood it has a *pulpitum* from which the Gospel is proclaimed, and the drawing indeed shows two coped clergy standing at a lectern. The screen was provided with fine metalwork gates and grilles. Other drawings and tracings show the plan and elevation of the screen, which was in fact built, but was dismantled and re-erected behind the altar during post-Vatican II reordering'.[15]

Sebastian Pugin Powell: design for jubé screen, with ironwork, for St Cronan's church, Roscrea, Eire (JHAL)

Since its cathedrals and churches were already in place, the (Anglican) Church of Ireland did not need to launch a major programme of new building, but there were some major restorations of existing buildings. Among these was Christ Church Dublin, restored between 1871 and 1878 by G.E. Street, who turned to Hardman's for ten stained-glass windows.[16] All of them depict Old Testament subjects, a reminder perhaps that iconography was somewhat limited in the Church of Ireland, where stout resistance to 'popery' and Tractarianism also restricted the use of ornaments such as Hardman's were now supplying in abundance to mainland Anglican churches.

The English Gothic Revival had its impact on continental Europe, notably in France and many of the German States, but it was in Belgium that Gothic became something of a national style following the creation of this new independent kingdom in 1830, and the Belgian Gothic Revival was influenced more directly by Pugin and Hardman than any other. Pugin had been inspired by the medieval art of the Low Countries, where he acquired a good many of the artefacts which he brought back to England on his boat. He visited Belgium several times between 1844 and 1851 and continued to draw inspiration from its medieval buildings. 'I have just got a capital sketch of the chandelier at St John's Bruges,' he wrote to Hardman in 1851; 'we can make a very good one from it.[17] The names and addresses in the endpapers of Pugin's diaries include a number of contacts in Bruges, including the architect J. de Stoop, the engraver A. Verbecke, the English art-collector John Steinmetz and, most signficantly of all, another expatriate, Thomas Harper King (1822–92), who was a passionate advocate of the Gothic Revival movement. King published edited translations of Pugin's works for the benefit of an international readership, and as an architect he designed a number of churches in which the influence of Pugin was clearly to be seen. Pugin's relationship with King was problematical. While he admired King's enthusiasm for true-principles Gothic, Pugin had to give him a 'blowing up' for altering the prices of Hardman's goods which were being supplied through him to others.[18] King also managed to acquire tracings of stained-glass cartoons and casts for metalwork from the Hardman works. Pugin warned Hardman to be on his guard against those who might enter the studio for the purposes of industrial espionage. After one particular incident he wrote, 'I have no doubt that they have lots of tracings. as soon as they begin to design they will fail but it is abominable . . . they would stick at nothing to cheapen a few candlesticks.'[19]

Chief among Pugin's admirers was Jean-Baptiste Béthune (1821–92), Belgium's most prolific Gothic Revival architect. He first met Pugin in 1844 while sketching in the Church of Our Lady at Courtrai. Pugin took an interest in the young man's drawing, and gave him a guided tour of the church and town. Pugin's remarks and observations on Gothic architecture struck a chord with Béthune, so that 'between the two there sprang up an intimate friendship, which led to M. Béthune taking up the idea of devoting his life to art'.[20] He visited Pugin at Ramsgate, corresponded with him, and shared the Puginian belief in architecture as the expression of the Catholic Faith to the extent that he became known as 'the Belgian Pugin'. In the 1850s he was involved with E.W. Pugin's great pilgrimage church at Dadizele, and he took over the building of the castle of Caloen in Loppem, near Bruges, which Edward Pugin had designed in 1856.

Following the example of A.W. Pugin in England, Béthune gathered together a team of craftsmen whom he personally instructed and who were entrusted with the execution of his designs. Hardman's not only supplied glass to Béthune, but they also assisted with the setting-up of the stained-glass workshop which Béthune established in Bruges in 1854. This was a most unusual step, given Pugin's earlier warnings about the dangers of plagiarism and Hardman's general unwillingness to work with artists outside his direct control. The first glass to be made in the Béthune workshop, under supervision by members of Hardman's staff, was a window depicting the Annunciation, done in 1856–7 for the chapel of the St Mary's Congregation in Zottegem, near Ghent.[21] It may have been in connection with this project that Hardman's supplied Béthune with quantities of coloured glass, quills, brushes and pigments in February 1857, and there were further orders in May, September and November.[22] In 1858 Béthune moved his workshop to Ghent, but he remained in close contact with John Hardman, and continued to order materials from him.[23]

J.B. Béthune:
Reliquary of
Charles the Good,
St Saviour's
cathedral, Bruges
(photo: Ern. Thill,
Brussels)

Amongst Béthune's most spectacular achievements as a designer of gold- and silverwork was the shrine of Charles the Good in St Saviour's cathedral, Bruges (1883). The extent of Béthune's career and influence were such that the Belgian Gothic revival was the most Puginian of all, and if Pugin had lived to see it, he might well have considered it to be a more perfect realisation of his vision than the English one.[24]

In 1844 A.W. Pugin wrote to Lord Shrewsbury, 'It is quite delightful to start in the good style in the antipodes.'[25] He was referring to the appointment of their mutual friend, Robert Willson (1794–1866), to the new Australian see of Hobart Town, and the consequences of that appointment in the form of large quantities of Hardman church furnishings, and Pugin church-designs, being taken to Tasmania by Willson when he finally set sail in 1844. A mission-priest at Nottingham from 1824, Willson had caught the Gothic flame from his brother, the architect E.J. Willson (1787–1854), from Bishop John Milner (1752–1826), another early apologist for the revival of Gothic, and finally from Pugin, whom he engaged to build the new church (later cathedral) of

Robert Willson, first Bishop of Hobart, oil painting by Paul Dowling, 1853: Archdiocese of Hobart (photo: Tasmanian Museum & Art Gallery

Chalice presented to Bishop Willson by Pope Pius IX and remodelled by Hardman's; Archdiocese of Hobart (photo: Tasmanian Museum & Art Gallery)

St Barnabas at Nottingham.[26] Willson's episcopal regalia was made by Hardman's. Pugin donated the pectoral cross, Lord Shrewsbury contributed £10 to the cost (£16) of his pastoral staff, while one of Willson's protestant friends, Nottingham magistrate Thomas Close, gave the jewelled mitre which was probably the work of Hardrnan's sister, Lucy Powell.[27] The new bishop then proceeded to procure, through Pugin and Hardman, '. . . not less than 40 sets of vestments . . . Crosses, Chalices Ciboriums, Pixes [*sic*], holy oils stocks . . . models of churches constructed on proper scales'.[28]

This, of course, was only a beginning. As churches were built according to the Puginian models, so they were equipped with the correct metalwork furnishings supplied by Hardman's. In December 1847 ten chalices and patens were sent to Willson. Made with silver bowls but with only plated-metal bases, at a cost of £4 each, they were no doubt destined for poorer churches, but suffered nothing in terms of their design.[29] Quantities of 'sale-or-return' items were sent to Willson to show to Australian clergy, an arrangement which carried on at least until 1860.[30] At the other end of the scale there were individual and expensive pieces of metalwork such as the silver-gilt chalice presented to Willson by Pope Pius IX in May 1847. Since the chalice was in the Classical (or as Pugin would have put it, the 'revived Pagan') style, Hardman's melted it down, added some extra silver, and made a new one to Pugin's design, carefully reproducing the inscription recording it as the gift of the Pope.[31] Another silver-gilt chalice was presented to Willson by the clergy of his diocese in 1854. Though designed by John Hardman Powell, it is almost identical in design to the Sienese-style chalice made for St Giles's, Cheadle in 1845.[32]

141

The founder of the Australian Catholic hierarchy was Archbishop John Bede Polding (1794– 1877), who consecrated Willson in St Barnabas', Nottingham in 1842. Polding then left for Australia, to be joined by Willson in 1844. He was equally committed to Puginian Gothic, having attended the opening of St Chad's, Birmingham, in 1841. Hardman's made his metropolitan cross and mitre, while the countess of Shrewsbury paid for a cloth-of-gold cope ornamented with jewels and made by Lucy Hardman and Lucy and Winefred Brown.[33] Polding's coadjutor, Bishop Charles Henry Davis, likewise acquired his episcopal regalia from Hardman's prior to his consecration in February 1848, and over the ensuing months several other pieces were made for him, including a second pectoral cross, a chalice and paten, and a ewer and basin engraved with his episcopal arms.[34] Among the other bishops who acquired goods from Hardman's the most prolific was James Goold of Melbourne, who placed orders totalling £1,132 between 1852 and 1859 for various churches in the diocese.[35] Many sets of vestments made by Lucy Powell and the Brown sisters were bought by Australian clergy on their visits to England, and they provided the inspiration for Tasmanian makers to work in the Pugin style.

Hardman glass also found its way into Australian churches. The first was a gift by Pugin himself to Bishop Willson: a two-light window depicting the Annunciation, for St Joseph's church, Hobart.[36] The inscription bids prayers for 'the good estate of Augustus Welby de Pugin': a rarity since – outside his own church at Ramsgate – Pugin generally shunned any reference to himself. The Annunciation window was just the beginning.

Archbishop John Bede Polding with vestments and metropolitan cross by Hardman's; oil painting by Eugene Montague Scott: St John's College, University of Sydney (photo: Tasmanian Museum & Art Gallery)

Chasuble: woven ribbed cream and gold silk, woven cream, blue and gold silk orphreys, and appliqué. Made by Lucy Powell and Lucy and Winifred Brown, c.1853–4: Archdiocese of Hobart (photo: Tasmanian Museum & Art Gallery)

St Joseph's church, Hobart: the Annunciation window, 1847 (photo: Tasmanian Museum & Art Gallery)

As church-building schemes proliferated, so orders for Hardman glass increased, continuing into the 1940s. The firm's greatest single involvement was with St Mary's cathedral, Sydney, begun under Archbishop Polding and rebuilt after a fire in 1865. Between 1882 and 1936 Hardman's made over fifty windows for St Mary's, including three rose windows, and the great north window in the choir, which is of eight lights.

The architect of the new St Mary's was William Wilkinson Wardell (1823–99), a Catholic architect much influenced by Pugin, whose commissions included the church of Our Lady Star of the Sea, Greenwich (1849–51), before he emigrated to Australia in 1858. He was later joined by John Bunn Denny (c.1800–92), who had been Lord Shrewsbury's clerk of works at Alton Towers, and was deeply involved with the building of Pugin's churches at Cheadle and Alton in the 1840s. They ensured the continuation of the Pugin style – and Hardman furnishings – until the end of the century. Wardell's greatest achievement was St Patrick's cathedral, Melbourne (1858–1939), which also has a significant amount of Hardman glass. Among Wardell's other churches was St Mary's, East St Kilda (1859–71), where the priest, Fr James Corbett (later Bishop of Sale), was another devotee of Pugin. In November 1869 he placed a huge order with Hardman's for metalwork screens, communion rails, a Benediction crown, altar crosses, lamps and curtain cranes, all for St Mary's.[37]

The most prolific of Tasmania's architects was Henry Hunter (1832–92), who began life as the son of a timber merchant in Nottingham, emigrated to Australia in 1851, and was propelled into architecture by Bishop Willson, who provided him with the appropriate publications by Pugin. Hunter's Catholic churches, dotted all over Tasmania, gave full expression to Pugin's ideas in their furnishing as well as their structure, and Hunter was still working well into the 1880s, modifying and supervising other architects' churches as well as his own. With their rood-screens, painted furniture and complement of Hardman metalwork, they continued to 'give their nineteenth-century beholders an authentic experience of the Antipodean vision for which Willson and his bosom friend Pugin had so earnestly striven'.[38]

Bishop Willson died on 30 June 1866 while on a visit to England, and he was buried in Nottingham cathedral.[39] His vicar-general, Fr William Hall (1807–66), died less than three weeks afterwards. He too had been a friend of Pugin during his years in London, and he was a prolific patron of Hardman's. Both were commemorated in a five-light memorial window designed by John Hardman Powell and installed in St Mary's cathedral, Hobart, in 1869.[40] Fr Hall was also commemorated by a memorial brass designed by Powell and installed in the cathedral in December 1869. The figure closely resembles that of the priest on the 'Exhibition Brass' of 1851.[41]

In addition to the clergy who ordered directly from Hardman's there were a number of contractors and importers who bought in bulk. Among these was Wardell's contractor, John Young of Melbourne, who placed several large orders for the whole range of altar plate as well as gas fittings and *coronae*. A single order placed in February 1862 was for £670 worth of goods.[42] Andrew Lenahan of Sydney, who appears to have been a general import agent, was also on Hardman's books as ordering quantities of chalices, ciboria, monstrances and thuribles. Later in the century the Sydney firm of Trapp, Sterling & Co. were selling direct as church furnishers, and also processing orders on behalf of clients. The 1890 *Australasian Catholic Directory* contains a full-page advertisement for them as agents for Hardman Powell & Co., who are described as manufacturers of 'church requisites and ornaments of every description', and inviting inspection of 'the numerous Samples and Stock'. As late as 1947 Hardman's were themselves advertising in the *Directory* as artists in stained glass, mosaics and paintings,[43] and in the 1950s significant work was undertaken by the firm in New South Wales, Queensland and Victoria.

Although Pugin never referred directly to New Zealand, attempts were being made there as early as the 1840s to 'start in the good style' in that other country of the antipodes. Here it was the Anglicans who led the way, under the leadership of George Augustus Selwyn (1809–78), the first Anglican bishop of New Zealand, who supplied copies of Pugin's books to guide builders of new churches in North Island.[44] A few years later, Benjamin Woolfield Mountfort (1825–98), a young Birmingham architect, arrived in the south armed with

Pugin's publications, and eventually earned himself the title of 'Architect of Canterbury'.[45] On the Catholic side, it was John Edmund Luck (1840–96) who brought the Pugin influence to bear after his appointment as fourth Bishop of Auckland in 1882. Luck was one of several children born to Pugin's friend, the Revd Alfred Luck, before he became first a widower and then a Catholic priest. Hardman's supplied Edmund Luck's pastoral staff, and other items of Hardman metalwork and sets of vestments from Mesdames Powell & Brown are known to have been in his possession.[46] Between 1888 and 1940 Hardman's supplied windows to a dozen churches, but the scale of their New Zealand operation was slight in comparison with their work in Australia.

Hardman windows were exported in somewhat larger numbers to Canada, with some significant late commissions for the Rosary Church in Toronto (1927–40). Many large South African churches – Catholic, Anglican and Presbyterian – acquired large collections, including Durban Catholic Cathedral, St James's Cape Town, and the Church of the Immaculate Conception in East London. In countries outside British control or influence, however, the Gothic Revival – and hence Hardman glass and metalwork – made comparatively little inroad. An exception was the Catholic church in Montevideo (Uruguay), where five single-light windows were installed as early as 1869, and eight of two lights in 1874.[47]

In 1878 the *Catholic Directory* carried a full-page advertisement extolling the achievements of 'Hardman's abroad' over the preceding twenty-five years:

Messrs. Hardman & Co beg to draw attention to the fact that they received the Council Medal for Ecclesiastical Metalwork & The Prize Medal for Stained Glass at the Great Exhibition of 1851.

They also exhibited at the Dublin Exhibition of 1853.

Received the Prize Medal for Stained Glass at the Paris Exhibition of 1855.

Prize Medals for Metal and Stained Glass Work in the International Exhibition of 1862.

Prize Medal for Stained Glass in the Paris Exhibition of 1867.

The only Medal gained by an English firm for Ecclesiastical Metalwork in the Roman Exhibition of 1870, and

A Medal for Stained Glass in the Centennial Exhibition, Philadelphia U.S.A. of 1876.

These prizes were also recorded in a series of stained-glass panels, most of which are still at the studio. The most significant of all was the beginning of Hardman's activities in the USA, which soon outstripped all of their other overseas markets in the last quarter of the nineteenth century. Between 1878 and the mid-1930s Hardman's designed and made windows for over a hundred churches, their last recorded commission being a St Bernadette window for St Joseph's church, Kewanee (IL), in 1935. That, however, was not the end of the story, for new American commissions have been a key ingredient in the expansion of Hardman's stained-glass operations at the beginning of the twenty-first century.

In America as in the Antipodes, Pugin's 'Gothic Dream'[48] was firmly planted on American soil by migrant architects. These included Patrick Ford (1848–1900), Patrick C. Keely (1816–96)[49] and Frederick C. Withers (1828–1901), with two of Pugin's sons, Edward and Peter Paul, designing furnishings such as the spectacular altarpiece for Patrick Ford's Church of the Sacred Heart, East Cambridge (MA) done by P.P. Pugin in 1882, and perhaps even complete churches. Among the American-born architects influenced by Pugin's principles were James Renwick (1818–95) and John Hubbard Sturgis (1834–88), who took frequent trips to England and was drawn to the work of Pugin's followers.

Early American architecture developed along simple, boxy, Colonial, Georgian and Classical lines.[50] Gothic was just one of many European styles which influenced American architecture from the 1840s onwards, and for some the style was 'suspect' because of its associations with medieval Catholicism. In the field of stained glass, the seminal figures were John La Farge (1835–1910) and Louis Tiffany (1848–1933), who established the fashion for opalescent glass, very different in style from the traditional mosaic glass painted with enamels that was being revived in England. There was, after all, very little medieval glass to examine in US collections. It was the English Arts and Crafts Movement that had the greatest impact upon the revival of American glass-painting in the medieval tradition. One of the leading exponents was Charles J. Connick (1875–1935), who made a tour of major English and European churches, including Chartres, to study medieval glass at first hand. He established a studio in Bos-

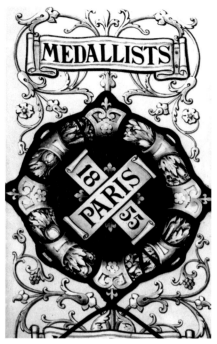

Stained-glass advertisement panel for Hardman & Co. (Hardman collection)

ton and was a leading figure in the Boston Gothic Movement. Connick was supported by the architect Ralph Adams Cram (1863–1942), who made a series of European tours, and in 1888 formed a partnership with Harry Goodhue (1873–1918), who also visited England and Europe to examine medieval glass *in situ*. Charles Wentworth (1861–97) joined them in 1892, and following Wentworth's death the firm became Cram, Goodhue & Ferguson as Frank Ferguson (1861–1926) joined the office as business and engineering partner.

All of this came rather late in the history of the Gothic Revival generally, and architects had to look to English and European studios as well as making tours of medieval buildings. Hardman's were particularly well-placed. Pugin's insistence on the close study of medieval glass *in situ* and close examination of his own collections of ancient glass ensured that Hardman's workforce became thoroughly familiar with the medieval methods of design and manufacture at every stage, and in the late 1800s and early 1900s the same standards were rigorously upheld by designers such as John Tarleton Hardman, Dunstan Powell and Elphege Pippet.

The Centennial Exhibition held in Philadelphia in 1876 brought Hardman's to the attention of US clergy, church-builders and patrons through their display of a large Gothic window depicting Jesus in the house of Mary and Martha at Bethany. After the Exhibition this window was returned to England and installed in the

Inscription on window made for Church Glass & Decorating Company, New York, 1907 (photo: JHAL)

parish church at St Neot's, near Cambridge (see above, pp.89-90). It was not until the 1880s, however, that Hardman's glass began to make a significant impact in the USA. The exhibiting of sample windows in a single location needed to be followed up by more vigorous promotion and salesmanship. In September 1885 John Hardman Powell's son-in-law, Roger Watts, undertook a tour in the US on behalf of the firm, taking with him a portfolio of 107 drawings of windows designed and installed by Hardman's in churches throughout Britain. Seven other drawings were added before Watts went on a second tour in April 1887.[51]

From the mid-1880's the number of windows executed by Hardman's for US churches grew steadily. The greatest concentration of work was, as might have expected, in the eastern states such as New York, Pennsylvania and Maryland, where Catholicism was strongest. Many Episcopal churches also ordered Hardman glass, and although iconography is not normally associated with Presbyterianism, in 1906 the North Presbyterian Church in Buffalo (NY) commissioned five Hardman windows containing representations of St Peter and St Paul, Martha and Mary, and other New Testament figures.[52]

To begin with, the commissioning of windows was done directly by the client, who would correspond with the firm in England, and submit his requirements. Hardman's would then provide a watercolour of the projected window for the client's approval. Correspondence in the Hardman Archive shows how the original design was sometimes modified, and the copies of watercolours retained by the firm are often annotated with comments received from the client. When the client was satisfied with the design, the full-size cartoon would be made, the glass cut and painted, and packed for export to the US, normally through the port of Liverpool.

Conducting business across the Atlantic raised obvious problems. Hardman's were generally unable to visit the buildings for which their glass was intended, and therefore had to rely on written descriptions, picture-

Corpus Christi Church, Baltimore
(photo: Abram Engelman)

Corpus Christi, Baltimore: St John the Baptist
window, 1901 (photo: Louisa Nielson)

147

Corpus Christi, Baltimore: panel in mosaic and opus sectile (photo: Abram Engelman)

Corpus Christi, Baltimore: one of the set of Stations of the Cross in mosaic and opus sectile by Gabriel Pippet (photo: Abram Engelman)

postcards and photographs, some of which are still filed in the archive. Given the eclectic nature of American church architecture, 'medieval glass' sometimes had to be adapted to settings that were in some cases only vaguely Gothic, and in others were not Gothic at all. Sketches and watercolours often made several journeys between Birmingham and the US before the client was satisfied, and even when a finished window was installed there could be complaints about tonality, and differences between the design as originally shown and the way in which it was finally interpreted. Some windows did not look sufficiently old, and there were requests for 'distressed' finishes, while other windows appeared much darker in reality than they did in the watercolour design. Then there were the inevitable delays in dispatch and shipment, and even on arrival in the US, glass could be held up in the Custom House pending the assessment and payment of import duty. Nevertheless, English 'medieval' glass was greatly sought after, and with their long experience in design and manufacture, Hardman's were well able to hold their own against other English companies such as Powells of Whitefriars and Clayton and Bell, and European ones such as Meyer of Munich.

An important set of commissions for the Church of the Holy Angels, Chicago, was initiated in 1897 by the Revd Denis Tighe, who was supplied with ten sanctuary windows with figures of saints, two windows for the side-chapels, and a rose window for the west gable, at a total cost of $3,600,[53] and further orders followed. The Glass Daybooks in the Hardman Archive record the details of each of the windows made for over 130 US churches over a period of fifty years, and in many cases watercolours, cartoons, and photographic records of completed windows have also survived. Single windows often led to further commissions from the same church; a testimony, surely, to the quality of the work and the satisfaction of the client. Some commissioning architects and clergy progressively filled the windows of their churches with large quantities of Hardman glass. An example of this is the Cathedral of the Immaculate Conception, Albany (NY), a large Gothic building designed by Frederick C. Withers. The first commission, completed in 1891, consisted of seven windows for the apse: traceried lancets with the Risen Lord at the centre, flanked by single figures of apostles and evangelists.[54] This was followed by two large seven-light windows for the transepts, the one on the north side costing $3,500.[55] By 1902 the cathedral had a set of forty-seven Hardman windows.

The Hardman contribution to Corpus Christi Church, Baltimore (MD), was even more remarkable, a total of sixty windows commissioned between 1889 and 1911 by the founder and patron, Michael Jenkins. The architect in this case was Patrick Keely. Hardman's also supplied many items of metalwork, stonecarving and mosaic. Begun in 1881, Corpus Christi is one of the most spectacular of American Catholic churches. It has a tall tower and spire set at the south-west angle of the building, and the overall style is of the mid-late thirteenth century, perhaps purposefully chosen as the period of the great Eucharistic saint, Thomas Aquinas (1227–74), who is closely linked with the feast of Corpus Christi, and who is celebrated in the stained glass and in the dedication of one of the side-chapels. The aisled nave has a triforium, large clerestories set with grisaille glass from Hardman's, who progesssively filled the windows of the nave, baptistery, side-chapels and vestibule.[56] The short apsidal chancel has five tall lancets with quatrefoil tracery. Here the Hardman glass includes figures of the Virgin and Child, Melchizedek and St Thomas Aquinas, Melchizedek representing the Old Testament 'types and shadows' spoken of by Thomas Aquinas in his great Corpus Christi hymn, 'Pange lingua'.[57]

Michael Jenkins' other gifts to the church and commissioned from Hardman's included an engraved brass plaque recording the consecration of the church, an expensive monumental brass in memory of his wife, Mary Isabella Plowden Jenkins, who died in 1911, and a pair of kneeling angels sculpted in white marble.[58] In addition, Hardman's were called upon to supply a set of Stations of the Cross and some decorative panels for the apse of the church in *opus sectile* and mosaic.[59] Unlike mosaic, which is made up of small cubes of coloured stone and glass of roughly regular size, *opus sectile* uses slabs of opaque glass or ceramic which are cut to a variety of shapes and sizes, and fitted together jigsaw-fashion. Hardman's also designed the High Altar and carved stone reredos, and a range of metalwork items including door-panels and a tabernacle. After the founder's death in 1917, Hardman's made a memorial brass, engraved with figures of St Michael, St Gabriel, the Blessed Virgin Mary and St Joseph.[60]

Corpus Christi, Baltimore, was in many ways exceptional. From 1904 to 1913 Hardman's glass was generally imported into the US through the Church Glass and Decorating Company of New York City, through whom Hardman's obtained commissions for eleven windows, some of which were very large, for the Episcopal Church of St Ignatius in New York. The architect was Charles Coleridge Haight (1841–1917), who had hitherto used the English firm of Clayton and Bell. Though designated as 'Protestant Episcopal', St Ignatius' was what in England would be deemed Anglo-Catholic, and was noted for its elaborate ritual. In May 1904 Caryl Coleman, President of the Church Glass and Decorating Company, wrote to Hardman's in connection with a large chancel window:

> St Ignatius' Church is extremely high, both in doctrine and in ritual; there is so little difference between it and a Catholic church that the non-Catholic cannot discover any difference.

> Both the rector and the architect are more or less affected with Anglo-mania, hence the window must be extremely English; there must be canopies and bases, and these canopies and bases must be treated in silvery and pearly tones, in conjunction with light yellow stain. The drawing of the architectural portion must be in keeping with the general architectural feeling of the church.[61]

Instead of the glass being dispatched in leaded-up sections as was usual with domestic commissions, it was the standard practice with CG&DC for the pieces of cut glass to be imported in an unleaded state, presumably with a cut-line to enable employees of CG&DC to undertake the leading-up and cementing in their own workshop prior to fitting the completed window on site. By the beginning of October 1905 the St Ignatius window was in place, and Caryl Coleman wrote to say that it 'had given great satisfaction, not only to the rector, but also to the architect', and that it ought to be of use in obtaining further orders, as indeed it was.[62] Coleman followed it up by publishing illustrations of the window in several church newspapers, and sending out circulars and travelling salesmen to promote the work of John Hardman & Co.[63] In June 1907 the CG&DC placed an order for a sample panel for trade purposes. It depicted Christ the Healer, standing under a Gothic canopy, and below it ran the telling inscription:

> Painted by John Hardman & Co of London and Birmingham for the Church Glass and Decorating Company of New York to illustrate their work which embodies the mediaeval principles of stained glass painting revived and taught by Augustus Welby Pugin and continued by them.

Thus were the memory and achievements of Pugin revered more than fifty years after his death in a country which he had never visited and for which he designed not a single building.

Arguably the most prestigious Gothic Revival building in the United States, the (Episcopalian) cathedral of St John the Divine in New York City is also something of an architectural chameleon. Begun in 1892 by the architects Heins & La Farge in the Romanesque style, it was taken over in 1912 by Ralph Adams Cram, who remodelled the chancel in Gothic style, and built the impressive spacious nave with aisles rising to the same height. Hardman's work dates from the earlier period, and it consisted of glass for St Saviour's chapel, the central one of seven apsidal chapels at the east end of the cathedral. The early medieval style was called for, and the donor, August Belmont, impressed upon Hardman the need for deep, dark, mosaic glass:

St John the Divine, New York: Belmont window cartoon for centre light (JHAL)

It will be evident to you at once that the opportunity is an unusually good one except in a single respect. The atmosphere of New York is so exceedingly transparent that unless dark colours are freely employed the strain upon the eyes of the congregation looking eastward is very severe.[64]

There were to be three windows in all: a large central one of three lights depicting the Transfiguration of Christ with the attendant figures of Moses and Elijah, with two windows either side consisting of canopy-work and ornament. In addition to Hardman's, August Belmont also sought designs from other firms, including Clayton & Bell, which did not particularly please Coleman, who adopted a somewhat abrasive attitude:

You know he (Belmont) is one of our wealthiest men . . . a man of arrogant and overbearing character, extremely close in all matters connected with money. Time for him means money, and he believes money can command time. Therefore there must not be any delay in getting this sketch here.[65]

In spite of Belmont's stipulations about dark glass, Hardman's still incorporated the thin white borders which they had always believed were essential to give sparkle to early glass, but they were overruled, and obliged to submit a new watercolour sketch with all white lines removed.[66] The completed windows were installed in 1908–9, and the central one is entered at $5,500, one of the most costly single commissions undertaken by Hardman's for a US church.[67] Caryl Coleman's hopes that it might lead to other work at St John's were unfulfilled. When Ralph Adams Cram took over as architect he chose members of a new generation of American glasspainters – such as Charles Connick – to make his windows.

In 1913 the Church Glass and Decorating Company went into liquidation. Roger Watts believed that the fault lay with Caryl Coleman's lack of sound business sense more than anything else: 'We have never impugned Mr Coleman's personal integrity, but his business capacity was about as rotten as it very well could be'.[68] The failure of CG&DC left Hardman's awkwardly placed, both with work already in progress through the Company and in respect of future commissions. Roger Watts continued to look after Hardman's interests in the US, carrying out some detailed enquiries about the reliability and solvency of another agency, Montague Castle-London of New York, and as a consequence Hardman's began to do business through them. Montague Castle – 'a straightforward respectable man' according to Roger Watts[69] – was the president, and F.M. London the secretary. Surprisingly, perhaps, Caryl Coleman was appointed a director, but this was no doubt because of his expertise in matters of glass, decoration and church furnishing, and he continued to champion Hardman's glass. Set out in ornamented Gothic letters, the new firm's company letterhead announced that they dealt in 'English stained glass from the Studios of John Hardman & Co., Birmingham'. In March 1914 Montague Castle requested a sample window-panel for the showroom at 247–249 West Thirty-Sixth Street, similar to one that Hardman's had done for St Ignatius' church. 'We have occasional customers who come into our showroom, and as we have no painted example of yours, it is at times a little embarrassing, as in quite a few instances out of town customers will not give us the time to visit with them examples of your work installed in many Churches in this City.'[70]

Given their established reputation, it might have been thought that Hardman's would have fared better than they did at St Patrick's Catholic Cathedral, New York City. Though built between 1856 and 1878 by James Renwick, much in the style of Cologne Cathedral, the Lady chapel was still incomplete at the beginning of the twentieth century. In 1910 a bequest of £30,000 was received from Mr Eugene Kelly, a member of a prominent Irish-American family, to finish the work. The glass for windows was to be paid for by other donors, but the Kelly family retained an interest, and they commissioned designs from Paul Woodroffe (1875–1954), an English stained-glass artist and book-illustrator based in Chipping Camden (Gloucestershire). Woodroffe had been taught in London by Christopher Whall (1849–1924), who also had a great influence on the work of the American artist-craftsman Charles Connick. Watts nevertheless hoped that Hardman's would actually execute the windows, and to this end he made direct approaches both to Eugene Kelly's brother, Thomas, and to Cardinal John Farley, Archbishop of New York, who would actually commission the windows.[71] On visits to England both of them had been to Arundel and seen the Hardman glass in St Philip's cathedral and at the castle. Roger Watts firmly believed that Thomas Kelly would favour Hardman's. Woodroffe also had his supporters, including other members of the Kelly family, and Monsignor Lavelle, the rector of St Patrick's. The other contenders for the work were the Munich firms of Meyer and Boucher. A suggestion that Woodroffe and Hardman might cooperate over a sample window was first accepted, but then Woodroffe pulled out and decided to go it alone. Hardman's produced their sample window, depicting the figure of Christ being crowned with thorns, in February 1912 at a cost of $1,022,[72] and this was displayed in the Lady chapel along with the others, all of whom had to interpret Woodroffe's preliminary sketch. Having seen them, Caryl Coleman wrote to Hardman's:

> The first Munich window (Boucher) is not worth considering for a moment. If it had been made with coloured tissue paper it could not be any worse than it is.

> The second Munich window (Meyer) does not look as well as it did before Mr. Woodroffe's window was put in position . . . It is conventional, flat and uninteresting.

> Mr. Woodroffe's window is very striking and has a certain artistic suggestion about it which cannot help hold the attention of the cultured observer, but when studied the good impression dissipated. Some of the colouring of the medallions is offensive and the drawing is not good, and it never has the charm of the archaic drawing of the 13th century.

> The Hardman window. The writer cannot see how there should be any hesitation on the part of the judges in making their choice between the Woodroffe window and the Hardman window . . . The clergy of the cathedral all agree that the Hardman window had the other windows skinned.[73]

There was, however, one dissenting voice amongst the cathedral clergy, namely Monsignor Lavelle, who favoured Woodroffe because he believed that the artist who made the design was best placed to interpret it.[74] The failure of the Church Glass & Decorating Company was a further complication, although Roger Watts continued to write vehement letters to Monsignor Lavelle and to the archbishop. Moreover, a delegation from the Association of American Workers in Ornamental Glass objected to the use of foreign firms on the grounds that 'money for the Lady-chapel windows was being collected from the people of the church who were largely artisans depending on the work they got in this country', to which Caryl Coleman retorted that the reason why no American firm had entered the competition was because there was none.[75] The matter dragged on for more than three years, but in the end Monsignor Lavelle had his way, and Paul Woodroffe designed and made all of the windows for the Lady chapel, completing them in 1930.

The most challenging commission undertaken by Hardman's in New York was almost certainly the Church of Our Lady of Guadeloupe, otherwise known as 'The Spanish Church' because it was built for Spanish residents of New York by 'a non-Catholic gentleman of large means who is deeply interested in everything that has to do with Spain in matters of literature and art'.[76] By the beginning of 1910 the church was almost complete; gifts of altar-vessels, vestments and other furnishings had been given by the King and Queen and other members of the Spanish Royal Family. 'Altogether it is going to be a very swell ecclesiastical edifice', wrote Caryl Coleman to Hardman's, 'and it is now settled that the windows shall come from John Hardman & Company.'[77] There were to be five windows in the sanctuary, four in the chancel, six aisle windows, six gallery windows and a skylight.

The main problem for Hardman's was that the style of the Spanish Church was Italian Renaissance rather than Gothic, and although English antique glass was wanted, it needed to be light in order to reveal the wall-decorations and other features. Unfortunately the result was far too dark, and after their installation Caryl Coleman complained not only about the colours but also about the treatment of some of the subjects:

> The windows you have sent to us are the darkest ones you have ever made for us . . . they are not only darker, they are muddy . . . My idea was to produce a Church in which every part was in exact harmony with the other parts . . . in other words a gem of a Church, but now everything is sacrificed to these windows . . . we are afraid that when the Archbishop sees it there will be a royal row. If it were not for the skylight, the Church would be like a cave.

> Moreover, the actual and traditional likenesses of some of the saints represented is so well known that some people, seeing the windows, remarked, concerning St Theresa for example, 'That St Theresa! That pretty doll-like girl! St Theresa was a woman, rather homely, and where are her moles?'[78]

In the end, however, things were by no means as bad as Coleman feared, and far from there being 'a royal row', the archbishop was full of praise for the Hardman glass when he saw it for the first time, along with a number of other clergy including an Italian cardinal. 'Luckily for us,' Coleman wrote, 'the day was very clear, we had almost an Italian sky and an abundance of sunshine, so the church was seen at its best.'[79]

At City College, New York, Hardman's were faced with a slightly different problem when it came to making a ten-light window for the Faculty Room. First of all the clients wanted American glass, but they were persuaded by the Church Glass and Decorating Company to have English glass because it would harmonise better with the medieval English character of the building. The subjects for the window were full-length figures of Greek philosophers, with their faces as shown on the busts already at the college, but they were to be 'treated in such a way as to harmonize with the architectural lines',[80] i.e. Hardman's had to portray the Classical figures of Aristotle, Plato and Socrates in the manner of saints, in manifestly medieval surroundings.[81] Much more in the Hardman style of things was a set of a dozen or more windows – including some very large transomed ones – for the chapel of Williams College, Williamstown (MA), filled with figures from the Old and New Testaments. The total value of this commission, carried out between September 1904 and March 1907, ran to over $12,000.[82]

Among the commissions undertaken at this time for educational establishments, one of the most interesting is the Cornaro window installed in 1906 in the Thompson Memorial Library at Vassar College, Poughkeepsie (NY), a new addition to the college built in the Gothic style by Francis Richmond Allen, of the Boston firm of Allen and Collen. The window is of five lights with tracery. The glass, designed by Dunstan Powell, depicts the conferring of the first doctorate in philosophy upon a woman, Elena Lucrezia Cornaro Piscopia, by the University of Padua in 1678.[83] Both the donor, Mary Clark Thompson, and Caryl Coleman of CG&DC emphasized the secular nature of the window and urged Powell to avoid the use of ecclesiastical imagery.[84] Nevertheless, the central figure of the Lady Cornaro standing in front of a Gothic throne, with the semblance of a halo behind her head and surrounded by adoring figures, bears an uncanny resemblance – albeit a secularized one – to the Coronation of the Virgin. The design is executed in the painterly style, treating the whole window area as a single canvas, taking little note of the vertical divisions of the mullions. The composition of the scene and the brilliant colours of the glass elevate and glorify the event which the window depicts.[85]

Given the eclectic nature of American church architecture, Hardman's had to adapt their designs to a wide variety and mixture of architectural styles. A significant number of orders were for single-light round-headed windows without mullions or tracery. Yet Hardman's designers were able to adapt figure-work and ornament

Vassar College (NY): the Cornaro window (photo: Vassar College)

St Patrick's Seminary, San Francisco: the chapel. (courtesy of Joseph Fegan)

to produce a satisfactory composition in which Gothic elements were blended with neo-Classical ones. A particularly good example is the set of twenty-six windows made between 1904 and 1915 for the chapel of St Patrick's Seminary, Menlo Park, San Francisco. The chapel is of the Roman basilican type, with a semicircular apse, and tall, round-headed windows which have a hint of Gothic tracery in the heads. The design of the glass reflects the eclecticism of the architecture, with the Biblical scenes and figures framed in a thoroughly Renaissance manner under rounded arches flanked by Classical columns and ornament.[86] These windows are particularly well-documented in the collection of watercolours and photographs at Lightwoods House. A statement from Dunstan Powell, a copy of which is also in the Lightwoods Collection, explains his ideas for the general scheme of the windows, and the choice of 'type and anti-type' in which each Old Testament subject is paired with its fulfilment in the New:

> The great and high purpose of a Seminary, the teaching of men to make them 'Priests for ever according to the order of Melchisedek', at once surely demanded for its pictorial scheme of windows that story of Sacrifice in Type and Anti-Type, the fulfilment of the New Law of the Promise in the old, culminating in the entrance 'into heaven itself' of the Great High Priest to 'Appear now in the Presence of God for us' as expounded to us by St Paul in his Epistle.[87]

This letter, written just fifty years after the death of Pugin, shows that the firm of John Hardman maintained a strong Catholic ethos, that its designers had a thorough grasp of the theological principles involved in the design of windows for particular locations, and that it was not always the client who determined the choice of subject-matter.

A paddle-steamer may seem an unlikely location for a Hardman window, but in 1912 the Detroit and Cleveland Navigation Company built a large side-wheeled steamboat, the *City of Detroit III*, for sailing the Great Lakes. Designed by the naval architect Frank E. Kirby, the luxurious salons included a lounge called the Gothic Room which had a profusion of medieval-style columns and traceried arches. A prominent feature of this room was a large five-light window commissioned from Hardman's through the Church Glass & Decorating Company. Executed in a painterly style, the window depicts the seventeenth-century French explorer, La Salle, landing at the site of the present-day Detroit.[88] When the *City of Detroit III* was scrapped in 1956 the entire Gothic Room, including the Hardman window, was fortunately recovered and preserved in the Dossin Great Lakes Museum, Detroit.

Orders for Hardman glass slackened off, almost inevitably, during the First World War, a notable exception being a large commission for the Cathedral of the Holy Name, Chicago (IL), built to the design of Frederick Withers, who had ordered the first window from Hardman's in 1893. The glazing of this church continued after Withers' death in 1901. A set of twenty- two windows for the aisles, sanctuary, baptistery and side-chapel was shipped out in July 1918 at a cost of $13,346. This was the largest single commission ever to have been placed with Hardman's for an American church.[89] The subject-matter of these windows embraced the complete panorama of the Christian Faith, from the Presentation of the Blessed Virgin Mary to her Coronation, with most of the significant events in the life of Christ placed in between.

In the 1930s the number of windows commissioned from Hardman's declined rapidly, then in 1935 they ceased altogether. By this time the US had well-established stained-glass designers and manufacturers of their own. There was stiff competition too from James Powell & Sons, of the Whitefriars glassworks in London, whose chief designer, James Hogan, made a number of personal visits to the US, beginning in 1926. There were economic considerations, then the onset of World War II, and the general decline in popularity of the Gothic idiom in which the firm specialised. Powell's were also affected by this, although they managed to struggle on until 1948,[90] and other firms, on both sides of the Atlantic, also declined and disappeared. Hardman's held fast to their inherited traditions and methods of glass-painting, remaining in business through the difficult period of the 1960s and '70s. By so doing they were uniquely well-placed to take advantage of the revival in popularity of English stained glass which began towards the end of the twentieth century, and the opening up of new world markets.

The La Salle window, formerly on the paddle-steamer City of Detroit III (photo: Dossin Great Lakes Museum, Belle Isle, Detroit, MI)

8. GOTHIC FOR EVER!

Advertisement leaflet for John Hardman Studio, c. 1925 (JHAL)

In the early part of the twentieth century some significant changes took place in the organisation of the Hardman company. Since 1883 the firm had effectively been divided in two, with Hardman Powell & Co. undertaking all the metalwork except memorial brasses, the latter being looked after by John Hardman & Co. along with stained glass and decoration. Hardman Powell & Co. operated from King Edward's Road, Birmingham, with London offices in King William Street, while Hardman & Co. continued at 43 Newhall Hill, Birmingham, with a London office first at 24, Haymarket, and then at No. 1 Albemarle Street, Piccadilly. John Tarleton Hardman (1873–1959) took charge of Hardman & Co. after the death of his father, John Bernard Hardman, in 1903, while his younger brother, Gerald James (1875–1953), assumed responsibility for metalwork and church furnishings at Hardman Powell & Co., which, from 1916, traded as Gerald J. Hardman & Co., with a new assay mark – GJH&Co – replacing the old JH&Co. The growing separation of the two parts of the firm may be linked to a disagreement between the two Hardman brothers, the exact nature of which has not been ascertained.[1] Be that as it may, in December 1919 the stained glass and decoration business was formally reconstituted as a private limited company under the name of Messrs John Hardman & Co. Ltd., with John Tarleton Hardman and Dunstan Powell as managing directors.[2] A photograph taken around this time of J.T. Hardman and staff indicates that the total workforce then numbered about sixty-five. The designer Elphege Pippet became a director, and by 1928 the name of Donald Taunton appeared on the letterhead. Unlike most other members of the firm, Donald Battershill Taunton (1885–1965) had not received a conventional Catholic education but had attended Saltley College School, and afterwards studied at the Birmingham School of Art. Taunton was an extremely talented watercolourist and became chief designer at Hardman's from 1935 until his retirement in 1964. When John Tarleton Hardman retired in 1936, Taunton took over the running of the firm along with Patrick Feeny, Tom Farrell and Vincent Durk.

Artists at work in the cartoon room at Newhall Hill (JHAL)

John Tarleton Hardman and the staff of John Hardman & Co., c.1920 (JHAL)

It had been hoped that the younger Hardmans might continue the family interest in the firm, but this was not to be. Edmund Hardman (1888–1961), elder son of John Bernard Hardman by his second marriage, embarked on a career in the RAF and became a Squadron Leader. His younger brother, Bernard Joseph, served with the 5th Lancers during the First World War, and subsequently worked for the Anglo-Persian Oil Company in Mesopotamia where he died of heat stroke in 1921, aged only twenty-seven. The last hope was Edmund's son, Gordon, who intended to enter the business, but was killed in 1943 while serving as a pilot in the RAF. His death, at the age of twenty-three, effectively marked the end of the Hardman dynasty.[3]

Some of the most important commissions undertaken by Hardman's in the period between the turn of the century and the Second World War concerned buildings with which they had been involved since the days of Pugin and which were now, sixty or more years on, in need of redecoration and repair, or requiring significant additions. In the Catholic Midlands, some major work was undertaken at St Barnabas' cathedral, Nottingham, and St Mary's, Derby, between 1929 and 1935. At Nottingham the repainting of the nave, aisles, transepts and side-chapels was instigated by Bishop Thomas Dunn (1870–1931) as a part of his drive to 'restore all things in Pugin' following the depredations carried out by his predecessor, Bishop Brindle, which had included the removal of the rood-screen and the replacement of Pugin's high altar with one which, according to Bishop Dunn, was 'enough to make the angels weep by its unsightliness'.[4] The designs were made by Elphege and Oswald Pippet, and the name of E. Skuse appears as the principal decorator, with Manders of Wolverhampton supplying the paint.[5] Alternative designs were submitted for the decoration of the south-east chapel, then known as the Chapel of the English Martyrs. Most of the decoration was painted out in the 1960s, with the notable exception of the Blessed Sacrament chapel, where Elphege Pippet's richly coloured painting and stencilling was cleaned and renewed by Hardman's under the supervision of Patrick Feeny. During the 1993 re-ordering and redecoration of the cathedral, the Pippet decorations behind the altar of St Hugh's chapel were uncovered and conserved.

At St Mary's, Derby, a set of eight large windows designed by Dunstan Powell was installed in the Lady Chapel in 1931–2.[6] A major restoration scheme was undertaken in 1927–8 because of deteriorating stonework on the outside and unstable plasterwork on the interior. Hardman's undertook almost the complete restoration and redecoration of the interior, including twenty large medallions in the spandrels of the nave arcades representing subjects from the Old and New Testaments. They were designed by Elphege and Oswald Pippet, who also decorated the Lady Chapel.[7] New figures were supplied for the rood, Bridgeman's of Lichfield undertaking the carving and Hardman's doing the decoration.[8]

St Chad's cathedral, Birmingham, had the closest connection of all with the Hardman family. John Bernard Hardman shared his father's interest in the

St. Barnabas' cathedral, Nottingham: Decorative scheme for the English Martyrs' chapel, c.1929 (JHAL)

Interior of St. Mary's, Derby, during the restoration of 1927 (JHAL)

cathedral choir, adding £500 to the original endowment. His younger son, Gerald James, served as church-warden for many years, and he supervised the first major restoration of the cathedral, done in 1903–4 to mark the silver jubilee of Bishop Edward Ilsley's episcopal ordination. He also designed the war memorial shrine in the south aisle, over which is a Hardman window depicting a Requiem Mass being offered for the fallen of the Great War.[9] In 1911 the golden Jubilee of Bishop Ilsley's ordination to the priesthood coincided with the eleva-tion of Birmingham to the dignity of a metropolitan see, with Ilsley as the first archbishop. It was decided to present him with a set of pontifical vestments, and these were commissioned from Hardman's in April 1911.[10] Elphege Pippet undertook the complete design, and nuns in various communities made up the vestments and carried out the embroidery. The set comprised the archbishop's cope, a priest's cope, a chasuble, four dalmat-

ics, stoles, maniples, chalice veil and burse, humeral veil and gremial veil, all made of cloth-of-gold and richly embroidered.[11] This was the last major tex-tile commission in which Hardman's were involved, thus bringing to an end – spectacularly – a tradition which had begun in the 1840s when Lucy Powell started to make vestments to Pugin's Gothic pat-terns. Gerald Hardman designed a gilt-metal metro-politan cross for the new archbishop. The base of the cross has figures of saints in canopied niches, the front of the cross has a silvered figure and emblems of the four evangelists at the extremities, while the reverse is set with glass cabochons.[12]

When Archbishop Ilsley died in 1926, it was decided to build a memorial chapel at the north-west corner of the cathedral, dedicated to the archbishop's patron saint, Edward the Confessor. It was designed

Chasuble from the Ilsley vestment set, St. Chad's cathedral, Birminghan (photo: Dr. John Davis)

by Sebastian Pugin Powell, A.W. Pugin's grandson, and the youngest surviving son of John Hardman Powell, who had taken over the firm of Pugin and Pugin after the death of Peter Paul Pugin in 1904. Donald Taunton of Hardman's designed a set of stained-glass windows which included representations of the discovery of the relics of St Chad in 1840, and lifelike portraits of archbishops Ilsley and Williams in their pontificals. Gerald Hardman was responsible for the altar and baldachino, and also for the cylindrical reliquary flanked by angels which stood above the tabernacle for the exposition of one of St Chad's bones.[13] St Edward's chapel was consecrated in May 1933. Gerald Hardman also embellished Pugin's original reliquary over the high altar by adding angel supporters and a pinnacled Gothic canopy containing an image of St Chad.[14]

Even more spectacular than Archbishop Ilsley's metropolitan cross was the processional cross made in 1922 for St Peter's church, Roath (Cardiff). It was given by the parents of Reginald Wolstan Lewis in memory of their son, who had been killed in action in the closing weeks of the First World War. Like the Ilsley cross, the metal staff is made in sections so that it can be packed in a carrying-case, and there is a pair of matching processional candlesticks. The original design, and the detailed working drawing – almost certainly by Gerald Hardman – are currently (2007) in the Lightwoods collection. The crucifix, of gilt metal, is of superb quality, with pierced work, enamelling, and figures of saints in niches at the base and extremities. Figures of Our Lady and St John are carried on flanking brackets, much as Pugin did it in the 1840s. The cross, candlesticks and fitted case are entered into the Glass Rough Daybook – which was the usual practice for metalwork items commissioned at this time through Hardman Powell & Co. – at £213.17s.6d, and the Lewis family were billed for £350, a mark-up of about 40%.[15]

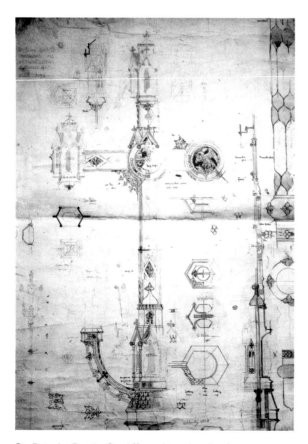

St. Peter's, Roath, Cardiff: working drawing for processional cross (JHAL)

St. Peter's, Roath, Cardiff: the Lewis memorial cross

Dunstan Powell: Turnbull memorial window, St. Peter's, Roath, 1926

Hardman's involvement with St Peter's, Cardiff, dates back to the late 1860s. It was one of a number of churches built in South Wales by Charles Hansom, but although it was begun in 1860 it remained unfinished until Cardiff's principal landowner, the Marquess of Bute, undertook to complete it, and also to build a school and presbytery, following his conversion to Catholicism in 1868. The decoration of the roof and walls of the chancel, and the painting and gilding of the altar, were carried out by Hardman & Co. in 1869 at Lord Bute's expense, and they also supplied figures of Our Lady and St John for a new triple-arched wooden rood-screen of simple design, to complement a large crucifix already in the church.[16] In 1897 Lord Bute donated a new rood-screen: a triplet of stone arches with delicate pierced tracery above. In 1904 the chancel was redecorated by Hardman's, and figures of saints painted on canvas were placed in the arcading either side of the altar.[17] Stained glass was added: first the apse windows were done by one of Hardman's chief rivals, Meyer of Munich, then, starting in 1904, Hardman's progressively glazed the remaining windows in the aisles and side-chapels, the final window being added in 1926.[18]

In the 1960s St Peter's suffered drastically from post-Vatican II 're-ordering' which included the demolition of the screen, even though its central arch was broad enough and tall enough to give an uninterrupted view of the altar, or to have accommodated a forward altar. It was broken up, and the rubble was used as hardcore for the new forward sanctuary. The high altar was demolished, the paintings in the apse were destroyed, and other decorative work was obliterated. Recent (2000–7) redecoration and refurnishing has restored something of the church's pre-1960s character, replacing what the parish priest describes as a 'Stalinist' altar with a Gothic one salvaged from a redundant church.[19] A peaked brass tabernacle of about 1870–80, set with stones and enamels, and unmistakably by Hardman, has been acquired for the high altar, and Hardman's are progressively cleaning and restoring some of the church's other metalwork items.

Many outstanding decorative schemes designed by Elphege and Oswald Pippet were carried out by Hardman & Co. in various parts of the United Kingdom in the first three decades of the twentieth century, most of them involving richly-coloured stencilling work, figure-work, diapering and gilding, and reminiscent of the intense colouring applied by A.W. Pugin to many of his churches. The Hardman (Lightwoods) archive contains many coloured drawings for such schemes, notable examples being the Church of Our Lady of Good Aid, Motherwell (Scotland), St Mary's, Llanelli, Our Lady and St Patrick, Maesteg (both South Wales), and St Cuthbert's College, Ushaw (Durham). The Hardman involvement with Ushaw dates back to Pugin's time, and subsequent architects continued to use Hardman's for further additions of metalwork, stained glass and decoration for their extensions to the college and chapel. The last of these was Sebastian Pugin Powell, who added a two-bay fan-vaulted extension to the ante-chapel in 1925–8, with painted decorations by Elphege Pippet.[20] At the same time Powell and Pippet decorated the south chapel of St Gregory the Great.

Although it did not achieve cathedral status until 1976, the church of St John the Baptist, Norwich (1884–

St. Cuthbert's College, Ushaw: design for decorations and stained glass. Elphege Pippet 1925 (JHAL)

1910), was of cathedral-like proportions from the beginning. Built in the Early English style, with a massive central tower and a ten-bay nave, St John's was 'probably the grandest Catholic parish church in England . . . a huge and dominating presence'.[21] The architects were George Gilbert Scott junior (1839–97) and his brother, John Oldrid Scott (1841–1913), and it was the second cathedral to be financed by the Duke of Norfolk. Hardman & Co. made most of the glass, with the nave windows by John Hardman Powell and the chancel windows by Dunstan Powell. The great north window, of five lancet lights, was destroyed in the Second World War, and subsequently recreated by Hardman's from the original designs and cartoons. New glass was designed in 1955 for the north transept and side-chapels, including a representation of Our Lady of Walsingham.[22] Very different from St John's, Norwich, is St Joseph's, Sheringham (Norfolk), by Giles Gilbert Scott (1880–1960), George junior's son. Though still recognisably Gothic, it is in a much freer style, and built of brick. Dunstan Powell designed the tall 'Jesse tree' west window which belongs to the original build of 1908–10, and was relocated when a westward extension was added in 1934–6.

The largest and most important commission carried out by Hardman's in the mid-twentieth century was the restoration of stained glass at the Palace of Westminster following wartime bomb damage. A total of 407 individual lights, comprising almost 5,600 square feet of glass, came under the scope of the contract placed

Palace of Westminster:
detail of window in
St. Stephen's Hall,
c. 1949 (JHAL)

with John Hardman & Co. by the Ministry of Works in 1947.[23] Some heraldic glass had been removed before the bombing, and a quantity of damaged glass was either in store or still *in situ*, but not all of it was sent to Hardman's. Members of both Houses were allowed to collect souvenirs of damaged glass, and it is difficult to know exactly how much was dispersed in this way.[24] Many of the original cartoons survived in Birmingham, but some were in a poor condition, sometimes wrongly labelled, and some were specimen cartoons which had never been actually used. Surprisingly, perhaps, there was no detailed guidebook listing the windows and what they contained.

The Commons' Chamber had been completely destroyed in the bombing. Sir Giles Gilbert Scott's replacement had only leaded lights of plain tinted glass; likewise the scheme for the Central Lobby. This work was carried out by Powell's of Whitefriars. Hardman's first task was the restoration of the ten large windows in St Stephen's Hall. Each was of five lights with transom. The lights were filled with the heraldic shields of 150 cities, boroughs and towns; in all probability an accurate restoration of what had been there before the war, although Pugin's original intention – for which drawings existed – was to have figures as well as arms.

The Royal Arms in the twenty-eight windows of the Royal Gallery was the next series to be undertaken. The old glass had been drastically altered in the 1860s because it competed too strongly with the painted murals, and such as remained was in poor condition. All the windows were redesigned and remade; 'the new design being based upon the old but with a more lively setting. It was essential that the windows should let in plenty of light and in no way overpower the elaborate and matured decoration of this Gallery'.[25]

The twelve transomed windows of the Lords' Chamber had originally contained figures of kings and queens standing in two tiers under Gothic canopies, designed by Pugin but actually made by Ballantine and Allen of Edinburgh,[26] but in 1947 it was stipulated that the new windows were to contain coats of arms of peers of the realm. The contract was not automatically placed with Hardman's. An anonymous donor, later identified as Lord Kenilworth, had offered £20,000 to defray the cost of the windows, and designs were invited from several prominent artists, including Donald Taunton of John Hardman & Co. Eventually a design submitted by Carl Edwards was approved, and the windows were made by Powell's of Whitefriars. Hardman's were no more successful in obtaining the contract for the Great South Window in Westminster Hall, although they had originally made it, and had restored it from the original designs following the Fenian bomb attack in January 1885. The glass having been destroyed for the second time by a bomb, a completely new design was commissioned from Sir Ninian Comper as a memorial to parliamentarians killed in the war.

Elsewhere in the Palace, Hardman's undertook the restoration of the windows of the Grand Staircase, which include a figure of the Black Prince in armour, with his family and his military campaigns in France represented heraldically. The sixteen windows in the Peers' corridor, containing various Royal Arms, were considered by Patrick Feeny to be some of the best in the building in terms of the vigour of their design,[27] and the last major task was the re-designing of the windows of the Peers' Lobby, which were set with the arms of various peers. Though nothing more has been undertaken since 1955, there may yet be scope for further additions. 'With the John Hardman studios still at work in Birmingham,' writes Sir Robert Cooke, 'the Palace could be much enhanced by a revival of stained glass at Westminster.'[28]

Though Hardman's were kept busy with post-war restoration work, the number of new commissions being placed with the studios was considerably less than it had once been. Whereas at the turn of the century Hardman's were completing an average of 120 jobs per year, for the whole of the period 1945–61 there were only 146 new commissions, i.e. an average of nine a year.[29] This was no reflection on the quality of Hardman's work, but rather a comment on the decline of church-building in post-war Britain compared with the earlier period, and post-war economic constraints. New churches there were, principally in areas severely damaged by wartime bombing and in areas of new population growth, but the revived Gothic style, with which Hardman's had been primarily – though not exclusively – associated, had run its course and Modernism was on the ascendant. The design and production of metalwork ceased altogether with the closure of Gerald J. Hardman

Donald Taunton: watercolour design for west window,
St. Patrick's, Glasgow 1951 (JHAL)

Ltd in 1959, although ever since 1933 the manufacture of Hardman's metalwork had been undertaken by A.E. Jones Ltd. of St Dunstan's works, Pemberton Street, Birmingham, Albert Edward Jones having earlier served his apprenticeship with Hardman Powell's.[30]

Though fewer in number, some important commissions were undertaken by the Newhall Hill studios, and a single job might involve several windows in the same building. Much was done in and around Birmingham, for example the seven-light east and west windows of St Martin's in the Bull Ring (1952–4), another seven-light window for St Mary's, Moseley (1954–5), and a series of fourteen single lights for the church of St Faith and St Laurence, Harborne, where Philip Chatwin, one of a dynasty of Birmingham architects was, along with his nephew, Anthony Chatwin, adding a chancel, sanctuary and Lady Chapel to a building which he had begun in 1937.[31] Nor was it only Christian places of worship. Between 1958 and 1961 Hardman's made a series of twenty-seven round-headed windows for Singers Hill Synagogue in Birmingham, built in the Italianate style in 1855–6 by Yeoville Thomason and considered to be the earliest surviving so-called 'cathedral synagogue' in Britain.[32] The subjects include Jewish festivals, and scenes from the Pentateuch including the figure of Moses with the Tablets of the Law, but all faces are concealed in deference to the Second Commandment. Further afield, a full complement of eighteen windows was made for St Patrick's church, Langley Moor (Durham) in 1954, while at the same time Hardman's returned to the Church of Our Lady and the English Martyrs, Cambridge, for which John Hardman Powell had designed the west window and other glass in the 1880s, to install seventeen new windows in the chancel, aisles and side-chapels.

Forty of the jobs carried out between 1947 and 1961 were overseas commissions. The established links between Hardman's and the United States had, for the time being, been severed in the mid-1930s,[33] but work was still being done for a number of churches in Canada and other Commonwealth countries. In South Africa, thirty-four windows were made for Holy Trinity, Durban, and twenty-eight for St John's, Fish Hoek, between 1951 and 1960. The strongest connection, however, was with Australia, where Pugin and Hardman had first established the 'good style' in the 1840s. The most important commissions were in and around Sydney, where earlier twentieth-century commissions had included twelve windows for the chapel of St Ignatius' College, Riverview (1909–19), thirty-five windows for the Ceretti chapel at Manly (1934–5) and continuing work at St Mary's cathedral. The designs were principally by John Tarleton Hardman and Donald Taunton,[34] then, in the 1950s, Patrick Feeny came to the fore, undertaking a two-month business trip to Australia in 1955, visiting Adelaide, Melbourne, Perth, Sydney and other cities before flying on to New Zealand. It was a successful trip which generated several new commissions, including windows for the Church of Our Lady of Fatima, Eglinton (NSW), the Royal Prince Albert Hospital, Camperdown (NSW), and the Methodist Homes in Melbourne.[35]

Patrick Feeny (1910–96) was the seventh son of Felix and Marie Feeny of Beckenham, Kent. He attended Stonyhurst College, and it was there that he came into contact with John Tarleton Hardman, who admired some of Feeny's prize-winning sketches and drawings, and invited him to join the firm when he left Stonyhurst in 1928. There he worked alongside Dunstan Powell, the Pippet brothers and Donald Taunton, eventually taking over the firm when Taunton retired in 1964. Elected a Fellow of the British Society of Master Glass Painters, Feeny was a regular contributor to the Society's journal, and was for a time its Treasurer.

Under Feeny, Hardman's experimented with new materials and new techniques as well as carrying on the traditional work of glasspainting and restoration. This included the use of *dalles de verre* or slab glass, a French invention in which window panels were made from thick slabs of glass. Traditional leading-up was impossible with slabs, and so resin or concrete was used to bind them together into panels which were strong and heavy. The new resin glues also facilitated the development of appliqué work, in which coloured glass shapes are stuck onto a background panel. Feeny designed a set of five *dalles de verre* for the Catholic church at Dolgellau (Gwynedd), where he and his family worshipped while on holiday, and secular commissions in this medium were undertaken for branches of the Halifax Building Society in Blackpool and Fleetwood (1971–3), and the Trustee Savings Bank in Stafford (1972). Feeny also used GRP (Glass Reinforced Plastic) for mouldings on reredos panels and other relief work in place of wood or plaster. Some would argue that by tilting towards Modernism and abstract compositions, Feeny was moving away from some of Hardman's established traditions, but it was either that or lose out to rival companies at a time when commissions were scarce.

Decorative schemes continued to be carried out by Hardman's, Feeny having been trained in this aspect of the company's work by Elphege and Oswald Pippet. His mosaics in the church of the Sacred Heart, Droitwich (Worcs.), compare well with Gabriel Pippet's earlier and more famous ones. Feeny undertook important decorative work in Scotland – at St Andrew's cathedral, Glasgow, and St Mirin's cathedral, Paisley, for which he also designed fifteen apse windows – and he carried out the re-ordering of the sanctuary at St Mary's, Pollokshields to accord with the new liturgical requirements following the Second Vatican Council. A project of which he was particularly proud was the painted decoration of the wooden tunnel-vaulted

St. Edmund's, Beckenham: Feeny memorial window, 1946

ceiling of the Birmingham Oratory (1952–60), wholly in the Italian style, and which consumed over a mile of gold leaf in the gilding of the ribs. Dunstan Powell had earlier (1903–9) designed the high altar, the bronze canopy for the font, and a set of copper-framed Stations of the Cross.

Each summer, Feeny organised a works outing, the main idea being to visit buildings where Hardman's workforce could see the earlier achievements of the firm in their context. On one occasion they visited Tewkesbury, with its many windows by John Hardman Powell and Dunstan Powell. As they were looking at the great west window of 1886, depicting the life of Christ, the vicar came in, and on discovering that the party was from Hardman's, told them that a young girl had recently noticed an error in the scene showing the Last Supper. Instead of there being eleven disciples seated at the table with Christ, there were only ten, with Judas just about to leave the room. The local press had got hold of the story of the 'missing apostle', which worried the abbey clergy somewhat. Feeny agreed to check the records of the window – given in 1886 by the Revd Charles Grove in memory of his wife – to see if there was a particular reason for the omission. It turned out to be a design fault, and so Hardman's agreed to supply the missing figure free of charge. The story appeared in the national press, as a consequence of which Hardman's received three unexpected orders for new windows.[36] Surprisingly, perhaps, when the great west window was dismantled, cleaned and releaded in 2003, the work was given to Richard Green of Hull, rather than to Hardman & Co.

In the 1960s, when there were generally fewer stained-glass commissions to be had, Hardman's were faced with stiff competition from rival firms such as Clayton & Bell and Goddard & Gibbs, and from individual artists and glassmakers such as Patrick and Joseph Nuttgens, Patrick Reyntiens and John Piper. It was Reyntiens and Piper who did the glass for major new Catholic buildings such as the cathedral of Christ the King, Liverpool (1962–7), with the exception of an abstract window designed in 1967 by Patrick Feeny for the St Thomas Aquinas chapel. Reyntiens made 36 panels of *dalles de verre* for St Mary's, Leyland, Lancashire (1962–4), while at Kitts Green on the outskirts of Birmingham Richard Gilbert Scott's astonishing Church of Our Lady Help of Christians (1966–7) had all of its glass designed by John Chrestian, a friend of the architect. The glass for the most important Anglican building of the period, Basil Spence's new Coventry Cathedral, was given to Piper and Reyntiens.

Patrick Feeny nevertheless succeeded in getting his glass into some of the fifty or so new Catholic churches built in the archdiocese of Birmingham between 1945 and 1970. A set of eight windows was designed for the extension to All Souls', Coventry (1970–2), complementing his three earlier ones for the original building of 1924. A project in which he took particular delight was a set of six windows for St Edmund's Catholic church in his home town of Beckenham, including the nine-light west window and a memorial window to Feeny's parents.[37]

The Hardman archive contains many of Feeny's coloured drawings for the re-ordering and redecorating of churches following the Second Vatican Council, and for the furnishing of new ones in accordance with modern liturgical practice. At least one of these was controversial, namely the alterations carried out at Belmont Abbey (Herefordshire), which involved the destruction of E.W. Pugin's high altar. The carved stone reredos was left in place, and to fill the now vacant space below it, Feeny designed a set of slate panels carved with Eucharistic symbols picked out in gold leaf, and a tabernacle set on a free-standing pedestal. He also designed the new forward altar, and oak stalls for the monks.[38] This was the last major job which Feeny oversaw before his retirement from Hardman's in 1974, although two years before his death in 1996 he designed a set of windows for the chapel of his old college, Stonyhurst, to commemorate the 400th anniversary of the founding of the college.

On the night of Friday 13 February 1970 a fire broke out in the studios at Newhall Hill. The whole of the centre of the building, including the cartoon room, visitors' room and the glaziers' shop, was gutted. Fortunately the office, the painters' shop and the area where all the earlier cartoons were kept escaped severe damage, so it was possible for the time being to carry on working in reduced circumstances. It was obvious, however, that

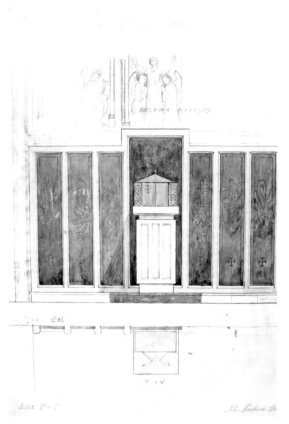

Patrick Feeny: design for panelling and tabernacle, Belmont Abbey, 1974 (JHAL)

the firm would have to find other premises, and Patrick Feeny visited a number of local buildings which were for sale or rent. One that he particularly liked was Lightwoods House, set in an attractive park on Hagley Road, and which he had known since childhood visits to an aunt and uncle who lived in Edgbaston. Until 1902 Lightwoods was the home of the Adkins family, who had made their fortune in soap-manufacturing. It was subsequently taken over by Birmingham City Council and put to a variety of uses, including café facilities for the adjacent park and gardens. By the 1970s, however, these activities had ceased. The Council had no use for the house, and the fabric was rapidly deteriorating. Feeny negotiated a long lease and in 1972 Hardman's moved in, having carried out some urgently-needed repairs to the upper floors and roofs, thus saving this important Georgian house from further deterioration, vandalism, and – perhaps – eventual demolition.

Although there was ample room at Lightwoods House for the working studios, there was insufficient space for the huge archive which had largely survived the fire: the daybooks, volumes of business letters, watercolour drawings and cartoons. Eventually the greater part of the archive was sold to the Birmingham Museum and Art Gallery and the Birmingham City Archive, thus ensuring that the collections would be kept locally and made readily accessible to the public.[39] Material still needed by the firm for day-to-day reference was retained at Lightwoods House.

Amongst Hardman's regular customers at this time were Edgar and Margaret Phillips, who regularly brought in stained-glass panels, salvaged from redundant churches, for repair or alteration. They showed great interest in the firm and its history at a time when the established traditions that Hardman's represented were severely undervalued, and when many of the church interiors created by Hardman, Pugin, Powell and the Pippets were being ruthlessly destroyed in the welter of iconoclasm which resulted from over-zealous interpretations of the Constitution on the Sacred Liturgy (1963) of the Second Vatican Council, and parallel movements within the Anglican Church. When Patrick Feeny decided to retire in 1974 he advertised the firm in both *The Times* and *The New York Times,* but there were no takers. Edgar and Margaret Phillips were amongst the few who understood how uniquely important Hardman & Co. was, and why it was necessary to maintain it as an active studio, and for his part Patrick Feeny was aware of the need to find the right people to take it over. The Phillipses therefore bought the Studio, having agreed to keep the name of John Hardman & Co., and it is they who were responsible for the firm's survival and the preservation of skills such as figure-painting which would one day enable it to grow again. They were later joined by their son, Neil, who, having been convinced by his parents of just how important Hardman's is, chose to enter the firm rather than pursue an independent career, took charge charge of the business after Edgar Phillips' death and is the present custodian of the firm.

In the decade 1970 to 1980, before and after the fire, Hardman's were undertaking an average of eighteen new jobs per year, including work in mosaic, slab glass and GRP. Restoration work at this time included the large pictorial windows originally designed and made in 1719–21 by Francis Slater and Joshua Price for the Baroque church at Great Witley (Worcs.), described as 'the most Italian ecclesiastical space in the whole of England'[40]. Amongst the overseas commissions undertaken at this time was a chandelier in slab and plate glass, and ten applique panels, for the Al Am Hilton Hotel in Abu Dhabi, and a set of heraldic GRP panels for Government offices in Muscat.

It was indeed work in the Far East that revived the fortunes of John Hardman & Co. in the design and manufacture of figurative stained glass windows. Paradoxically, perhaps, the impetus came not from Catholic Europe but from predominantly Shinto Japan where there has been a growing fascination with European culture and the great Gothic buildings of the Middle Ages. Quite specifically, a movement towards western–style wedding ceremonies has spawned a fashion for large Gothic chapels, and neo-Classical ones too, in the style of wellknown European buildings such as St. Mark's, Venice, St. Paul's, London, and Notre Dame, Paris. The architecture is serious, the buildings are constructed out of fine materials, the furnishings are authentic, and the Church has been very actively involved in their development, principally through the late Revd. Ben Abe. The Japanese company responsible for the various building projects – Trader Al of Shimonoseki directed by Mr Kanda, Mrs Kanda, and Mr. Kaneshiro – commissioned all their stained glass from John Hardman & Co. This includes a huge seven-light east window with figures of saints for the Notre Dame project in Sakai City, Osaka, an east window depicting the Coronation of Our Lady for 'San Marco' basilica, Moji, and a set of very tall lancets in the apsidal chancel at Holy Zion's Park, Fukuyama, a building of cathedral-like proportions. Through these buildings, thousands of people are being brought into contact with Christian iconography who might otherwise never experience it, and for those who wish to make a study of European stained glass, the Stained Glass Museum at Nasu, Tokyo, has excellent facilities. These Japanese buildings reveal the power of Gothic to reinvent itself, to inspire people of different cultures and traditions, to integrate art and faith; and once again Hardman's have been in the forefront, as they were in the 1840s when the first crateloads of metalwork and glass made their way from Birmingham to Tasmania.

Although some attempt was made in the 1970s to secure new work in the U.S.A., it was scarcely worth the effort. Fred L. Stuart, a New York agent, produced an advertisement leaflet listing some of Hardman's earlier work in the States, but Patrick Feeny suspected that Stuart was handing over American stained–glass enquiries 'to a rival of ours in London' and so gave him up[41]. An interesting story from this time concerns the relocation of a Hardman window in a new building. Between 1890 and 1893 Hardman's had made a set of windows for the chapel of St. Francis de Sales Industrial School, Eddington (PA), consisting of a series of worker—saints to act as role models for boys being trained at the school. One of these showed St. Dunstan of Canterbury (c.908–998) in the role of patron saint of metalworkers – the English equivalent of the French St. Eligius who had been adopted by Pugin and Hardman on their advertisement-board back in the 1840s. Below the figure of Dunstan a rectangular panel showed him at the anvil forging a piece of metal, and surrounded by various items of ecclesiastical metalwork. In 1981 the window was moved to the new church of St. Anselm, Philadelphia, with the inscription changed from St. Dunstan to St. Anselm but retaining, incongruously, the metalworking scene underneath[42].

It was nevertheless the building of churches like St. Anselm's which led eventually to the commissioning of new Hardman windows by clients in the USA. Though antique figurative glass was becoming popular again at the end of the twentieth century, there were few American firms capable of making it to the standards of Charles Connick (d. 1945) and Lawrence Saint (d. 1961). Acquiring old glass from redundant buildings could supply only a part of the needs of church-builders at a time when it was estimated (2005) around 900 new churches a year were being opened in the U.S.A. Though by no means all of them required stained–glass windows, it was in the context of these new buildings that the persistence of Hardman & Co. in training designers and glassmakers in the traditional techniques of figure painting began to pay dividends. In 2006 a significant breakthrough came with the commissioning of a large window for the Church of the Sacred Heart, Peoria

San Marco project, Japan (Trader Al Shimonoseki)

San Marco project, Japan (Trader Al Shimonoseki)

San Marco project, Japan (Trader Al Shimonoseki)

Mr Shindo

Mr Kaneshiro

Mr Kanda

Notre Dame project, Japan (Trader Al Shimonoseki)

Mrs Kanda

The late Revd. Ben Abe

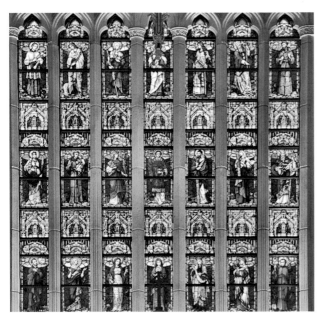

Detail of east window Notre Dame project, Japan
(Trader Al Shimonoseki)

Shimonoseki project, Japan
(Trader Al Shimonoseki)

Ubé project, Japan (Trader Al Shimonoseki)

Kurashi project, Japan
(Trader Al Shimonoseki)

(IL) to replace a somewhat indifferent abstract composition of 1960s date. Set high above the organ loft at the west end of the church, the new window consists of three round-headed lights with no vertical divisions or tracery. The subject is the Ascension of Christ who, with the Apostles and the Blessed Virgin Mary, occupies the central light, with hosts of angels in the sidelights. The figure-drawing and painting is superb: more naturalistic and soft-faced than either the medievals or Pugin would have done them, but with the figures dramatically posed as in the mature style of John Hardman Powell. Much of the ornament is clearly inspired by patterns in the Hardman archive, and

Church of the Sacred Heart, Peioria: west window (JHAL)

the colours are stunning. Above all, the subject is instantly recognisable for what it is. The purpose of figurative stained glass, according to Pugin, was to provide instruction in the Faith and to inspire devotion, so a composition which needs a screed of written commentary to explain its content and significance may be said to fail in its primary function of connecting directly with faith and worship.

The Ascension window may not be the end of the Peoria story. On a visit to England in 2006, the parish priest of Sacred Heart Church, Father Larry Zurek, was taken to see the Pugin masterpiece, St. Giles's Cheadle, where every inch of the building is covered with coloured decoration, and he returned full of ideas for future projects.

In designing a large rose-window for Syon Abbey (VA), in 2006-7, Hardman's adopted a more strictly historical approach. This newly-built church is wholly in the early medieval style, the architects being HDB/Cram & Ferguson, the successors of the firm established in the 1890s by Ralph Adams Cram, and now headed by Ethan Anthony who has done much to promote the revival of Hardman's work in the U.S.A [43]. Like Cram before him, Ethan Anthony has a love of early glass which he has studied at close quarters, working in close collaboration with Neil Phillips and his team of designers at Hardman's on the Syon project. The figures and ornament for Syon have been inspired by the thirteenth-century glass at Chartres cathedral and Cluny (France), and also at Canterbury cathedral. Here the emphasis in on glowing colours, with the jewel-like quality enhanced by narrow lines of white glass and ornament which Pugin believed to be essential to give sparkle and brilliance to deeply- coloured windows. Pugin, it should be remembered, made a special journey to Chartres to obtain both accurate details and some medieval glass so that Hardman could match the tints exactly. Pugin's efforts were not directed towards making copies of medieval windows, but the creation of new work on the basis of the 'true principles' of Gothic design and manufacture, and the same is true of the Syon window in which late-medieval saints such as St. Thomas More have been depicted in the Early style, with the appropriate symbolism worked into the design.. The use of mouth-blown glass made in England has captured the vibrant colours and brilliance of the medieval glass which inspired it, the whole ensemble proving the age-old maxim that originality should derive from tradition.

The rapid expansion of Catholic churches in the U.S.A. and the planting of new ones is illustrated by the church of All Souls', Sanford (FL). The original church dates back to 1882, making it one of the oldest in the Catholic history of Central Florida. The original church burnt down in 1932 and was replaced with a fairly plain stuccoed building with a red tiles roof and rectangular windows which were filled with windows of coloured

Peoria

John Hardman & Co. Ltd. (Estb 1838)

Church of the Sacred Heart, Peoria: details of west window (JHAL)

Rose Window, Syon Abbey 2007

dalles de verre. These are now to be replaced, and Hardman & Co. have been chosen to design, manufacture and install fourteen new windows in traditional style. In 1987 there were thirteen families worshipping at All Souls'; in 2007 there were 1,400. The consequence has been the building of a new church under the leadership of Fr. Richard Trout who has been parish priest since 1993, and Mass was celebrated there for the first time in January 2008. It is intended that the windows – over fifty of them – presently glazed with clear glass will eventually be filled with stained glass designed and made by Hardman & Co.

The largest commission received during 2007 was for a set of windows for the church of St. Peter Chanel, Rosewell, Atlanta (GA), which began life as a mission established in 2000 from St. Ann's in Marietta. Another story of remarkable growth in a short period of time, membership of St. Peter's has grown from the original six families to over 2,200 by the summer of 2006, under the leadership of their priest, Fr. Frank McNamee. Having won the contract in competition with the German firm, Mayer of Munich, Hardman's will undertake the glazing of up to 68 windows. These, along with other furnishings, are being financed by subscription, and ten windows have already (2008) been subscribed. They consist largely of life-size figure-work including representations of Blessed Teresa of Calcutta ('Mother Teresa') and Pope John Paul II. Another exciting project is Holy Trinity, Chicago, for which eight square-headed windows are being made, all with figures of saints, and screenwork of etched glass at the west end of the building, commissioned by Fr. de Salvo.

The changed political climate in China has enabled Christian congregations to worship freely again. In Shanghai the Anglican church of Holy Trinity, or 'The Red Church' as the brick-built edifice is known, is being restored. Built in 1871 to designs by George Gilbert Scott, Holy Trinity was gutted during the Cultural Revolution when organised religion was suppressed. The congregation intend to replace the original mahogany furnishings to match Scott's design, and Hardman's have submitted plans for new windows based on the original drawings and watercolours which are preserved in the Birmingham archives.

As Hardmans enters its 170th year, it is entirely appropriate that a firm which was founded at the beginning of Queen Victoria's reign and helped to furnish her new Palace of Westminster should also have made the stained-glass panels for Cunard's prestigious new liner, *Queen Victoria,* with its 990 staterooms and a guest capacity

All Souls' Church: details of window panels

Sanford new church
designs for window panels

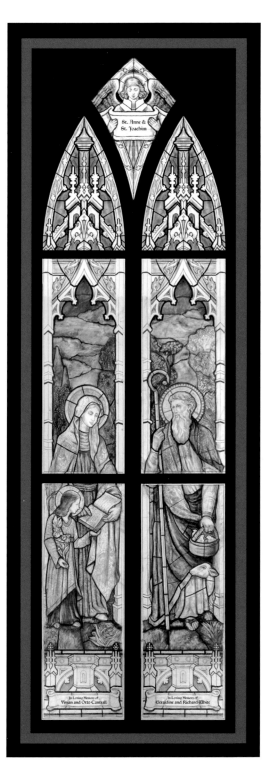

St. Peter Chanel, Atlanta: memorial window with figures of St. Joachim and St. Anne (JHAL)

St. Peter Chanel, Atlanta USA details of St. Joachim and St. Anne window

St. Peter Chanel, Atlanta USA: Cartoon progress for Pope John Paul II and Blessed Mother Teresa window

St. Peter Chanel, Atlanta USA designs in progress

Holy Trinity Chicago: panels with figure of
St. Thomas Becket (JHAL)

183

of over 2,000. The key areas in which Hardman's were involved are the Queen's Room, Casino and Library. The Queen's Room is based on the interior of Osborne House, the Isle of Wight summer retreat for Queen Victoria and Prince Albert, whose gilded portraits are set into stained glass panels.

A contemporary of John Hardman Jnr. was the pioneer tour-operator Thomas Cook, who in July 1841 arranged the world's first publicly advertised excursion train, and whose name was to become synonymous with foreign travel. In 1851 Cook organised excursion trains to take visitors to the Great Exhibition. Later the firm developed a special relationship with the operators of the Cote d'Azur Pullman Express, which catered for the luxury end of the market and was exclusively First Class. The

Ready for restoration: the English Church in Shanghai (JHAL)

dining car was adorned with three cast glass panels by the celebrated French artist Rene Lalique, and after it had been taken out of service the panels were presented to Thomas Cook's chairman to mark the fiftieth anniversary of the two firms' association in 1979. Necessary restoration and conservation work was undertaken by John Hardman & Co. With their deeply-cast Kingfisher design, the panels are now located in the executive dining room at the company's headquarters in Peterborough.

A significant commission undertaken during 2007 was a memorial window for the museum at the North Weald Airfield, which was the front-line airfield in the Battle of Britain. The window commemorates airmen of 7 nations and 42 squadrons who took part in the battle, and contains reprentations of Hurricane and Spitfire aircraft. By contrast, a private commission for a large country house in the Cotswolds (2008) consists of a stunning window in the style of Christopher Whall and Edward Burne-Jones. Consisting of three lights, it

Detail of Battle of Britain window, North Weald Air Museum (JHAL)

portrays the archangels Gabriel, Uriel and Michael, the faces of whom are based on those of the client's children. These two undertakings help to illustrate the diversity of Hardman's work, and the wide-ranging skills of the firm's designers and glasspainters.

Ecclesiastical commissions from within the United Kingdom towards the close of the twentieth century included the restoration of the magnificent five-light east window at the church of the Sacred Heart, Henley-on-Thames (1994) designed originally by John Hardman Powell and shown at the London International Exhibition of 1862. Conservation work in the historic buildings at Alton Towers, Staffordshire (1999-2006) comprised the repair and releading of a set of six Pugin windows in the Armoury, and earlier glass by William Raphael Eginton (1778-1834) in the Music Room. A scheme is to be put forward for the restoration of the huge oriel window in the banqueting hall with its vast array of Pugin-Hardman heraldic glass, fully documented in the Hardman archive which includes the original watercolour design.

Stained glass panels for the Cunard liner *Queen Victoria* (JHAL)

Domestic commission 2008 with figures of archangels (JHAL)

Though now more famous as the location of the most popular theme-park in the United Kingdom, Alton Towers was once the largest Gothic-revival mansion in the country and it contains many important survivals of historic glass by Hardman's and other artists of the period.

In 2005 a new window was designed for the baptistery in the Catholic church at Harvington (Worcs.), for which Hardman had already made glass in the nineteenth century. It incorporates the figures of St. Anne, St. Margaret Clitherow, the Venerable John Henry Newman and Nicholas Owen, the seventeenth-century carpenter who created the many 'hides' inside Harvington Hall for the concealment of Catholic priests in the days of persecution. The figures are composed in a naturalistic way, with the face of St. Anne taken from a photograph of one of the persons commemorated in this memorial window. Other commissions have ensued for Harvington: a 'Jesse tree' and a third window depicting the life of the Blessed Virgin Mary which is still (2007) at the design stage. At the twelfth-century church of St. Chad, Stafford, Hardman's artists employed the glowing colours of early glass, but avoided the obvious course of representing the seventh-century patron saint as a medieval bishop in full pontificals, portraying him instead in a style which reflects his Celtic origins, and using the Romanesque details of the church to inspire the surrounding ornament (2003).

Modern computer-generated graphics are of only limited use in the design and making of stained-glass windows. The design of a window depends, initially, on the knowledge, skill and imagination of the artist in creating, first a pencil sketch, and then a watercolour which may go through a number of revisions as a result of discussions with the client and the studio manager. Once the design and the palette of colours have been agreed, the window proceeds to cartooning, that is the preparation of the full-size working drawing and then the cutline which gives the shapes of the individual pieces of glass as they are to be cut. The processes of cutting, painting, firing and assembly then proceed as previously described[44]. The actual production of the glass is also an area in which mechanisation and modern processes of sheet-glass production are of little value. 'Antique' glass was never uniformly clear and transparent; the sheets were thick and uneven, never perfectly flat, and they were full of bubbles and striations. The coloured glass was not uniform in colour, but showed gradations even in a small sheet. It was these very imperfections, as they would be called in modern glass, which gave antique glass its character, causing light to be refracted at different

St. Mary's, Harvington: baptistery window, 2005

Work in progress at the Hardman Studio

angles, like the facets of a jewel, so that the glass glowed and sparkled[45]. By contrast, glass of uiniform thickness, colour and translucency produces windows that are flat and uninteresting. Antique glass has still to be made by the centuries-old mouth-blowing process, whereby a large bubble of molten glass is formed, using an iron blow-pipe. The glass bubble is converted into a cylinder which is then heated and unrolled to produce a flat sheet embodying all the essential characteristics of medieval glass. Since the closure of Hartley Wood of Sunderland, the firm which Hardman's had dealt with almost from the beginning of their stained-glass enterprise, mouth-blown glass is sourced from English Antique Glass Ltd. of Alvechurch (Worcs.), the only makers of this material, and thus essential to the continuation of the traditional glassmaking crafts.

The fire at Newhall Hill in February 1970 destroyed many of the artefacts in the Hardman collection which had been built up since the 1830s: woodcarvings, metalwork, medieval glass, as well as a library of reference works on art and liturgy. Such items as survived were relocated at Lightwoods House, and the collections have been augmented with Hardman items acquired from redundant churches, or which have been disposed of because of liturgical changes. A fine example is the lampadarium which hung in front of the altar in the chapel at Oscott College. As part of the 1970s reordering of the sanctuary, this carved and richly-decorated wooden beam was taken down and put into storage before being offered, along with its seven hanging brass lamps, on loan to the Hardman Studio. The process of acquisition continues as historic artefacts and documents which appear from time to time in the salerooms are purchased and added to the collection. A set of early drawings by A.W. Pugin was bought in 2003. It consists of furniture and metalwork designs, and some architectural studies, dating from between 1829 and 1834, i.e. before Pugin and John Hardman met, and they illustrate Pugin's skills as an artist and draughtman while yet a teenager, and his early interest in ecclesiastical metalwork and the rituals of the Catholic Church. Hardman's have also acquired a set of superb cartoons executed in the 1920s and '30s by the stained-glass artist A.E. Lemmon (1889-1963) of the Bromsgrove Guild, and archive material from the now-defunct Birmingham metalworking firm of A.E. Jones.

In October 2006 the American singer, Cher, sold the contents of her Malibu mansion, including a large collection of Gothic-Revival items. Hardman's were able to buy back a part-volume of drawings by J.H. Powell to re-unite with detached pages from this volume already at Lightwoods House. At the same sale they purchased a pair of *coronae* which had formerly hung in the Bishop's House in Birmingham prior to its demolition in the 1960s, and a pair of standard candlesticks which had been converted into electric lamps. Though made of polished brass, both the *coronae* and the candlesticks had been painted black, in accordance with the late-twentieth misconception based partly on a certain genre of rock music and horror films that 'Gothic' is necessarily dark, sinister and nightmarish. The removal of the paint will demonstrate that the opposite is true, and that Gothic whether of the Middle Ages or of the nineteenth century has always been about beauty and truth, light and colour, brilliance and sparkle.

Corona formerly at the Bishop's House, Birmingham

Another significant return to Hardman's (2007) was a quantity of archive material which had earlier gone missing. This included some fine drawings by J.H. Powell for memorial brasses, a quantity of decorative schemes designed by J.A. Pippet and his sons, and various drawings and watercolours of woodwork, metalwork and stained glass. Hardly had these items been unpacked and sorted when a drawing of the Presentation of the Virgin Mary was put to immediate use by one of Hardman's artists who was seeking inspiration for a new window on precisely that theme. This exemplifies the value of the archive not just as a vehicle for historical research, but also as a working collection in constant use by glassmakers and metalworkers as a reference-point for their own creations, and in the restoration of historic glass and other artefacts which is an integral part of the firm's operations. In 2004, for example, Hardman's began the restoration of some of their earliest windows, at St. Mary's church, Wymeswold (Leicestershire). Other important restoration schemes include the huge Immaculate Conception window in St. Chad's cathedral Birmingham, originally installed as a memorial to John Hardman Jnr. also, the nine light 'Jesse Tree' window of 1913 at the church of the immaculate Conception, Farm Street, London, was recreated at the Hardman Studio for a church in Japan. In either case, the original cartoons, watercolours and other working drawings enabled the glass to be restored accurately to its initial design and condition.

The carefully-preserved stencilling patterns from the many decorative schemes undertaken by Hardman's have also been the inspiration for new work. They were, for example, used in 2003 to create new decorations for the interior of the chapel at St. Mary's convent, Handsworth, opposite the former Hardman house in Hunter's Road, which was undergoing a complete restoration at that time. It was with reference to the original metalwork drawings in the Birmingham Museum that Hardman's were able to reinstate the painted metal shields on the fireplaces at The Grange, Ramsgate, as part of the restoration of Pugin's home carried out by the Landmark Trust in 2003-6, while items in the metalwork collection at Lightwoods House provided patterns for the manufacture of door-furniture and light-fittings to replace those which had been lost or destroyed. The revival of Hardman's metalworking was taken a stage further with the making of a pair of standard candlesticks for the chapel of Jesus College, Cambridge to replace the missing Pugin ones which had stood either side of the lectern. The Pugin corridor at Chirk Castle (Clwyd) now has a full set of brass gasoliers, Hardman's

Immaculate
Conception
window, created
from original
1913 cartoon for
a church in Japan

metalworkers having made new ones, identical to those of the 1840s, to complete the set (2007).

Though there has been no corresponding revival in Birmingham of traditional needlework as designed and made at Hardman's and in their associated workshops, the important collection of vestments at St. Chad's cathedral, Birmingham, has been catalogued and recorded under the supervision of Textile Consultant, Jane Dew, while a NADFAS textile group have made their own meticulous survey. Many of these items date back to the time of Pugin and John Hardman Jnr. and some incorporate much older fabric and embroidery[46]. The fact that these items are now better cared-for is a reflection of the renewed interest in Gothic-Revival art which was stimulated by the exhibitions, *Pugin: A Gothic Passion,* held at the V&A Museum in 1994, *A.W.N. Pugin, Master of Gothic Revival,* held a year later at the Bard Graduate Center for Graduate Studies in New York, and the Australian touring exhibition, *Creating a Gothic Paradise: Pugin and the Antipodes* (2002-3). Examples of the many and varied products of John Hardman & Co. were prominently displayed in all three exhibitions and shown in the lavishly illustrated publications which accompanied each one.

At a more local level, an exhibition in the vast crypt of St. Chad's cathedral in 2003 brought together many items from the Lightwoods collection with the cathedral's own Hardman treasures, demonstrating also the great potential of the crypt as a heritage centre and exhibition area for the cathedral and archdiocese. Chirk castle was the summer venue, in 2007, for the exhibition, *Hardman: A Passion for Gothic,* containing examples of the diverse aspects of the firm's historic and current work, and in the following November these displays formed the centrepiece of the *Antiques for Everyone* Fair at the National Exhibition Centre, Birmingham, where Hardman's attracted widespread public and media attention. Events such as these, and the proposed development of Lightwoods House into a working museum, not only highlight the past achievements of John Hardman & Company, but demonstrate too that the crafts and design-skills which Hardman and Pugin fostered in the nineteenth century are still thriving in the twenty-first. Through the tenacity and dedication of Patrick Feeny, and, latterly, of the Phillips family, the firm has outlasted many of its former rivals which have, sadly, closed through lack of vision, knowledge and appreciation of the importance of the craft, and with consequent dispersal of their collections and archive material. With its international team of artists and designers ready to meet any challenge, the Hardman Studio is once again an expanding centre of excellence for education and training in the decorative arts. Trainees are no longer bound by the same conditions as applied in 1853 when John Hardman Jnr. took on Edmund Bradshaw as an apprentice glass painter, and his widowed mother Sarah Bradshaw had to agree that her son would not 'commit fornication nor contract Matrimony... play at Cards or Dice Tables or any other unlawful Games.. haunt Taverns or Playhouses' during the term of his apprenticeship'[47]. Nor is it a requirement, as it was in the nineteenth century, that Hardman's employees should be

exclusively Catholic. However, the same high standards of professional training and supervision which put John Hardman & Co. on the world stage in the mid-Victorian period still apply, enriched by many decades of experience across the broad field of design and manufacture. 'Let then the Beautiful and the True be our watchword for future exertions'[48]. Gothic For Ever!

The Hardman chantry, St. Chad's cathedral, Birmingham: Justin Hardman and Neil Phillips at the 2003 exhibition

NOTES TO CHAPTERS

Abbreviations:

BAA	Birmingham Archdiocesan Archives
BCA	Birmingham City Archives
BMAG	Birmingham Museum & Art Gallery
HLRO	House of Lords Record Office
ML	Metalwork Letters (BCA)
JHAL	Hardman Archive: Lightwoods House Collection
MWDB	Metalwork Day Book (BCA)
RDB	Rough Glass Daybook (BCA)
RIBA	Royal Institute of British Architects
SGL	Stained Glass Letters (BCA)
V&A	Victoria & Albert Museum

Andrews	Brian Andrews, *Creating a Gothic Paradise: Pugin at the Antipodes.* Hobart: Tasmanian Museum & Art Gallery, 2002.
Belcher 1987	Margaret Belcher, *A.W.N. Pugin: An Annotated Critical Bibliography.* London: Mansell, 1987.
Champ	Judith Champ (ed.), *Oscott College: A volume of commemorative essays,* Birmingham 1988.
BOE	Nikolaus Pevsner, *The Buildings of England,* Harmondsworth: Penguin, 1951–74.
Ferrey	Benajmin Ferrey, *Recollections of A.N. Welby (sic) Pugin and his father, Augustus Pugin,* London: Edward Stansford, 1861.
Glossary	A.W.N. Pugin, *Glossary of Ecclesiastical Ornament and Costume,* London: Henry Bohn, 1844.
GP	*Pugin: A Gothic Passion.* ed. Paul Atterbury & Clive Wainwright. New Haven: Yale University Press, 1994.
Letters I	*The Collected Letters of A.W.N. Pugin,* vol. 1, 1830 to 1842, ed. Margaret Belcher. Oxford: Oxford University Press, 2001.
Letters II	*The Collected Letters of A.W.N. Pugin,* vol. 2, 1843 to 1845, ed. Margaret Belcher. Oxford: Oxford University Press, 2003.

Meara   David Meara, *A.W.N. Pugin and the Revival of Memorial Brasses.* London: Mansell 1991.

O'Donnell   R. O'Donnell, The *Pugins and the Catholic Midlands,* Leominster 2002.

Powell   J.H. Powell, *Pugin in his Home,* ed. Alexandra Wedgwood. Ramsgate: The Pugin Society and Thanet District Council, 2006.

Present Staste   A.W.N. Pugin, *The Present State of Ecclesiastical Architecture in England,* London: Charles Dolman, 1843. (First published in Dublin Review, May 1841 and February 1842).

Shepherd   Stanley Shepherd, 'The Stained Glass of A.W.N. Pugin, c. 1835–52'. Unpublished PhD thesis, University of Birmingham 1997.

Stanton   Phoebe Stanton, 'Welby Pugin and the Gothic Revival', unpublished PhD thesis, University of London, 1950.

TP   *True Principles: the Journal of the Pugin Society.*

Trappes-Lomax Michael Trappes-Lomax, *Pugin: A Medieval Victorian,* London 1932.

Wedgwood 1985 Alexandra Wedgwood (ed.), *Catalogues of Architectural Drawings in the Victoria & Albert Museum: The Pugin Family,* London: V&A Museum, 1985

Notes to Chapters

Chapter 1 – Pugin's Candlestick Maker

1   Pugin to William Osmond, 30 January 1834? *Letters I*, p. 23.

2   *Orthodox Journal*, 9 November 1839, p. 320.

3   John Hardman's indenture is kept in the Lightwoods archive. For the toy trade of Birmingham, see Timmins (ed.), *Birmingham and the Midland Hardware Dustrict*, 1866.

4   For a history of Oscott see Judith Champ (ed.), *Oscott College, 1838–1988*, and Judith Champ, *Oscott College Chapel: A Temple of Living Stones*, 2002.

5   The exact date and location of Pugin's first meeting with Lord Shrewsbury are uncertain. *Ferrey* gives 1832, but this seems unlikely. The first reference to Lord Shrewsbury in Pugin's diary is on 3 October 1836. Daniel Rock, the earl's domestic chaplain was in contact with Pugin by then, and he could well have been the intermediary.

6   Pugin to John Hardman Jnr, 10 June 1837, *Letters I* , pp. 77–8.

7   The order was valued at £15. Booker & Dolman were based in New Bond Street, and they had published Pugin's controversial book, *Contrasts*, in 1836.

8   See below p.188

9   *Present State*, p. 8

10 For Pugin's influence at Oscott, his role as Professor of Ecclesiastical Antiquities, and the significance of the museum, see R. O'Donnell, 'Pugin at Oscott', in Judith Champ, *op. cit.*, pp. 45–66.

11 Pugin to E.J. Willson, 6 November 1834, *Letters I*, p. 43.

12 A. W. Pugin, *Some Remarks Relative to Ecclesiastical Architecture and Decoration*, 1850, p. 15.

13 Pugin to J.R. Bloxam, 3 April 1843, *Letters II*, pp. 35–6.

14 W.C. Aitken, 'The revived art of metalworking in the precious metals, brass and iron, on medieval, or true principles', in Samuel Timmins, *The Resources, Products and Industrial History of Birmingham and the Midland Hardware District*, 1866, p.539

15 *TP* p. 29.

16 Pugin to J.R. Herbert, July 1845? *Letters II*, p. 418.

17 Pugin, *True Principles,* p. 22.

18 Pugin to John Hardman Jnr, June 1845? *Letters II*, p. 402. Hardman is described as 'Gold Smith' in the 1851 census return.

19 *Glossary*, p. 60.

20 Shirley Bury, Pugin and the Tractarians', *Connoisseur*, January 1972, p. 16.

21 *Apology*, p. 40

22 Henry Weedall to John Hardman, 23 February 1845, ML February 1845, *Letters II*, p. 253.

23 *Orthodox Journal* LX, 1839, p. 36. A large order for Uttoxeter is entered in MWDB at 16 August 1839. For the history and significance of St Mary's, Uttoxeter, as a seminal 'true-principles' church, see M.J. Fisher, *Pugin-Land*, 2002, pp. 43–51. Both Hardman and Lord Shrewsbury (who contributed to the building) were present at the opening of St Mary's on 22 August 1839, but they had not yet been introduced. A few days later Shrewsbury wrote to Hardman saying that if he had known he was there he would have asked for an introduction 'as I should be happy to number amongst my acquaintances a Gentleman who is doing so much good to religion' (BAA Hardman Correspondence, no. 141).

24 Undated letter from Hardman to George White of London, BCA clients' letter box 1839–44.

25 BAA Hardman Correspondence, no. 81.

26 *Andrews*, Appendix C, pp. 222–3.

27 Pugin to John Hardman, 27 December 1844, *Letters II*, p. 308.

28 MWDB 22 February 1845; MWDB 3 August 1846.

29 MWDB 30 June 1849, entered (with paten) at £50. John Hardman wrote a statement about the making of this type of chalice for the first catalogue of the Museum of Manufactures at Marlborough House (later the V&A Museum), in 1852. 'The chalices were made entirely by hand: the bowls being beaten up from circles of sheet silver, the knops and feet were made in sections and soldered together; the patterns upon them were then chased. Chalices in this style, during the mediaeval period, were principally executed by the Florentines, whose works have been carefully studied, in order to produce this kind of metalwork.' See also Brian Andrews, 'Some sources of A.W.N. Pugin's chalice designs', TP vol. iii no. 1, 2004, pp. 18–20.

30 Pugin to John Hardman, 27 December 1844, as above, n.27.

31 Pugin to John Hardman, 16 October 1844, *Letters II*, p. 257.

32 Shirley Bury, *op. cit.*, as n.19 above.

33 An altar cross and candlesticks made for Pugin's church of St George's, Southwark, were of plated German silver. MWDB 16 July 1846.

34 Pugin to Lord Shrewsbury, 5 June 1843, MS V&A L.525-1965/11, *Letters II*, p. 72. The first attempt failed, and Weigall had to make a new wax model.

35 *TP*, p. 27

36 M. Fisher, *Alton Towers: A Gothic Wonderland*, pp. 41, 63, 145–7.

37 *GP*, pp. 96–7.

38 Fisher, *op. cit.,* pp.148 & 150.

39 *TP*, p. 21.

40 *ibid.*

41 W.C. Aitkin, Timmins *op. cit.,* p. 548.

42 Eatwell & North, 'Metalwork', *GP* p. *176.*

43 BAA Hardman Correspondence no. 158.

44 *ibid.,* no. 166.

45 *ibid.,* no. 144.

46 ML 13 November & 21 December 1843.

47 ML 6 March 1842.

48 ML 25 February 1842. Jewitt was at that time based at 45 Broad Street, Oxford. In September 1843 he moved to 49 High Street. In another letter to Hardman he encloses an engraving of a chalice which his brother, Orlando, had produced from a fourteenth-century monumental brass, and asks the cost of making one to that pattern. The pattern is no longer attached to the letter. ML 19 January 1843.

49 ML 11 February 1842.

50 Advertisement in *The Tablet*, 18 January 1851.

51 Pugin to Lord Shrewsbury, 13 February 1846, HLRO PUG3/15.

52 *Dublin Review*, 1839, p. 244.

53 Pugin to J.R. Bloxam, 24 October 1840, *Letters II*, p. 154.

54 Pugin to Lord Shrewsbury, 5 December 1841, *Letters 1*, p. 298.

55 *ibid.*

56 RDB 27 January 1854.

57 Dunstan Powell designed glass for the nave and Lady Chapel.

58. Trappes Lomax, *op. cit.*, p. 201 M. Trappes Lomax, *Pugin, A Medieval Victorian*, 1932

59 Before the restoration of the hierarchy in 1850, English Catholics were organised into four geographical districts or vicariates, each with its vicar apostolic who was in bishop's orders. The bishops took the titles of extinct extra-territorial sees, and Walsh was Bishop of Cambysopolis. When the vicariates were increased to eight in 1840, Walsh was translated into the new central district which was centred on Birmingham.

60 Charles Robert Blundell of Ince Hall, Lancashire, died in October 1837. A loyal Catholic, Blundell left the residue of his estate – mounting to more than £200,000 – to the London and midland districts in the names of their respective bishops. The will was challenged by relatives, and it was not until March 1839 that a compromise was reached. In the end Walsh received £42,000 from which he contributed £13,852 to St Chad's out of the total cost of £18,583. See *Letters II*, p. 117 & 171–2.

61 E.g. W. Greaney, *A Guide to St. Chad's Cathedral Church, Bath Street, Birmingham*, 1877; The Cathedral Clergy, *A History of St. Chad's Cathedral, Birmingham, 1841–1904*, 1904; M. Hodgetts, *St. Chad's Cathedral, Birmingham*, Archdiocese of Birmingham Historical Commission no. 4, 1987; R. O'Donnell, *The Pugins and the Catholic Midlands*, 2002, pp. 18–21, 57–65.

62 Pugin to John Hardman Jnr, 10 June 1837, *Letters 1*, p. 77. Pugin was referring here to his original 1837 scheme for St Chad's.

63 Pugin to J.R. Bloxam, 13 September 1840, *Letters 1*, p. 143.

64 Pugin to Daniel Rock, 13 December 1840, *Letters 1*, pp. 173–4, and Pugin to Ambrose Phillipps, 18 December 1840, *Letters 1,* p. 175.

65 Pugin to Lord Shrewsbury, 5 January 1841, *Letters I*, p. 188

66 Pugin to J.R. Bloxam, 7 February 1841, *Letters I*, p. 205.

67 Brian Doolan, 'St. Chad's Cathedral in the Twentieth Century', *Midland Catholic History*, Number 10, 2004, pp. 43—6, and Gavin Stamp, 'Ambonoclasm Redeemed', *True Principles:The Journal of the Pugin Society,* vol. 2, No. 4, Summer 2002. The Birmingham screen was not the only issue over which Pugin and Wiseman clashed. See below, p.48.

68 This was also a controversial issue, see below p.41

69 A.W. N. Pugin, *An Earnest Appeal for the Revival of the Ancient Plain Song*, 1850, p. 8.

70 For the fascinating history of these relics, see M. Greenslade, *Saint Chad of Lichfield and Birmingham*, Archdiocese of Birmingham Historical Commission, No.10, 1996.

71 R. O'Donnell. *op. cit.,* p. 60.

72 HLRO PUG/1/639. The Glassworkers' window is entered in First Glass Daybook at 20 December 1853 at a cost of £27.15s.5d.

73 Pugin to J.R. Bloxam, 13 September 1840. *Letters I*, p. 143, and see below pp. 122-3

74 See Brian Doolan, 'The Hardman Vault in St. Chad's Cathedral Crypt' *Midland Catholic History*, No. 10, 2004, pp.50–2.

75 Pugin, *Present State*, 1843, pp. 101–3. Pugin had very definite ideas as to the kind of residence appropriate for clergy. They should, he believed, exhibit *'a solid, solemn, and scholastic character that bespoke then at once to be the habitations of men who were removed far beyond the ordinary pursuits of life'*, and he drew a sharp contrast between surviving examples of medieval ecclesiastical residences and 'the drawing room of an Anglo-Protestant prebendary, with its piano, nick-nacks, mirrors, and ottomans' (pp. 99 & 100). As with most other things, fitness for purpose was Pugin's guiding principle, and the design of ecclesiastical residences presupposes a Catholic understanding of the office and work of a priest or a bishop.

76 *Powell*, pp.39–40.

77 *Present State*, p. 30.

78 Pugin to Lord Shrewsbury, 28 November 1841, *Letters I*, p. 280. In this letter, Pugin consistently mis-spells Croxden as 'Croxton', which is the site of a medieval abbey in north-east Leicestershire of which nothing remains above ground. Croxden, however, is a very substantial ruin, and the west front and south transept with their tall lancets are quite evidently the source from which Pugin took his inspiration for St Barnabas'. Unlike St Chad's, St Barnabas' was built entirely of stone, and is cruciform in shape with a central tower and spire. Lord Shrewsbury was the principal benefactor, contributing £7,000 to the total cost of £20,000. Bishop Walsh contributed £3,500. For a full history of St Barnabas see M. Cummins, *Nottingham Cathedral*, 3rd edn, 1994, and R. O'Donnell, *op. cit.*, pp. 102–4 which also takes account of the Mercy Convent built by Pugin, 1844–6.

79 Pugin, *Some Remarks*, 1850, p. 12. He says that 'even the width of the lights was regulated' (presumably by the dimensions of the lancets at Croxden) and 'the result has been what might be expected, the church is too dark, and *I am blamed for it.'*

80 MWDB June–August 1842. The church was consecrated on 27 August.

81 See below, pp. 140-145

82 JHA Decoration Cost Book, August–December 1930 and September–November 1932. Elphege Pippet was at this time chief designer at Hardman's in succession to his father, Joseph Aloysius Pippet (1841–1903).

83 The decorations and Pugin–Hardman furnishings at St Baranabas' have had a chequered history. The ex-Oratorian Bishop Brindle (1901–15) demolished the rood-screen and high altar. Bishop Dunn (1926–32) wished to 'restore all things in Pugin' and so brought back Hardman's and the Pippets. Bishop Ellis (1944–79) unpicked a good deal of Dunn's work in the wake of the Second Vatican Council at which Ellis was present. The most recent re-ordering (1994) has restored a balance between historicism and present liturgical needs.

84 Brian Doolan, *The Pugins and the Hardmans*, Archdiocese of Birmingham Historical Commission, No. 18, 2004.

85 Pugin, *Present State*, p. 104.

86 *Powell*, p. 40.

87 Pugin to John Hardman, 6 December 1842, *Letters I*, p. 398.

88 See below p.124

89 See below, pp.63-5

90 Pugin to John Hardman, 14 November 1844. *Letters II*, p. 290.

91 Pugin to John Hardman, 12 January 1845. *Letters II*, p. 321.

92 Pugin to John Hardman, 27 December 1844? *Letters II*, p. 308.

93 Pugin to John Hardman, mid-February 1845. *Letters II*, p. 342. In this as in other extracts from Pugin's letters, his erratic spelling, punctuation and use of capitals have been preserved.

94 Pugin to John Hardman, 26 December 1845. *Letters II*, p. 487.

95 Pugin to John Hardman, HLRO PUG/1/399.

96 Pugin to John Hardman, HLRO PUG/1/404 & 59.

97 See below, p.146

98 *Pugin in his home: Two memoirs by John Hardman Powell*, edited with an introduction by Alexandra Wedgwood. New Enlarged Edition. Ramsgate: The Pugin Society and Thanet District Council, 2006. Appropriately, Powell was buried in the Pugin Chantry at St Augustine's, Ramsgate.

Chapter 2 – Complete Church Furnishers

1 *Catholic Directory and Annual Register*

2 ML 18 January 1841.

3 Pugin to John Hardman, 14 January 1845, *Letters I*, p. 325.

4 *ibid.*

5 Megan Aldrich, *The Craces: Royal Decorators, 1768-1899*, (1990).

6 As note 2.

7 *Letters II*, annotations on p. 402.

8 Pugin to John Hardman, mid-June 1845, *Letters II*, p. 402. Eligius (c.588–660) was both an artisan and a bishop. He had a great talent for engraving and silversmithing, and some reliquaries made by him still exist. He was appointed bishop of Noyon and Tournai in 641.

9 Pugin recounts the story of the censuring of the vestments in an indignant letter to Ambrose Phillipps, *Letters I*, pp. 127–9.

10 ML 15 February 1841.

11 'We are greatly indebted to the ladies of the Middle Ages for much beautiful church needlework; but pure taste was then generally diffused and *all worked in accordance with the regulations and traditions of the Church*, which were strictly enforced; and we may hope that such will again be the case, when Catholic art is better and more extensively understood.' *Present State*, p. 9.

12 Pugin to John Hardman, 5 March 1845, *Letters II*, pp. 355–6. Pugin also expects Hardman to send him a chalice, paschal candlestick and a herse-light in time for Holy Week and Easter.

13 Pugin to E.J. Wilson, 6 November 1834, *Letters I*, p. 43.

14 Bishops generally had three mitres: a plain one made of white linen (*simplex*), a gold embroidered one (*aurifrigiata*) made of simple cloth of gold or white silk with gold embroidery, and the precious mitre (*pretiosa*) adorned with metalwork and precious stones.

15 MWDB 30 June 1848.

16 See also *Letters I*, p. 180.

17 As note 15.

18 Drawing in the JHAL.

19 It appears that these designs were never executed.

20 George Mostyn to John Hardman, ML 25 November 1840.

21 BCA Copy Bill Book, 23 December 1879. Hadfield paid £9/9/6 for it.

22 MWDB 20 June 1848, cf. ML 22 December 1841: Lady Arundell requests Hardman to send her 'twelve of the smallest Pugin's metal crosses made to sew upon church ornaments and six of the next largest size. Burns later became a partner in the Catholic publishing company of Burns & Oates.

23 See below, p.72

24 MWDB 11 April 1849.

25 A gold enamel chain and cross is entered to Pugin on 21 December 1843 at £47.15s and a pair of gold earrings on 1 December 1842 at £8.15s.

26 The headband and one of the brooches from the parure are in the V&A, along with the cross and chain made for Louisa.

27 Pugin to John Hardman, undated but probably late February 1848, *TP*, p. 170.

28 So Pugin wrote to his friend, The Revd James Hornby, on his wedding day in August 1848. M. Trappes-Lomax, *Pugin*, p. 280.

29 Drawings in JHAL. A bracelet of similar pattern was made for Powell's wife, and this is currently in a private collection.

30 C. Webster & J. Elliott (eds), *A Church as it should be: the Cambridge Camden Society & its influence*, Stamford: Shaun Tyas, 2000. This is the definitive study of the work of the Ecclesiologists.

31 ML 16 September 1843.

32 Pugin to Ambrose Phillipps, 1 December 1839, *Letters I*, p. 128.

33. *Ibid.*

34 E.g. J.M. Capes, the Catholic editor of *The Rambler,* wrote, 'We have been shocked by Mr. Pugin's sympathy with the Anglican heresy. We have ever regarded Puginism as identical with Puseyism' (*The Rambler*, 8, 1851, pp. 45–6). Edward Pusey was one of the leaders of the Oxford Tractarians.

35 MWDB 25 March & 8 June 1843.

36 Pugin to J.R. Bloxam, 7 February 1841, *Letters I*, p. 205. The furnishings for Dudley are listed in MWDB 26 December 1840.

37 18 December 1840, *Letters I*, p. 175. There was also a move to pull down Pugin's rood-screen, *Letters I*, p. 201.

38 MWDB 30 June 1848: parcel-gilt pax on saw-pierced base, large enamel in centre £35.

39 MWDB. It is illustrated in *GP* p. 173 where it is wrongly described as a pyx.

40 For a history of Cheadle see M.J. Fisher, *'Perfect Cheadle'* (2005) and *Pugin-Land* (2002), and R. O'Donnell, *The Pugins and the Catholic Midlands* (2002).

41 The tabernacle is mentioned in a letter from Pugin to Hardman, January 1845, *Letters II*, p. 316. There is also a drawing for it in BMAG L.122.84.

42 Letter as in note 37.

43 *Ibid.*

44 A paschal candlestick of this type is illustrated in the *Glossary*, p. 51.

45 Undated list in HLRO PUG/1/889.

46 *Letters II*, pp. 311–3 gives comprehensive lists of goods ordered for Cheadle. A good many of these items are no longer at the church.

47 The *coronae* were removed in the mid-1930s but they appear in several old photographs of the church.

48 See below, p.60

49 Pugin to Lord Shrewsbury, 19 March 1842, *Letters II*, p. 328.

50 See below, pp.68-69

51 MWDB 16 April 1851. A letter from Gambier-Parry to John Hardman dated 30 June 1850 refers to coronae for the nave, standards, candelabra, and windows for the south aisle and side-chapel. BCA ML.

52 MWDB 24 July 1851.

53 MWDB 22 July 1851. Undated letters HLRO PIG/1/727

54 *Letters II*, pp. 191–3. See also K. Tiplow, 'St. Lawrence Church, Tubney', *TP* vol. 1, no. 5 (1997–8).

55 Charles Fuge Lowder was one of the great figures among Anglo-Catholic clergy working in slum areas. He joined the Ecclesiological Society in 1852.

56 MWDB 11 May 1848.

57 In the Prayer of Consecration (1662) the rubric instructs the priest to 'lay his hand upon every vessel (be it Chalice or Flagon) in which there is any Wine to be consecrated'.

58 MWDB 24 August 1843.

59 MWDB 31 March 1849. This may be identical with the one exhibited at the Birmingham Exposition in 1849. See *Stanton*, p. 168.

60 MWDB 6 June 1851. This may be the one currently at St Editha's church and illustrated in *Stanton*, p. 168.

61 BCA Decoration Daybook 1845–50, 26 August 1848.

62 See *Letters II*, pp. 372–3, and below p.66

63 Pugin to Lord Shrewsbury, 2 February 1846, HLRO PUG/3/15.

64 Brian Doolan, *The Pugins and the Hardmans,* p. 11.

65 When Pugin saw the church which Hansom had built for Ullathorne in Coventry, he 'not only commended its solidity, but considered it to be a pure revival of the style of the thirteenth century'. *Belcher 1987*, D604.

66 MWDB 22 March & 18 May 1850.

67 MWDB 29 April 1850.

68 *Ibid.*

69 *Ibid.* (tabernacle) & 18 May 1850 (crucifix).

70 For a history of the church see M. Hodgetts, *Erdington Abbey*, 2000

71 This lectern was one of three exhibited by Hardman in the Great Exhibition. Alexandra Wedgwood describes the device of two kneeling angels carrying the bookrest as 'unPuginian'. *GP*, p. 244.

72 *Glossary*, p. 168.

73 The Ushaw lectern is still in the college chapel but the whereabouts of the one made for Southwark is unknown.

74 The lectern and candlesticks are pictured in *GP*, p. 180. The candlesticks were later stolen from the chapel, but exact replacements have been made (2006) in the Hardman Studios, see below p.174

75 MWDB 18 October 1861.

76 Clive Wainwright, 'Book Design and Production', *GP*, pp.153–4.

77 Letter dated 9 June 1841, BCA ML. William Riddell (1807–47) was elected in 1843 as co-adjutor to the vicar apostolic of the northern district, and succeeded him in 1847 only three months before his death.

78 *Letters II*, pp. 143–4.

79 It is illustrated in *GP*, p. 154.

80 Revd Robert Richmond to John Hardman, ML 12 March 1844. MWDB enters repairs to the cross and the provision of a new staff at 25 March 1844.

81 MWDB 25 March & 26 April 1844. This statue should not be confused with that known as 'Our Lady of Brewood' which is in the north aisle. Pugin was impressed by the survival of Catholicism in the area, and the devotion of Fr Robert Richmond. He gave a stained-glass window to the church, and Hardman donated the tabernacle. For an account of Brewood see *Pugin-Land* , pp. 135–44.

82 *Letters II*, pp. 130–1.

83 Pugin to John Hardman 22 November 1843, *Letters II*, pp.135–6.

84 Pugin to Lord Shrewsbury, 6 November 1840, *Letters I*, p. 161.

85 *Present State* (1843 edn), p. 89.

86 For an account of St John's and the thinking behind it, see *Pugin-Land*, pp.52–79.

87 BMAG Loans Collection

88 *Letters II*, p. 310.

89 MWDB 17 July 1846: 'An Iron Hexagon Corona, with Gilt Inscription, richly pierced & Chains &c & brass pans with Pierced Borders'.

90 The text reads, around the hexagon: *tuam crucem/adoramus domine/gloriosam passionem/recolimus etiam/miserere nobis/qui passus es pro nobis* (we adore your cross, O Lord, and we honour your glorious passion; have mercy upon us for whom you have suffered).

91 *Staffordshire Advertiser*, 5 September 1846, & *Illustrated London News*, 9 January 1847.

92 For Wardell's later career, see below, p.144

93 MWDB 23 April 1851.

94 Undated letter in the archives of Jesus College, Cambridge quoted in *Belcher 1987*, D318.

95 *Journal of Design and Manufactures*, 2 October 1849 p. 54. *Belcher 1987*, p. 262.

96 Letter from Pugin to J.G. Crace, quoted in *GP*, p. 238.

97 Earley to John Hardman, 16 April 1851, ML.

98 MWDB enters several items to Sidney Herbert in December 1849.

99 There is a list of these in HLRO PUG/1/102.

100 Quoted in *GP*, p. 180.

101 They were loaned in December 1852 for the funeral of the 16th Earl of Shrewsbury. See below, p.127

102 They are entered to Henry Cole in MWDB 5 December 1851, and most are now in the V&A.

103 See below, p.104

104 After the Exhibition the tabernacle was taken to St Augustine's, Ramsgate. Removed from there during 're-ordering' in 1969–71, it is now in the Harvard chapel at Southwark cathedral. See Alexandra Wedgwood, 'Pugin's Tabernacle in Southwark Cathedral, *TP*, vol. 2 no. 4 (2002).

105 *Illustrated London News*, 18 May 1851.

106 *Illustrated London News,* 20 September 1851, p. 362.

Chapter 3 – Pugin's Glasspainter

1 See Jim Cheshire, *Stained Glass and the Victorian Gothic Revival*, 2004 and Martin Harrison, *Victorian Stained Glass,* 1980.

2 Pugin to Lord Shrewsbury, 28 August 1841. 'Warrington . . . has become Lately so conceited that he hs got nearly as expensive as Willement . . . Warrington is a wretched herald'. *Letters I*, p. 269.

3 *Letters II*, p. 343. By 'shop' Pugin meant a workshop rather than an emporium.

4 J.H. Powell, 'The Art of Stained Glass in Birmingham', in Samuel Timmins (ed.), *The resources, products, and industrial history of Birmingham & the Midland hard ward district,* 1866, p. 252.

5 Timmins, *op. cit.*, p. 524.

6 Pugin to Lord Shrewsbury, 13 February 1846, HLRO PUG/3/15.

7 A.W.N. Pugin, Third lecture on ecclesiastical history to students at Oscott, *Catholic Magazine*, vol. LII no. xxv, February 1839, p. 92.

8 *Ibid.,* p. 93.

9 *Powell,* p. 23.

10 Pugin to J.R. Herbert, *Letters II*, p. 418.

11 *ibid.,* p. 419.

12 *Ferrey*, p. 189.

13 Flashed glass has a thin layer of colour fused to the surface only, whereas pot metal is coloured all the way through.

14 HLRO PUG/1/986.

15 Pugin to David Read, 14 January 1841, *Letters I*, p. 193.

16 *Powell*, p. 34. It should be remembered that surviving letters written to Pugin are few, because of his tidy habit of destroying incoming correspondence once it had been dealt with.

17 6 February 1845, *Letters II*, p. 336. Dr Acquarone got no better. In July 1845 Pugin wrote to Hardman, '. . . this afternoon he positively insulted me in the very chapel. I am so sick of everythings that I am determined no ecclesiastick shall ever live in my house again. I would rather go 20 miles to mass'. *Letters II*, p. 421.

18 Pugin to Hardman, ?20 July 1845. The sign was for Hardman's new showroom in Birmingham (see above p.36-7). *Letters II*, p. 423.

19 HLRO PUG/1/855.

20 Pugin to John Hardman, HLRO PUG/1/784.

21 *Powell*, p. 22.

22 Pugin to John Hardman, mid-1850, HLRO PUG/1/179.

23 Pugin to John Hardman, 1847, BCA.

24 When N.J. Cottingham (1787–1847), the architect in charge of the restoration of Hereford cathedral, wanted to send his own designs to Hardman for glass for the Lady chapel, Hardman replied that he would only work from cartoons prepared by Pugin. *Shepherd*, p. 43.

25 *Shepherd*, p. 18.

26 *Ibid.*, pp. 20–25.

27 Pugin to John Hardman, 1849. HLRO/PUG/1/406.

28 Pugin to John Hardman, September 1849. HLRO PUG/1/982.

29 Hartley to John Hardman, 30 August 1852. *Shepherd*, p. 30.

30 Timmins, *op.cit.,* p. 525.

31 BCA undated letter, 1847 box. *Shepherd* Appendix 1, p. 530.

32 HLRO PUG/1/394.

33 Earley to John Hardman, 12 September 1847, BCA.

34 E.S. Purcell, *Life & Letters of Ambrose Phillipps de Lisle,* 1900, vol. 1, pp. 340–1.

35 See M.J. Fisher, 'A.W.N. Pugin and the Restoration of St. Mary's Church, Wymeswold', *Ecclesiology Today*, Issue 34, January 2005, pp. 3–15.

36 First Glass Daybook, 22 April 1848. In April Alford wrote to Hardman, 'The window has arrived safe . . . I like it very much, all but the face of the child which is not pleasing', *Shepherd*, Appendix 1, p. 537.

37 Pugin to Lord Shrewsbury, 28 August 1841, *Letters I*, p. 268.

38 Pugin to John Hardman, HLRO PUG/1/985: possibly mid-May 1848 when he returned from Liverpool and Chirk castle via Birmingham.

39 Pugin to John Hardman, undated, but the windows are entered in the First Glass Daybook at 19 November 1851. Jane, of course, is Pugin's third wife.

40 Pugin to Lord Shrewsbury, 28 August 1841, '. . . the most beautiful effect of stained glass is from the *setting sun.* is it not so in the state apartments at Alton. the reflection thrown from the west window up the church is glorious.' *Letters I*, p. 269.

41 Stanley Shepherd, *GP*, p. 201.

42 G.E. Street, 'On glass painting', *Ecclesiologist* 13, August 1852, pp. 245–6.

43 Canon G.B. Blumfield to John Hardman, 10 May 1850, BCA. *Shepherd*, Appendix 1, p. 265.

44 Pugin to John Hardman, 1850, HLRO/PUG/1/693.

45 Pugin's third lecture to students at Oscott, *Catholic Magazine*, January 1839, p. 29.

46 Pugin had already carried out work for the Sutton family, and he continued to work for them to the end of his life, e.g. St Mary's church, West Tofts, Norfolk.

47 HLRO PUG/1/406.

48 Pugin to John Sutton, letter in Jesus College Archive.

49 Pugin to John Hardman, HLRO PUG/1/686.

50 Pugin to John Hardman, HLRO PUG/1/688. Pugin's diary tells us that he went from Birmingham to Fairford on 29 July 1850.

51 Pugin to John Hardman, HLRO PUG/1/692.

52 Randall Burroughs to John Hardman, 18 October 1851. BCA.

53 Pugin to John Hardman, postmarked 20 November 1851, HLRO PUG/1/665.

54 Pugin to John Hardman, HLRO PUG/1/446.

55 Caroline Paine to John Hardman, 26 December 1851. BCA. The Paine family were the principal benefactors at Farnham.

56 Pugin to John Hardman, 1 October 1847, HLRO/PUG/1/127.

57 *Shepherd*, pp.194–5. The case was reported in *The Ecclesiologist* LXXXII, February 1851, p. 46, and a copy of Pugin's letter to the *Manchester Guardian* is in HLRO PUG/1/418.

58 John Elliott, 'A Trusted Disciple: Richard Cromwell Carpenter', Webster & Elliott, *A Church as it should be*, 2000, pp. 149–72.

59 Stanley Shepherd, 'The West Window of Sherborne Abbey', *Journal of the Society of Master Glass Painters*, vol. 19., 1989–95, pp.315–22.

60 *Shepherd*, Appendix 1, pp. 296–303.

61 Danesfield was demolished in 1908.

62 *Shepherd,* Appendix 1, pp. 236–42.

63 See below, pp.101-112

64 Both Phillipps and Scott-Murray were executors of the earl's will, and beneficiaries.

65 First Glass Daybook, 27 August 1851, 18 October 1852, and 14 February, 2 April and 26 November 1853; also correspondence with the Hartopps in BCA letter bundles 1850, 1851 and 1852.

66 *Powell*, p. 36, and see David Meara, 'The Death of A.W. Pugin, *TP*, vol. 1 no. 3, 1997.

67 HLRO PUG/1/651.

68 HLRO PUG/1/650.

69 A moving account of Pugin's final illness is given in Jane Pugin's journal, published under the title, *Dearest Augustus and I* (Caroline Stanford, ed., Spire Books, 2004).

70 Alfred Barry to A.W. Pugin, 1851, but marked 1852 by Hardman's clerk. *Shepherd*, Appendix 1, p. 838.

71 Alfred Barry to John Hardman, 30 March 1852.

72 John Hardman to R. Wilson, 27 May 1853. BCA.

73 *Reports by the Juries on the Subjects in the Thirty Classes into which the Exhibition was Divided*, London 1852, vol.4, section C, division C2. Cheshire, *op. cit*, p. 44.

Chapter 4 – After Pugin – Personalities and Projects

1 HLRO/PUG/1/58.

2 HLRO/PUG/1/631.

3 C. Stanford (ed.), *Dearest Augustus and I*, p. 79.

4   BCA: Copy Letterbook, 16 November 1856.

5   Letters in private collection.

6   Wilfrid Ward, *Life and Times of Cardinal Wiseman*, 1912, p. 357.

7   Undated letter in private collection.

8   MWDB December 1854 enters a carved oak prie-dieu and brackets to John Hardman Powell, Hunter's Lane, also an umbrella stand, and wallpaper of 'green gothic pattern on green ground'.

9   First Glass Daybook, 31 December 1851. Included in this figure are two sets of 24 windows for the Commons Lobby entered on 20 February (£644) and 3 October (£722).

10 J.H. Powell, 'The Art of Stained Glass in Birmingham', Timmins, *op. cit.*, p. 525.

11 From the detailed report on the consecration of Langley church in *Kentish and South-Eastern Advertiser*, 11 December 1855. The rector, the Revd William Pusey, was brother of the more famous Edward Bouverie Pusey, one of the leaders of the Oxford Movement. I am grateful to Anne Clinch of Maidstone for sending me the press-cutting, and for pictures of the windows.

12 J H. Powell, *Some Stray Notes on Art*, published originally in 1889 and reproduced in *TP*, vol. 2 nos. 1 (Winter 2000), 3 (Summer 2001) and 5 (Summer 2003).

13 *TP*, vol. 2, no. 1 (Winter 2000), pp.13–24.

14 Information from Mr. M. Maycock, per Fr Brian Doolan.

15 Bill Covington, 'J.A. Pippet and Hardman, Powell & Company', *TP* vol. 2 no. 3 (Winter 2001).

16 BCA Decoration Letter Book, 14 August 1882.

17 BCA Decoration Letter Book, 14 August 1882.

18 Covington, *op. cit.*, p. 14.

19 The Masfen window is an unusual example of an A.W. Pugin design executed nearly twenty years after his death. RDB 12 June 1871, and *Shepherd*, Appendix 1, pp.667–8).

20 Jim Cheshire, *op. cit.*, p. 166.

21 S.P. Powell had a fine collection of antique sculpture and metalwork, some of which had been in A.W. Pugin's collection. It was sold at auction in 1960. *GP* p. 100.

22 Quoted by R. O'Donnell, 'Edward Pugin's Kentish Obituary', *TP* vol. 1 no. 10, Summer 2000.

23 MWDB October 1856, December 1857.

24 BCA Glass Cost Sheet no.74, 25 September 1856.

25 For an assessment of Michael Trappes-Lomax, see Anthony Symondson, SJ, in *TP*, vol.2 no. 1 (Winter 2000), pp. 4–6.

26 MWDB 20 March 1858. The monstrance is no longer at the church.

27 Stained Glass Cost Sheet 26 October 1860, nos 92, 93 & 94.

28 I am greatly indebted to Mr. J. Bernard Phelan of Great Harwood for information about the church, and for photographs of the windows.

29 MWDB 7 December 1863, entered at £120.

30 MWDB 29 January & 22 July 1853.

31 For a detailed account of Belmont, see R. O'Donnell, *The Pugins and the Catholic Midlands*, 2004, pp.52–7.

32 According to Stuart Marsden who is currently (2007) writing on Edmund Kirby. Information from Barbara Howell, Salford.

33 BCA Copy Bill Book, 15 July 1879. Many large private houses were built by Kirby in the Liverpool area, some of them with Hardman metalwork and glass, e.g. The Towers, Rainhill, built for a Mr. H. Baxter, had a staircase window of 20 lights and stained glass in the library; RDB 19 April & 20 October 1880.

34 O'Donnell, *op. cit.*, p. 98.

35 RDB 28 April 1903.

36 BCA Copy Bill Book, vol. 5, 1902–5, 6 June 1903.

37 A.W. Pugin, Third lecture on ecclesiastical architecture delivered to students at Oscott, and published in *Catholic Magazine*, February 1839, p. 92.

38 *Letters I*, p. 141.

39 The Princethorpe archive contains copies of some 200 letters from P.P. Pugin.

40 RDB 22 March 1900 (8 chancel windows and west window) 15 June 1900 (centre chancel window and clerestories) 19 September 1900 (4 choir windows)

41 Information from the Revd Canon Roger Arguile, who kindly sent me a copy of his researches into the Rowley family and the St Neots windows.

42 He is listed as a Tractarian clergyman in G.W. Herring's D.Phil. thesis, 'Tractarianism to Ritualism', Oxford 1984.

43 It is entered into the glass daybook at 16 May 1876, and invoiced to Hardman at £200. See below, p.147.

44 *BOE* Worcestershire, 1968, p. 298.

45 MWDB 28 February 1874.

46 RDB 26 August 1875, and Cost Sheet no. 104/75.

47 Glass Letterbook, vol. 8, 30 June 1910, and see below, p. 189. Installed in 1912-13, the window was restored by Hardman's in 1949 following wartime damage.

48 RDB 27 January 1884, and correspondence (2007) with Mrs Kathleen Aikman of Dyffryn Ardudwy, who sent in an enquiry about this window and kindly supplied photographs of it.

49 It cost him £788, RDB 13 November 1886. Groves' other gifts included five windows in the south aisle (£1118, RDB 3 August 1888), and five north aisle windows (£1440 RDB 8 September 1892)

50 See J. Mordaunt Crook, *William Burges and the High Victorian Dream*, London, 1981.

51 MWDB 29 June 1860. The chalice cost £35, paten £9.10s, flagon £18.10s.

52 MWDB 23 July 1864. The chalice is entered at £64.7s which, for the time, was very expensive.

53 MWDB 29 August 1862.

54 MWDB 22 April 1863.

55 BCA Metalwork Letters.

56 Burges tells Powell, 'You have now been so long in the making of silver work that you must have surely had sufficient experience to be able to estimate a small thing like the foot of this vase'. BCA ML 4 June 1863.

57 J. Mordaunt Crook, *op. cit.*, p. 139.

58 Burges to James Powell, ML, 13 May 1863.

59 Burges to James Powell, ML, 13 July 1863.

60 Quoted by J.M. Crook, *op. cit.*, p. 139, from *Art Journal*, 1886, p. 180.

61 Burges would, of course, have known of the figure of St Eligius on the sign-board outside Hardman's premises in Great Charles Street.

62 Burges to J H. Powell, ML, 29 May 1863. The lecture would have been one of many that Powell gave at the Birmingham School of Art.

63 ML 10 October 1863 and 28 December 1863. In 1866 he commissioned a ciborium, Powell's drawing for which is in the Lightwoods collection. While at St Barnabas', Pimlico, Bennett had commissioned a rich chalice and paten, engraved and gilt all over (MWDB 5 June 1850) which would doubtless have been to Pugin's design.

64 MWDB 14 April 1870.

65 J.S.S. Hansom to his brother George, ML 6 May 1868. George Hansom was working for Hardman's at this time.

66 Drawing in Lightwoods Collection.

67 RDB 13 January 1879, entered at £500. The window was destroyed during World War II.

68 MWDB 20 December 1858.

69 Powell's drawings for this are in JHAL.

70 MWDB 19 December 1862 enters it at 16 guineas.

71 MWDB enters Stuart Knill's cup on 30 November 1893 at £85, and John Knill's on 17 March 1910 at £100. There are references to letters concerning details of the second cup from S.J. Borsinge, who appears to have been the designer. I am very grateful to Andrew Ford, Plate Butler at the Mansion House, for supplying photographs of the cups.

72 Information kindly supplied by Miss Pamela Taylor, archivist at Arundel Castle. The metalwork daybook for 1897 is, unfortunately, missing.

Chapter 5 – Domestic Work: Villas, Palaces and 'Brass Castles'

1 Rosemary Hill, *Gods Architect*, 2007, p.378

2 See Caroline Stanford, *The Grange, Ramsgate*, The Landmark Trust, 2006 [NOTE TO BE AMENDED?]

3 E.g. *Letters II*, pp. 254–6 (14 October 1844).

4 Hill, op.cit., p.444

5 MWDB 27 May & 27 June 1870. A silver claret jug, beaten, engraved and set with stones and enamels is entered to Walter Carew Cocks at £40 on 9 July 1856.

6 Drawings in RIBA, and reproduced in Stanton, *Pugin*, 1971, pp. 178–80.

7 A.W. Pugin, *True Principles,* 1841, p. 51.

8 See M.J. Fisher, *Alton Towers: A Gothic Wonderland*, 1999, and 'In the Shadow of Fonthill', *TP*, vol. 2 no. 1 (Winter 2000), pp. 7–9.

9 MWDB 13 June 1840 enters the *coronae* at £47 each, and charges £85.10s for the reliquary, mounted with ivories and enamels, which stood on the altar of the Towers chapel.

10 MWBD 30 June 1842, and Fisher, *Alton Towers*, pp. 116–7.

11 Pugin to Lord Shrewsbury 30 July 1847, *Wedgwood 1985*, no. 52. Pugin estimated the total cost at £2,271, *Wedgwood 1985*, p. 121.

12 MWDB enters all fourteen dishes to 'The executors of the late Earl of Shrewsbury' on 31 December 1853 – more than a year after the earl's death – at £260.10s.

13 M.J. Fisher, 'Abney Hall, Cheshire, and the great sideboard mystery', *TP*, vol. 3 no. 2 (Summer 2005), pp. 18–25.

14 MWDB enters the chandelier to Lord Shrewsbury on 20 November 1851 (i.e. after the close of the Great Exhibition) at £150, and the chain on 26 July 1855 at £18.10s. The charge of £5.12s.6d for hanging the chandelier is entered at 15 April 1859.

15 It was discovered by the late Professor Clive Wainwright of the V&A who oversaw its restoration and relocation.

16 Pugin to Hardman, 1851, HLRO PUG/1/197. The window is entered in the daybook at 10 October 1853 and charged at £147.

17 HLRO PUG/1/956.

18 Glass Cost Sheet, 16 February 1856, gives £311.19s 6d. as the total cost, deducting £32.10s for the work completed in 1852.

19 Staffordshire County Record Office, Shrewsbury Papers, D240/G/4/1.

20 MWDB 20 November 1851.

21 MWDB 15 April 1869. This further demonstrates the unfinished state of this part of the house at the time of the deaths of the last Catholic earls and the succession to the Alton estate in 1860 of the Anglican branch of the family, following a prolonged legal battle over the titles and properties. See Fisher, *Alton Towers*, pp.157–60.

22 *Report from the Select Committee on Fine Arts*, 18 June 1841.

23 The school buildings, now demolished, were in New Street.

24 C. Brooks, *The Gothic Revival*, 1999. Brooks brilliantly analyses the social and political significance of the Gothic style as expressive of Britain's medieval past, a reformed Church, a constitutional monarchy, and individual liberty.

25 Barry to Pugin, 3 September 1844, *Letters II*, p. 209.

26 The dispute was waged very publicly in the Press. *Belcher 1987* gives a total of 118 extracts.

27 Sebastian Pugin Powell to Shane Leslie, 23 February 1921. Original letter in Georgetown University Library, Washington DC.

28 M. Port (ed.), *The Houses of Parliament*, 1976, p. 121.

29 A.W. Pugin, *True Principles*, 1841, p. 22.

30 *Ibid.*

31 BMAG L.98.83.

32 Pugin to Hardman, 31 January 1845, *Letters II*, p. 333.

33 BMAG L.57.83.

34 Pugin to John Hardman, 1847, HLRO PUG/1/124.

35 HLRO PUG/1/126 (1847).

36 M. Port, *op. cit.*, p. 261.

37 MWDB 30–31 December 1847 enters those at the throne end at £595, and the four at the bar end at £333.

38 MWDB 8 January 1847 enters these to Webb, the enamels at 9s each and the crystals at 7s. Two large crystals set in enamels for the arms of the throne are entered at 26s each on 24 February. The throne and its surroundings underwent several changes in design as Pugin and Barry exchanged ideas. One set of drawings, showing a scheme very different from the one finally carried out, is in BMAG L.101.83. See also *GP*, pp.225–8, and Alexandra Wedgwood, 'The throne in the House of Lords and its architectural setting', *Architectural History*, 27, 1984, pp. 59–68.

39 Queen Victoria's Journal, quoted by Sir Robert Cooke, *The Palace of Westminster*, 1987, p. 129.

40 They are entered into the daybook at 18 February 1847 at a cost of £802.8s.

41 MWDB 2 February 1847. The star is made of eight separate pieces of brass and is entered at £70. The enamelling has since worn away.

42 The idea of gilding cast iron ran counter to Pugin's principles, although brass was eventually incorporated into the design; Port, *op. cit.*, p. 262. The gasoliers were removed at a later date, but in 1987 it was stated that the remains of one of them had still been in the basement 'within living memory' (R. Cooke, *op. cit.*, p. 147).

43 Port, *op. cit.*, pp. 263 & 266.

44 They are entered in MWDB at £600.

45 MWDB 17–18 January 1871.

46 MWDB enters it at 21 March 1870 and 13 December (statue), at a total cost of £212.

47 RDB.

48 Port, *op. cit.*, pp. 255–6.

49 HLRO PUG/1/228.

50 *Shepherd*, Appendix 1, p. 423.

51 For an account of Hardman's work at the Palace of Westminster in 1947–55 see below, pp. [XREF]

52 Postmarked 15 February 1846. Letter in private collection. Information from Dr. M. Belcher.

53 MWDB 10 February 1854 enters grates and andirons to the value of £56.8s. Glass Order Book, 8 July 1846 enters eight lights with different shields in each, and six lights for the Library.

54 Pugin to Myddelton Biddulph, 8 May 1849. Letter in a private collection which includes eleven other letters from Pugin formerly kept at Chirk but sold as Lot 502 in the Chirk Castle Sale (Christie's) on 21 June 2004.

55 MWDB 8 December 1854. In the Pugin–Crace accounts for 1847 the cost of 'work done' at Chirk is given as £2,650 (*Wedgwood 1985*, p. 190). E.W. Pugin's east window in the chapel was replaced with a new one by Arthur Blomfield in 1890.

56 Pugin to J.G. Crace, 1846; *Wedgwood 1985*, p. 190. A significant number of wallpaper designs for Chirk are in the Pugin collection at the V&A.

57 HLRO PUG/1/126.

58 Pugin to Lord Shrewsbury, 1847; *Stanton*, Appendix VIII, p. 19.

59 First Glass Daybook, August 1847 to June 1848; *Shepherd,* Appendix 1, pp. 695–700.

60 Like Lord Shrewsbury, Scarisbrick bought furniture from Edward Hull of London, and it may have been in this connection that he first encountered Pugin, who designed furniture for Hull. For a full account of Scarisbrick Hall see Rosemary Hill, 'Scarisbrick Hall', *Country Life*, 8 & 15 August 2002.

61 MWDB March–May 1861 and January–October 1862.

62 MWDB 31 May 1861.

63 MWDB 4–6 June & 1 August 1861.

64 i.e. Anne Scarisbrick's initials. MWDB 31 July 1861 enters 'brass perforation for grand stairs'.

65 MWDB 26 September 1863.

66 The 'Cher' sale also included a painted panel in a Pugin Gothic frame which had come from the chapel at Grace Dieu, Leicestershire, *coronae* formerly at the Bishop's House in Birmingham, and a volume of drawings by J H. Powell. The *coronae* and the drawings were purchased for the Hardman Collection, Lightwoods House.

67 RDB 16 April 1861.

68 RDB & letters from EW. Pugin to Powell 12 June & 10 October 1862.

69 RDB 7 Aprilm1865. the window is entered at £110.

70 Mark Girouard, *The Victorian Country House*, 1979, p. 119.

71 RDB 15 December 1888.

72 MWDB November 1869. The house was demolished in 1964.

73 MWDB 21 April 1855.

74 ML 25 March, 8 June & 14 July 1869.

75 MWDB 7 October 1869.

76 MWDB 22 & 28 February 1870 (decorations) & 16 September (shields).

77 MWDB S & 6 April 1871.

78 MWDB 28 April & 14 June 1871. I am extremely grateful to Andrew McLean, archivist at Mount Stuart, for providing me with information, and photographs of these items.

79 A.W. Pugin, *Apology*, pp. 38–9

80 'Every building that is treated naturally, without disguise or concealment, cannot fail to look well' (*ibid.*).

81 Rosemary Hill, 'Pugin's Small Houses', *Architectural History*, 46 (2003), pp.165–6.

82 MWDB February–November 1855. For a full account of Burton Manor see M.J. Fisher, 'Burton Manor: The Staffordshire Grange', *TP*, vol. 3 no. 4 (Summer 2007).

83 RDB 27 March & 13 June 1865.

84 Simon Jenkins, *England's Thousand Best Houses*, London 2003, p. 75.

85 It is also the title of a book by George Sheeran: *Brass Castles. West Yorkshire new rich and their houses, 1800–1914*, Ryburn 1993.

86 MWDB 15 January, 8 & 12 December 1853.

87 MWDB 30 April 1857 enters them at £50.

88 MWDB 28 May 1853, and see above, n. 13.

89 Abney Hall is in corporate ownership and not generally open to the public. Much of the furniture was removed and sold in 1958 when the hall was put to civic use. See E. Mostyn, 'Abney Hall, Cheshire', *Country Life*, 18 & 24 April 1963.

90 ML 'B' bundle, 29 April 1863.

91 *Powell*, p. 33.

92 ML 3 March 1865.

93 MWDB 29 August, 29 September, 30 November & 2 December 1865.

94 Kennedy to Hardman, ML 31 August 1865.

95 Kennedy to Hardman, ML 26 September 1865.

96 Kennedy to Hardman ML 7 September 1865. In a letter to Powell he writes, 'There is a battle about who is to execute the Hudson window . . . But I am determined to have it all my own way'. ML 27 September 1865.

97 RDB 4 April 1867. The two-light window is entered to Kennedy at £70 including fixing, and the smaller one to Wood at £12. Wood also paid for '100 copies of the Matterhorn window printed by the Anastatic process', RDB 24 May 1867. I am grateful to the Revd Dr Hilary Geisow for enabling me to visit Skillington church and photograph the windows.

98 Kennedy to Hardman, ML 5 October 1865.

99 ML 27 September 1865.

100 ML 19 December 1865.

101 See above, p.101

102 Kennedy to Hardman's, ML 11 April 1865. 'Mr Pugin has designed a sideboard with recesses for silver or other objects'.

103 MWDB 13 August & 5 November 1869.

104 MWDB 19 October 1869 & 12 January 1870.

105 ML 30 January & 6 February 1867.

106 RDB 14 January 1873 enters the dining-room windows at £77.

107 RDB 22 December 1873

108 I am most grateful to Jane Hedley of NADFAS for arranging to visit the house on my behalf, and for taking a large number of photographs.

109 Prince Albert had arranged for Schulze to provide an organ for the Great Exhibition, thus setting a fashion. The Meanwood organ, with over 3,600 pipes, was one of the largest ever built. Kenneth Johnstone's publication, *The Armley Schulze Organ*, is currently (2007) out of print, but detailed information about the instrument may be found at www.armley-schulze.freeserve.co.uk/OrgHist.htm.

110 RDB 22 October 1868.

Chapter 6 – Memorials and Funeral Furnishings

1 Published in *Dublin Review* in May 1841 and reprinted in 1843 as a separate volume along with his second article of May 1842.

2 *Ibid.*

3 Pugin to J.R. Bloxam, 13 September 1840, *Letters I*, p. 143.

4 The chapel was redecorated by Hardman & Co. in 1878, and the scheme was restored in 1998. Brian Doolan, 'The Hardman Vault in St. Chad's Cathedral Crypt', *Midland Catholic History*, no.10, 2004, pp. 50–2.

5 MWDB 26 January, 2 March & 1 May 1844.

6 *Ibid.* MWDB 10 September 1844 enters the coffin plate and handles, and sixteen candle-shields for the herse-lights.

7 *The Tablet* 21 September 1844 p.597

8 HLRO PUG/1/640, undated but a reference to the post-natal illness of Anne Powell suggests early December 1851.

9 Fisher, *Pugin-Land*, pp.63–5.

10 MWDB 18 September 1852. See also *GP* p. 283 for David Meara's account of the opening of the Pugin burial vault in October 1992: Pugin's coffin still retained 'most of its brass fittings made by Hardmans, including a fine brass floriated cross running along the top ridge'.

11 See R. O'Donnell, 'No "maimed rites": the Funeral Obsequies of the 16th Earl of Shrewsbury', *TP* vol. 2, no. 4, Summer 2002; also Fisher, *Alton Towers,* pp. 154–5 and *Pugin-Land,* pp. 41–2.

12 Hatchments to both the earl and the countess were removed from St. John's in the 1960s. One is now in Alton Castle, and another was sold in 2004 at the Olympia Fine Arts and Antiques Show.

13 Fisher, *Alton Towers,* p. 154.

14 MWDB 26 November 1853.

15 BCA Brass Order Book vol. 2, p. 5, March 1855, and MWDB 25 April 1856.

16 O'Donnell, *op. cit.*, p. 19.

17 BCA Copy Bill Book, 9 July 1879.

18 BCA Copy Bill Book, 21 August 1879.

19 Edward Blore, *Monumental Remains,* 1826; Richard Gough, *Sepulchral Monuments of Great Britain,* 1786–99.

20 Now in the British Museum, it is illustrated in *Meara 1991*, p. 12.

21 *Orthodox Journal*, 12 May 1838, pp.289–92.

22 A detailed price list is given as a footnote in *Present State*, p. 54.

23 Pugin to John Ringrose, priest of the church of St James, Reading, which Pugin had designed in 1837. *Letters I*, p. 139.

24 *Letters I*, p. 239.

25 Pugin, *Apology*, p. 36.

26 At Pugin's request, Roddis's memorial was placed in St Giles's church, Cheadle, where he had done almost all of the interior stonecarving. The cross is no longer there, but the inscription plate survives.

27 Pugin, *Apology*, p. 34.

28 20 December 1842, *Letters I*, p. 405.

29 6 November 1842, *Letters I*, p. 390.

30 HLRO PUG/1/175.

31 *Ibid.*

32 It is illustrated in *Meara 1983*, p. 58.

33 Pugin to John Hardman, June 1845, *Letters II*, pp. 402–3.

34 BCA Brass Estimate Book, 26 July 1864.

35 *Ibid.*, 26 & 27 October 1863.

36 *Ibid.*, 14 January 1860.

37 ML, 24 July 1863.

38 *Meara 1983* lists sixteen other firms who made memorial brasses.

39 BCA Brass Sales Ledger, 18 May 1908.

40 *Ibid.*, 2 June 1904 and 25 February 1905.

Chapter 7 – Hardman's Abroad

1 *Tablet,* 13 October 1852, p. 630.

2 Willson recalled this reaction some years later when writing to Dean John Fitzpatrick of Melbourne. *Andrews* p. 54.

3 BCA Hardman Letters, 1841 bundle.

4 ML 4 July & 5 August 1850.

5   MWDB 8 & 23 April & 6 May 1858.

6   *Powell* p.26.

7   R. O'Donnell, *GP*, p. 71.

8   *St. Mary's Cathedral, Killarney*, Geraldine Press, Tralee, 1973.

9   MWDB 5 November 1855. The brass was engraved with figures of the Blessed Virgin Mary, St Patrick and St Bridget, and a full-length figure of the Earl.

10 MWDB 27 June 1859.

11 RDB 7 August 1863, 29 June 1867 & 2 February 1874.

12 Ray Carroll, 'Notes on the Restoration of St. Mary's', in *St. Mary's Cathedral, Killarney*, 1973.

13 Benjamin Ferrey, *Recollections of A.N. Welby Pugin*, London, 1861, p. 125.

14 Mr Maurice O'Keeffe of Tralee, Co. Kerry.

15 Information kindly supplied by Fr Laurence, Mount St Joseph Abbey, Roscrea.

16 RDB 9 November 1877.

17 Pugin to John Hardman. HLRO PUG/1/772, not dated.

18 ibid.

19 Pugin to John Hardman, HLRO PUG/1/800

20 W.H.J. Weale, 'The School of St. Luke at Ghent', Building News xxxvi, 1879, p.350. Pugin's diary shows that he was in Courtrai at the end of May 1844, so this was probably the time of this first encounter with Bethune.

21 Information kindly supplied by Professor Joost Caen, University of Antwerp. The archive of the Béthune family is situated in Kortrijk Courtrai) and contains letters from Hardman.

22 They are entered on a separate foolscap sheet bundled with the stained glass cost sheets for 1856-7 (BCA).

23 e.g. RDB 15 September 1864 enters to Béthune a quantity of pencils, quills, brushes, silver stain and other pigments.

24 C. Brooks, The Gothic Revival, 1999, p.371.

25 30 January 1844, *Letters II*, p. 161.

26 See above, p.34

27 MWDB 22 & 27 October 1842. See also *Andrews* pp. 38–40, 47–50.

28 Draft of a speech by Willson to a meeting of clergy in Hobart, 23 October 1844, quoted by Brian Andrews in *GP*, p. 247.

29 MWDB 6 December 1847.

30 *Andrews* pp. 110–12.

31 MWDB 2 December 1847. *Andrews* p. 96.

32 MWDB September 1854 enters it at £38. The one for Cheadle, with its copper-gilt foot, had cost £25.

33 Polding's was the only metropolitan cross ever designed by Pugin. It is entered in MWDB at 13 October 1843 at a cost of £30.12s. For the cope, see *Andrews* pp.167–8. Both were destroyed when the pro-cathedral of St Mary, Sydney, burned down in1865.

34 MWDB 24 February, 11 March, 15 June, 15 & 20 July 1848.

35 *Andrews* p. 162.

36 ECA First Glass Daybook, 13 December 1847.

37 MWDB 30 November 1869. The order was valued at £290.5s.6d.

38 *Andrews* p. 144.

39 Plans are well advanced at the time of writing (2007) to remove the bishop's coffin to Hobart.

40 For a detailed account of this window see Brian Andrews, 'Aspects of Hardman's Glass Studio practice in the late 1860s', *TP* vol. 3, no.3, Summer 2006.

41 See above, pP.129-30

42 MWDB 13 February 1862.

43 Information and copies of advertisements kindly sent by Brian Andrews.

44 Selwyn was a graduate of St John's College, Cambridge, but although he showed sympathy with the Camden Society his name does not appear on the lists of members.

45 Margaret Belcher, 'The Good Style at the Antipodes', *TP,* vol. 2, no. 4, Summer 2002.

46 Nick Beveridge, 'A Pugin Link with New Zealand – The Benedictine Bishop', *TP,* vol. 2, no. 5, Summer 2003.

47 RDB f.51/1869 & f.183/1874.

48 See James Patrick, *Chronicles,* vol. 29, no. 12, December 2005.

49 For an illustrated survey of Keely's work see Edward H. Furey's article in *TP* vol. 1, no. 10, Summer 2000.

50 J. Gall, 'Pittsburgh 1893–1912: Five Artists', *Journal of Stained Glass,* vol. 26, 2004, p.47.

51 Between ff. 187 & 188 of RDB 1885 there is a finely—written list of these drawings, noting that a copy was sent to London House on 28 August.

52 RDB 29 June, 1 December 1906 & 25 June 1907.

53 RDB 3 June 1897.

54 RDB 21 December 1891.

55 RDB 2 March 1892, 2 March 1897.

56 RDB 7 & 26 March 1890, 25 September 1890, 18 October 1891, 21 June 1911.

57 RDB 26 March 1890.

58 BCA Copy Bill Book 13 May 1912 & August 1913.

59 RDB 5 June 1896, 1 October 1896, May–July 1914.

60 RDB 11 August 1917.

61 Caryl Coleman to John Hardman & Co. 20 May 1904, JHAL. The window is entered in RDB 29 July and 26 August 1905 at a total of $2,141 – less than Hardman's had anticipated, but Coleman played up the advertisement value of the window as a compensating factor.

62 Coleman to John Hardman & Co., 6 October 1905, JHAL.

63 Coleman to John Hardman & Co., 26 October 1905, JHAL.

64 August Belmont to John Hardman & Co., 24 April 1906, JHAL.

65 Caryl Coleman to John Hardman & Co., 13 May 1906, JHAL. Coleman's remarks about Belmont are shockingly peppered with anti-Semitism, e.g. 'Although M. Belmont is a Christian by religion, he is a Jew by blood. As you no doubt know, he is a left-handed member of the Rothschild family'.

66 Coleman to John Hardman & Co., 16 April 1907, JHAL,

67 RDB 2 September 1908 and 11 November 1909.

68 Roger Watts to John Tarleton Hardman, 25 January 1914, JHAL.

69 Roger Watts to John Tarleton Hardman, 29 January 1914, JHAL.

70 Montague Castle to John Hardman & Co., 1 July 1914, JHAL.

71 Correspondence between Roger Watts and John Hardman & Co., in JHAL April-August 1910.

72 RDB 10 February 1912.

73 Colcman to JH & Co., 19 August 1912, JIIAL.

74 Coleman to JH & Co., 12 August 1912, JHAL.

75 Coleman to JH & Co., 19 April 1910, JHAL.

76 Coleman to JH & Co., 18 February 1910, JHAL.

77 ibid.

78 Coleman to JH & Co., 14 October 1910, JHAL.

79 Coleman to JH & Co., 20 October 1910, JHAL.

80 Coleman to JH & Co., 1 April 1909, JHAL.

81 The window is entered in RDB, 25 November 1909, at $1,100.

82 RDB September-November 1904, January-May 1905, February 1906 and March 1907.

83 The choice of subject reflects the aim of the college, founded in 1861 by Matthew Vassar to promote higher education for women.

84 Correspondence in Vassar College Special Collections files 19.18 and 19. 19.

85 Lucy Cohen, Environmental Dissertation, Vassar College, December 2006. I am most grateful to Lucy Cohen for kindly providing me with a copy of her dissertation and photographs of the Cornaro window.

86 I am grateful to Joseph Fegan of St Patrick's Seminary for supplying me with photographs of the windows.

87 1 November 1902. JHAL.

88 MWDB 12 March 1912, entered at $550. When the City of Detroit 111 was scrapped in 1956 the entire Gothic Room including the Hardman window were recovered and preserved in the Dossin Great Lakes Museum, Detroit.

89 RDB 22 June 1918.

90 Dennis Hadley, 'James Hogan in the US: the Interwar Years', Journal of Stained Glass, 28, 2004, pp.95-113.

Chapter 8 – Gothic For Ever!

1   Information from Fr Brian Doolan.

2   Deed dated 2 December 1919 (JHAL).

3   There is an Australian branch of the family, among whom is Justin Hardman who was employed for a time by the present firm c.2003–5.

4   Martin Cummins, *Nottingham Cathedral*, Nottingham, 1977, p. 51.

5   BCA Decoration Cost Book, September to November 1932, January 1933, July to September 1935. The nave, aisles and transepts were not completed until 1941.

6   There is a detailed description of the windows in W.J. Lilley, *St Mary's Church, Derby*, 1996.

7   BCA Decoration Cost Book, 1927–56, ff. 43–44 (1929), August to December 1933 (Lady chapel).

8   *Ibid.*, January 1930. Hardman's paid Bridgeman's £100.10s for the figures.

9   JHAL contains a considerable number of coloured drawings for these.

10 BCA Decoration Day Sales Book, 1892–1920, f. 179. Brian Doolan, 'The Ilsley Vestments', *Midland Catholic History*, no. 9, 2002–3, pp. 35–8.

11 Several items – the humeral veil, chalice veil and one of the stoles – are now missing, but JHAL has a full photographic record of the complete set. It has been suggested that a High Mass set made in 1931 for Canon John Roskell in the Pugin style was designed by S.P. Powell or Dunstan Powell (Brian Doolan, 'St Chad's Cathedral in the Twentieth Century', *Midland Catholic History*, no. 10, 2004, p. 42).

12 The Ilsley metropolitan cross, and also his pectoral cross designed by Hardman's, were stolen from the cathedral in 1990. The metropolitan cross was recovered in 2007.

13 The bones were forensically examined in 1995. It was established that the five bones enshrined in the reliquary above the high altar were indeed of the seventh century, but that they belonged to two individuals. The single bone which had been kept in the cylindrical reliquary in St Edward's chapel since 1931 was shown to be of ninth-century date. Michael Greenslade, *St Chad of Lichfield and Birmingham*, Birmingham Archdiocese of Birmingham Historical Commission, 1996.

14 Bridgeman's of Lichfield appear to have made the canopy and figures at a cost of £158.15s. BCA Decoration Cost Book, 1927–57, f. 56.

15 RDB 6 and 19 April 1922.

16 MWDB 1869, f. 144.

17 RDB 27 January 1904.

18 RDB 4 March 1904 (6 windows), Copy Bill Book 21 September 1911 (2 windows), RDB 15 June 1914 (2 windows), RDB 31 March 1926 (Turnbull memorial window).

19 The Revd David Myers commenced the restoration of the interior of St Peter's (2000–2007), which has also included the reinstatement of a tiled floor incorporating encaustic tile patterns, stencilling in the side-chapels, a carved and painted reredos and a new organ.

20 *BOF County Durham*, 2nd edn, 1983, pp. 477–82, gives a concise account of the development of the buildings.

21 Christopher Martin, *A Glimpse of Heaven: Catholic Churches of England and Wales*, 2006, p. 138.

22 Watercolours and photographs in JHAL.

23 Patrick Feeny, 'The Heraldic Glass in the Houses of Parliament', *Journal of the British Society of Master Glasspainters*, 1955–7, pp. 142–7.

24 Robert Cooke, *The Palace of Westminster*, 1987, pp. 303–4. Cooke states that a list of those who had signed for quantities of glass had recently been discovered in the glazier's shop. A few were still alive but none of them could recall exactly what they had signed for.

25 Patrick Feeny, *op. cit.*, p. 145.

26 See above, pp.110-11. Ballantine & Allen were the firm originally engaged by the Fine Arts Commission to make the glass for the House of Lords. This was before Hardman had set up his stained glass operation.

27 Feeny, *op.cit.*, p. 146.

28 Cooke, *op. cit.*, p. 304.

29 *Stained Glass Windows by John Hardman Studios,* an extract from *A Directory of Stained Glass Windows* published in 1961 by the British Society of Master Glasspainters.

30 Arthur Sutton, *A. Edward Jones, Master Silversmith of Birmingham*, Birmingham 1980.

31 J.A. Chatwin (1829–1907), the founder of the dynasty, was the dominant figure in church architecture in Birmingham from the 1860s. One of his most spectacular churches is SS Peter & Paul, Aston, with five glorious windows by Hardman in the apse (1885).

32 Andy Foster, *Birmingham*, Pevsner Architectural Guides, 2005, p. 209. JHAL has some watercolours for these windows.

33 See Chapter 7.

34 Information from Karla Whitmore, Chatswood, NSW, who is researching the work of Donald Taunton in Australia.

35 Patrick Feeny, 'Fifty Years with Stained Glass and Colour', unpublished memoir, from which much of my information about Feeny's work has been taken. I am grateful to Patrick Feeny's daughter, Susan Fryer, for supplying me with a copy, and for other information about her father. Feeny's work is listed in K.G. Saur, *Allgemeines Künstler-Lexikon*, 2003, Band 35, pp. 468–9, and Feeny himself published lists of Hardman commissions in the *Journal of the British Society of Master Glasspainters.* See note 29 above.

36 Feeny, 'Fifty Years with Stained Glass and Colour', p. 7.

37 I am grateful to Miriam Power of Beckenham for information about Feeny's work at St Edmund's, and for photographs of the windows.

38 Feeny, *op. cit.*, as n. 35. See also R. O'Donnell, *The Pugins and the Catholic Midlands*, 2002, pp. 52–7.

39 See below, Appendix A.

40 *BOE Worcestershire*, 1968, p. 171.

41 Feeny, *op. cit.*, p. 6.

42 RDB 16 November 1893. The relocation of the window is documented in Farnsworth, Grace & Charpenning (eds.), *stained Glass in Cathoiic Philadelphia.* Philadelphia: St. Joseph's University Press, 2002, p.416.

43 Ethan Anthony is both a practising architect and an academic. In 1992 he merged his own incipient architectural practice with the remnant of the firm of Ralph Adams Cram, under the name of Hoyle Doran & Berry/Cram & Ferguson, performing a similar service to that of Edgar and Margaret Phillips in respect of John Hardman & Co., by saving a once–celebrated architectural firm from almost certain oblivion. Just as Neil Phillips had grown up without ever having heard of Pugin and Hardman, so Anthony emerged from architectural school totally unaware of Cram and his great legacy of American Gothic architecture and architectural publications: such was the impact of International Modernism in American architectural schools in the 1960s and '70s when the work of architects prior to Le Corbusier (1887–1965) was considered irrelevant. Anthony's own studies – which included six visits to Europe and extensive research in the Cram archives – stimulated a deep understanding of the principles of Gothic design and an ability to work within it in the modern age. 'Paradoxically, there is far more inventiveness in attempting a Gothic building than in the modern building that now can and often is ordered almost entirely from a catalog' (E. Anthony, *A Last Long Look at American Sacred Architecture*, The Institute for Sacred Architecture, Fall/Winter 2004). Syon Abbey is one of several new expressions of this reappraisal of sacred space, and of the need to re-integrate architecture and the arts. Anthony has also made a major contribution to American architectural history with the publication of his book, *The Architecture of Ralph Adams Cram and His Office* (2007) and he is a member of the INTBAU College of Traditional Practitioners, under the patronage of H.R.H. The Prince of Wales. Reappraisal of the liturgical landscape stimulated by Pope Benedict XVI (*Summorum Pontificum*, September 2007) will also impact on the architectural setting for worship as worldwide restrictions on the celebration of the Latin Mass are removed.

44 See above, p. 64-65

45 I am very grateful to Mr Cyril Easton, a former employee of Hartley Wood and now living in Stafford, for lending me his papers on English glass and the processes of manufacture.

46 Jane Dew has very kindly supplied me with a copy of her photographic record, carried out in collaboration with sacristan Frances Crockett, and Janet Waterhouse, Mary McGuire, Janet McKnight, Charlotte Garney and photographers Colin Birch and Mike Crockett. The Birmingham NADFAS survey was undertaken by Dr Margaret Davis, with photographs by Dr John Davis.

47 Indenture in JHAL

48 A.W.N. Pugin, *True Principles of Pointed or Christian Architecture*, 1841, p. 56.

APPENDIX A

THE HARDMAN ARCHIVES

The Hardman archive collections are the principal primary sources for the history of the firm, and for the most part they are accessible by the public. A private collection of over 1,000 letters from A.W.N. Pugin to John Hardman has been copied, and there is a microfilm copy in the House of Lords Record Office, collection PUG/1. Some are already in print in the first two volumes of Margaret Belcher, *The Letters of A.W.N. Pugin*, and the remainder (1846 onwards) will follow in due course.

The fire at the Hardman Studio at Newhall Hill, Birmingham, in 1970 destroyed surprisingly little of the archive material stored there, although many of the surviving items are in a fire- damaged condition. After the fire, and the subsequent relocation of the Hardman Studio, the bulk of the archive was acquired by Birmingham City Council, except for materials which, by agreement, were retained by the firm as being relevant to their continuing operations as designers and manufacturers of stained glass.

Part of the Hardman archive stack in Birmingham City Archives

Currently, the Hardman archive is split between four locations:

1) The Birmingham Museum & Art Gallery (BMAG) which holds most of the metalwork drawings, stained glass drawings, watercolours and cartoons, and brass-rubbings. There is also the Loans Collection consisting of metalwork and glass drawings, many relating to the New Palace of Westminster, in a private collection currently on loan to the Museum. The stained glass cartoons are held in the Museum Collections Centre, Dollman Street. They are largely uncatalogued and rolled-up in original wrappings, as most have remained untouched since their evacuation following the fire. A condition survey is due to be undertaken (2008) and it is hoped that the entire cartoon collection will thereafter be digitally photographed and put on-line. The work of cataloguing and recording material in the drawings and watercolours collections, begun by Glennys Wild, will also continue, with a view to making them more accessible for research

2) Birmingham City Archives (BCA), located on the sixth floor of the Birmingham Central Library, opposite the Museum. BCA holds the bulk of the written archive. A systematic programme of conservation has meant that some of the fire-damaged volumes are now accessible, but, inevitably, a few are awaiting the attention of the conservators and cannot in the meantime be issued to readers. The BCA collection includes 132 letters from Pugin to Hardman, and thousands of letters, boxed under the appropriate year, from customers, clients and suppliers. From the 1850s onwards letters for any one year are tied in alphabetical bundles according to the initial letter of clients' surnames, and this is noted on the outside of the neatly folded letters which are bundled in date order. They are also separated into the two main categories of metalwork and stained glass. Copy letter-books, with abstracts or (later) full copies of outgoing correspondence, occupy 167 volumes running from June 1866 to September 1979 with surprisingly few gaps. Each volume of letters is conveniently indexed.

The process of ordering, making and completing metalwork and glass can be traced though the Glass and Metal Order Books which run from 1846 to 1914 (glass) and from 1882 to 1914 (metal). Many of these volumes are either not indexed or only partially indexed. The Daybooks (1834–1910 for metal, 1845–1976 for glass) record the completion and billing of work. Bundles of cost-sheets, running from 1853 to 1914, give brief descriptions of each window made, and a breakdown of costs for the various processes. The Glass Daybooks are indexed by place and client name, but the early metal daybooks (up to the 1880s) are not. Monumental brasses are contained in a run of 30 estimate/order books, 1849–1912, and from 1913 onwards orders for brasses are entered into the Glass Order Books. Hardman's decorative work is contained in a series of daybooks, sales books and estimate books running from 1845 to 1968. Altogether the Hardman archive occupies about 100 metres of shelving in the BCA. A printed catalogue summarising the contents and what is accessible is available at BCA, and the reference to the collection is GB 0143 BCA MS 175.

3) Birmingham Archdiocesan Archives (BAA), Cathedral House, St Chad's Queensway, Birmingham. A file of correspondence (196 letters) addressed to John Hardman and other members of the Hardman family, 1844–1930.

4) The Lightwoods House Collection (JHAL), currently at the Hardman Studio, Lightwoods House, Birmingham, includes some important metalwork drawings and stained-glass designs by John Hardman Powell, decorative schemes for churches by J.A. Pippet and his sons Elphege and Oswald, and by Patrick Feeny, and cut stencils for some of these schemes. There is a collection of twentieth-century stained-glass watercolours by Donald Taunton, and an extensive photographic record of glass, metalwork and furnishing commissions carried out in Great Britain and overseas from about 1890 onwards. There is a card-index of churches for which Hardman's made windows in this later period, with annotated plans indicating the location of the windows in each building. Only part of the Lightwoods collection has been catalogued, but the drawings are filed together under their various categories and designers' names. The collection is not static. Additions have been made since 2000, principally material bought at auction. This includes a set of early A.W.N. Pugin drawings acquired in 2003, a quantity of metalwork drawings by J.H. Powell bought in 2006, and archive material formerly in the possession of the Birmingham silversmithing firm of A.E. Jones. The Lightwoods collection is very much a working archive, and is in constant use as a reference-point for the studio's team of designers and restorers.

The firm's own working indexes are an invaluable aid to locating particular commissions. There are copies of these indexes in BCA and at Lightwoods House:

a) Index of Glass 1845–1899. Locations of windows are given in alphabetical order down the left-hand side of each page, and the dates in vertical columns. The numbers in the columns enable each window to be located either in the First Glass Daybook (1845–53) or in the bundles of cost-sheets (1853–99).

b) Index of Windows 1866–1882 lists the locations of windows made, with a very brief description of each one.

c) Index of Windows 1883–1937

d) Monumental Brasses 1843–1937 lists all memorial brasses, inscription plates etc., giving both the location and the client, in alphabetical order. The price of each brass is also given, in the letter-code which is also used in many of the order books for metal and glass:

D = 0, E = 1, F = 2, G = 3, H = 4, J = 5, K = 6, L = 7, M = 8, N = 9, with Y as a repeat.

A brass costing £150. 10s would therefore be shown as EJD.ED

e) Index to Works, 1900–1940 gives dates and references to glass and decoration costs, the numbers in the columns referring to glass cost sheets up to 30 June 1914, and thereafter to the page of the appropriate daybook.

The indexes are a vital first resource in ascertaining whether or not a window or a memorial brass is by Hardman, and the date can be fixed precisely. There is, unfortunately, no corresponding index for metalwork commissions other than memorial brasses. The volume of work was too vast for this to be possible. Dating a piece of metalwork can therefore be quite difficult unless, of course, it is of gold or silver, in which case the assay-mark would pinpoint it. Most metalwork items, however, were made of brass, and unless they carry an inscription – as sometimes they did in the case of *in memoriam* gifts – or unless the date is otherwise known, locating a particular commission can prove very difficult, involving a trawl through the indexes of several daybooks; and not all of them are indexed. Once an item has been found in the daybook, it may be possible to build up a complete account of that commission by using the entry to locate correspondence, invoices, drawings, and in the case of stained glass, cartoons. The following example gives an indication of the process.

In 2006 an enquiry was received at the Hardman Studio about a set of windows at Holy Trinity Church, Mostyn Street, Llandudno (Gwynedd). A search in the index of stained glass revealed that five windows were made by Hardman's for that church between 1865 and 1886. The daybooks for those years were searched, and from these emerged the precise dates of each commission, a brief description of the subject-matter, the cost, and the names and addresses of the various donors. The cost-sheets gave a breakdown of the various processes from cartooning to the actual fixing of the windows, and the identification of the donors enabled correspondence about the windows to be traced in the stained-glass letters bundles. The precise dates of the windows pointed to the appropriate volume of watercolours in BMAG, and there was also an element of surprise. In August 2007 a set of preliminary pencil drawings by John Hardman Powell for three of these windows was discovered in a box of papers bought for the Studio at a sale. One of these was on the back of a piece of commercial stationery from a hotel in Llandudno, indicating that Powell visited the town in person to make the sketches. It was possible, therefore, to build up a very full account of the Hardman windows at Holy Trinity, to the delight of the Chairman of the Windows Appeals Committee.

Not all enquiries and searches prove so fruitful. A window may turn out not to be by Hardman's at all. Rarely is a Hardman window signed, and there were – even in the days of Pugin – many imitators. The index is the quickest way of establishing authorship and date, and once this has been done, the daybook will point the way to other documentation. Inevitably there are gaps: a volume may be missing or currently unusable, but since the order books, daybooks and cost-sheets contain similar information, the gaps can be largely filled, and so for most glass commissions a reasonably full picture may be built up. For metalwork commissions the task is somewhat harder, for reasons already given, unless the date and the name of the client are already known. Once a piece of work has been traced through the written archive, the next logical step is to consult the BMAG catalogues, and also JHAL to see if there are any drawings, watercolours or cartoons.

Useful Addresses

BirminghamMuseum&ArtGallery,

Chamberlain Square, Birmingham B3 3DH

Tel. 0121 303 2834

e-mail www. bmag. org. uk

Opening hours: Mon-Sat 10-30 a.m–4-40 p.m.; Sun 12-30 p.m– 4-30p.m.

Birmingham Museum Collections Centre,

25 Dollman Street, Nechells, Birmingham B7 4RQ

Tel. 0121 303 0190

e-mail www.bmag.org.uk

Visits by appointment only

Birmingham City Archives,

Central Library, Chamberlain Square, Birmingham B3 3HQ

Tel. 0121 303 4217

e-mail archives@birmingham.gov.uk.

Those wishing to use the archive need a CARN (County Archive Research Network) ticket. Registration can be carried out on the first visit, readers needing to produce official proof of identity, signature and address.

Opening hours: Mon-Sat 10 a.m.–5p.m., with extended opening on Thur until 8 p.m. Closed Mon.

Birmingham Archdiocesan Archives

Cathedral House, St. Chad's Queensway, Birmingham B4 6EU

Tel. 0121 230 6252

e-mail: archives@rc— birmingham. org

Opening hours: Wed–Fri 11a.m.–6p.m. by appointment only. Please remember to bring ID containing your address.

John Hardman Studio

Lightwoods House, Lightwoods Park, Hagley Road West, Birmingham B67 5DP

Tel. 0121 429 7609

e-mail: hardman.trading@googlemail.com

www. hardmantrading.com

Visits by appointment only

The Pugin Society

Hon. Sec. Pam Cole

33 Montcalm House, Westferry Road, London E14 3SD

Tel. 020 7515 9474

www.pugin-society.org

APPENDIX B

JOHN HARDMAN & CO. – USA COMMISSIONS
SUMMARY LIST OF LOCATIONS

This list is drawn from entries in the Glass Rough Daybooks. There may be some omissions and the list takes no account of windows which have been altered, moved or lost since the installation date. It does, however, give a broad picture of the scope of Hardman's work in the USA up to 1935, and their heavy involvement with a number of major churches and cathedrals.

ALBANY (N.Y.)

Cathedral of Immaculate Conception & Convent Chapel (Architect: Frederick C. Withers)

1891:   seven apse windows of 1 light & tracery each. Window of 1 light on N. side of choir. Window of 4 lights on N. side of Bishop's sacristy.

1892:   lower transom of 7 lights in N. transept window. 4 chancel clerestories of 2 lights & tracery each.

1897:   transept window, Gospel side, 7 lights transomed.

1899:   3 transept clerestories, 3 lights each

1900:   2 transept clerestories, 3 lights each.

1901:   10 nave clerestories of 3 lights & tracery each.

1902:   10 aisle windows of 3 lights & tracery each

1908:   (Convent chapel) 5 windows of 2 lights each & tracery

Vincentian chapel

1916:   2 windows of 1 light each.

ATLANTA (Georgia)

Calhoun Mausoleum Church

1911:   window of 1 light.

BALTIMORE (Maryland)

Mount Calvary Presbyterian Church

1883:   window of 1 lancet light.

1884:   window of 1 lancet light.

Grace Church (Architect: F.C. Withers)

1888:   3 windows of 2 lights & tracery, east aisle.

1888–9: 3 windows of 2 lights & tracery, west aisle.

1894:   2 windows of 2 lights in west aisle, & single light window in west aisle.

Corpus Christi Church (For Michael Jenkins, founder & patron. Architect: Patrick Keely.)

1889:   set of 6 windows, 2 lights & tracery, and lancets.

1890:   5 sanctuary windows of 1 light & tracery, 2 'moon' windows, 10 aisle windows of 2 lights & tracery.

1890:   rose window over main entrance. 2 lancets in Thomas Aquinas chapel, 4 lancets in Baptistery.

1895:   colour drawings for mosaic panels in apse.

1896:   five panels for apse in opus sectile & mosaic, 12 quatrefoil panels of opus sectile & mosaic to go under 'moon' windows.

1 opus sectile panel over porch; 4 quatrefoil panels of opus sectile & mosaic.

1901:   2 windows for front vestibule, 1 light each; 1 single light for tower entrance.

1911:   14 clerestory windows of 2 lights & tracery, grisaille.

1912–14: set of Stations of the Cross in opus sectile & mosaic.

Memorial brasses: Jenkins family, 1899–1917.

First Presbyterian Church
1886:   window of 2 lights on east side of nave.

Mount Calvary Church
1883:   window of 1 lancet light.

1884:   window of I lancet light.

Private chapel, 721 St Paul's Street
1894:   rose window, and 2 windows of 1 light each.

BOSTON (Massachusetts)
Church of the Advent
1888:   window of 4 lights & tracery on N. side of chapel.

1888:   design for window of 3 lights, south transept.

Trinity Church
1905:   2 windows of 1 light.

St Augustine's, South Boston
1898:   2 aisle windows, 3 lights each & tracery.

BROOKLYN (N.Y.)
St Anne's Church
1894:   window of 2 lights & tracery, N. side over gallery.

St Bartholomew's
1926–7: 3 round-headed windows of 1 light.

1931:   3 round-headed windows of 1 light.

Erasmus High School
1911–12: window of 9 lights & tracery for hall.

St James (pro-Cathedral)
1904:   3 sanctuary windows, 1 light each.

1904:   2 large transept windows, 1 light each.

1905:   1 large transept window, 1 light; 4 nave windows of 1 light.

1906:   2 square-headed windows of 1 light.

Church of the Messiah

1895:   window over gallery: 2 lights with tracery

1896:   3 panels in screen.

1897:   south window in south gallery: 2 lights & tracery; 2 panels for screen in partition.

1901:   panel for screen.

1922:   window of 2 lights.

SS. Peter & Paul Catholic Church

1902:   Vestibule window: 2 lights & tracery.

St Stephen's Catholic Church

1891:   aisle window of 3 lights & tracery.

Zenga Mausoleum, Calvary Cemetery

1922:   1 square window

BUFFALO (N.Y.)

The Ascension Church

1887:   window in apse, 2 lights & tracery centre window of chancel, over altar.

1894:   lancet window in S. transept.

St. Joseph's R.C. Cathedral

1893:   window of 2 lights, south aisle.

        (Convent) 1891: triplet window with tracery.

North Presbyterian Church

1906–7: 4 aisle windows of 3 lights & tracery.

1906:   transept window of 2 tiers of 7 lights each & tracery.

1934:   clerestory window of 2 lights & tracery.

St Paul's Church

1888–9: 2 windows of 1 light in S. aisle.

1890:   window of 2 lights & tracery.

1891:   south aisle lancet.

Trinity Church

1890:   south aisle window, 2 lights & tracery.

CARBONDALE (N.Y.)

Trinity Church

1900:   Baptistery window of 3 lights & tracery.

CARRIGART (Pennsylvania)

Protestant Episcopal Church

1898:   Window of 3 lights.

CHICAGO (Illinois)

Cathedral of the Holy Name

1893:   N. transept window, originally of 2 lights but with mullions sawn out.

1918:   22 windows for sanctuary, side chapel, aisles & baptistery. 1 light each & memorial inscription. Huge order: $13,346.

Convent of Mercy

1911:   aisle window for academy chapel, 2 lights.

1917:   window of 2 lights & tracery.

Church of the Holy Angels

1897:   2 semicircular windows over altars; 1 rose window in west gable; 10 sanctuary windows of 1 light each; 6 aisle windows, 3 lights each; 4 semicircular windows over confessionals & side chapels.

CHICOPEE (Massachusetts)

Convent of Notre Dame

1902:   6 windows of 2 lights each & tracery.

CHRISTCHURCH (N.Y.)

Pelham Manor, St Mary's Convent of Mercy

1911:   Rose window.

1911:   window of 3 lights & tracery.

CLEVELAND (Ohio)

Trinity Cathedral

1907:   chancel window, 5 lights & tracery.

1909:   5-light window with tracery.

COLD SPRING (N.Y.)

St Mary's Church

1890:   window of 2 lights & tracery.

CONCORD (New Hampshire)

Christian Science Church

1905:   traceries of 2 x 4-light windows.

1905:   figures for above windows.

CORNELL UNIVERSITY (N.Y.)

1908:   2 lancet lights.

CATONSVILLE (Maryland – suburb of Baltimore)

Catonsville – St. William's (Lanahan Memorial Church)

1915:   2 windows of 2 lights; rose window, transept windows, 2 of 3 lights; west window of 5 lights.

DETROIT (Michigan)

Trinity Methodist Episcopal Church

1924:   2 centre lights & tracery of 6-light window.

Faculty Building of Catholic University

1924:   6 round-headed windows of 1 light.

1931:   3 windows of 1 light each.

1932:   High School chapel. East window of 1 circular light.

Central Woodward Christian Church

1929:   Window of 3 lights.

DUBUQUE (Iowa)

St Raphael's, Catholic Cathedral

1888:   6 sanctuary windows of 2 lights each; 16 nave windows, 2 lights each & tracery.

1890:   2 windows at sanctuary end of aisles, 2 lights & tracery ornament to windows at entrance end of aisles, and to 2 transom windows over entrance.

EASTON (Pennsylvania)

First Presbyterian Church

1910:   window of 1 light, round-headed.

EDDINGTON (Pennsylvania)

St Francis' Home for Boys

1888:   2 sample panels.

1890:   (chapel) window of 2 lights.

1891:   window of 2 lights.

1892:   2 windows of 1 light, 3 rose window, window of 2 lights.

1893:   3 windows of 2 lights & tracery.

EDEN HALL (Torresdale, Pennsylvania)

Convent of the Sacred Heart

1888:   window of 2 lights.

1890:   2 windows of 2 lights.

1894:   2 windows of 2 lights.

1907:   2 windows of 2 lights & tracery.

1911:   window of 2 lights & tracery.

EDGE WOOD(Maryland)

Miss Jenkins' Country House Chapel

1909:   circular window & 2 round-headed windows.

ELLICOTT CTY (Maryland)

St Charles College

1910:   2 windows of 2 lights & tracery.

EUGENE (Oregon)

St Mary's Church

1912:   1 lancet light.

FAR ROCKAWAY (Long Island)

St John's Church

1909:   3 lancet lights

GLEN COVE (Long Island)

St Patrick's Church

1901:   6 single lights.

GOVERNORS ISLAND (N.Y.)

St Cornelius Chapel

1906:   window of 3 lights & tracery.

1911:   2 windows of 1 light for porch.

GREENWICH (N.Y.)

St Mary's Church

1905:   chancel window of 1 round-headed light.

1905:   8 nave windows, 1 round-headed light each.

1905:   6 nave windows of 1 round-headed light each.

HARTFORD (Connecticut)

Trinity Church

1901:   windows of 2 & 3 lights.

1902:   window of 2 lights.

1903:   4 aisle windows, 2 lights & tracery.

HENDERSON (Kentucky)

Church of the Holy Name

1890:   west window of chapel, 2 lights & tracery; 2 sanctuary windows, east window of 5 lights & tracery.

HYANNISPORT (Massachusetts)

St Andrew's Church

1907:   chancel window, 3 lights & tracery.

ISHPENNING (Michigan)Grace Church

1908:   window of 5 lights, side of chancel.

KEWANEE (Illinois)

St Joseph's Church

1914:   window of 5 lights.

1929:   window of 3 lights.

1935:   window of 3 lights *(This is almost certainly the last Hardman USA commission of the 20th century)*

LITTLE FALLS (N.Y.)

Emmanuel Church

1906:   window of 3 lights & tracery.

St Mary's Church

1914:   12 aisle windows of 1 lancet light; 1 3-light window & tracery for north transept; 3 trefoils for transoms over front door; 4 more lancets for aisle.

1915:   2 sanctuary windows of 2 lights & tracery; sacristy window, 3 lights & tracery.

1925:   2 lancets.

LITTLE ROCK (Arkansas)

Masonic Temple

1906:   window of 1 light.

LOWELL (Massachusetts)

St Peter's Catholic Church

1898:   5 single lights; 3 lights each, north transept & south transept; rose window, 8 single lights.

1899:   window of 2 lights.

1900:   window of 6 lights, 11 of 2 lights each.

Convent of Notre Dame

1904:   window of 2 lights.

LOWER MERION (Pennsylvania)

St John's Episcopal Church

1906:   4 windows of 2 lights, 1 window of 2 lights.

1914:   1 window of 2 lights.

MILL VALLEY (California)

Church of the Saviour

1905:   circular window.

MILWAUKEE (Wisconsin)

Catholic Cathedral

1897:   two windows.

1899:   two trial panels.

MONTAGUE (Massachusetts)
Hospital chapel

1900:   Circular window

MOUNT AIRY (Pennsylvania)
Episcopal Church

1891:   window of 2 lights.

NAZARETH (N.Y.)
Convent of the Sisters of Charity

1902:   south transept window.

NEWARK (New Jersey)
Jewish Synagogue

1915:   2 windows of 1 light.

1916:   1 window of 1 light; 1 window of 1 square light.

1917:   1 window of 1 square light; single light window with semicircular head.

1919:   single-light window, semicircular head.

NEW BRUNSWICK (New Jersey)
Dutch Reformed Seminary

1903:   6 windows for library.

1904:   10 windows for library alcoves.

1905:   2 windows of 1 light in library alcove.

1906:   2 windows for library alcoves.

NEWPORT (Rhode Island)
St Anne's Church

1894:   2 windows of 2 lights.

Convent of Mercy

1900:   rectangular window of 1 light.

St John's Church

1894:   east window of 5 lights & tracery; window on north side of chancel, 2 lights & tracery.

Zabriskie Memorial Church

1910:   1 window of 1 light, 2 of 2 lights, 1 of 3 lights.

NEWTON HIGHLANDS (Massachusetts)
Congregational Church

1906:   window of 3 lights.

NEW ROCHELLE (N.Y.)

St Gabriel's Church

1908:   Window of 3 lights with transom.

NEW YORK

Christ Church, 71st Street

1892:   chancel window of 3 lights.

1895:   12 single-light windows round apse & over west gallery; 1 light window on chancel S. side.

Offices of Church Glass & Decorating Co.

1907:   sample panel.

College of the City of New York

1909:   window of 10 lights in two tiers of five, in Faculty Room.

House of the Comforter

1906:   figures and inscriptions for 5 lights.

St John the Baptist's House, 233 East 17th Street

1885:   window of 1 lancet light.

1887:   window of 1 lancet light.

St Ignatius Episcopal Church

1900:   1 light window over side altar.

1905:   centre window in Lady chapel, 3 lights & tracery; Lady chapel window of 2 lights & tracery.

1905:   6-light window for chancel, transomed.

1906:   3-light window for choir.

1907:   2-light window for Lady Chapel.

1909:   5-light window, transomed with tracery, north transept.

1910:   single-light window with tracery, transept clerestory.

1921:   2-light window with tracery.

St John's Cathedral

1908:   window of 3 lights over altar in St Saviour's chapel.

1909:   2 windows of 3 lights: clerestories for St Saviour's chapel; 2 windows of 2 lights & tracery for St Saviour's chapel.

Church of St Matthew & St Timothy

1923: 1 lancet light

Our Lady of Guadeloupe

1910:   6 windows of 2 lights for aisle; 6 windows of 2 lights for gallery; skylight window of 3 openings; 2 windows of a light for chancel; 2 vestibule windows.

St Patrick's Cathedral

1912:   window of 2 lights.

Church of the Saviour

1914:   round-headed window of 1 light.

Church of the Transfiguration

1895:   2 lancet windows in chancel.

Trinity Church, Lancaster

1887:   central window in apse: 2 lights & tracery.

Trinity Chapel (Episcopal)

1886:   2 trefoil lights over west entrance.

Union Theological Seminary

1910:   window of 5 lights in 2 tiers of 5 lights each; window of 3 lights & tracery.

Women's Hospital

1906:   window of 3 lights & tracery.

Woodlawn Mortuary Chapel, Canandaigua

1910:   2 windows of 3 lights & tracery.

Church of Zion & St Timothy

1901:   2 windows of 2 lights & tracery, for chancel.

1902:   window of 2 lights & tracery, for chancel clerestory.

Vassar College

1905:   5-light window & tracery, for Library.

OCONOMOWE (Wisconsin)
Zion Church

1893:   east window of 3 round-headed lights.

OLEAN (N.Y.)
St Stephen's

1914:   window of 3 lights

OYSTER BAY (N.Y.)
St Dominic's

1900:   3 rectangular windows.

PHILADELPHIA (Pennsylvania)
Church of the Assumption

1890:   2 aisle windows, 2 lights each & tracery.

St Andrew's Church

1916:   window of 3 lights.

Convent of the Sacred Heart, Arch Street

1890:   window of 2 lights & tracery.

Church of the Incarnation

1890:   north aisle window, 2 lights & tracery.

1907:   north aisle window, 2 lights & tracery.

1909:   north aisle window, 2 lights & tracery.

1911:   south aisle window, 2 lights & tracery.

1921:   window in west wall, 2 lights & tracery.

1924:   window of 2 lights & tracery.

St James' Episcopal Church

1893:   cartoons for use of sculptors.

1907:   window in east wall for figures on tower.

St Mark's Church

1882:   window of 2 lights & tracery.

St Matthew's Church

1894:   1 round-headed light with transom.

Mount Airy Episcopal Church

1890:   window at west end of south aisle, 2 lights & tracery.

1891:   window at west end of north aisle, 2 lights & tracery.

Cathedral of SS. Peter & Paul

1903:   Window over great front entrance: one semicircular light.

Church of the Saviour

1903:   2 semicircular headed windows on north side.

1904:   2 semicircular headed windows.

1912:   1 semicircular headed light.

1912:   12 clerestory windows, 1 round-headed light each.

1914:   rose window.

1914:   12 clerestory windows.

1916:   transom window over side entrance at west end.

1920:   1 round-headed window of 12 lights.

1922:   7 chancel windows, 1 light each.

PITTSBURGH (Pennsylvania)

St Paul's Catholic Cathedral

1905:   15 chancel clerestories.

1911:   apse window: 1 light & tracery.

St Andrew's Church

1912:   4 windows of 3 lights.

POMEROY (Ohio)

Grace Church

1916:   chancel window of 3 lights.

PORTLAND (Oregon)

Bishop's Oratory

1911:   3 lancet lights.

PROVIDENCE (Rhode Island)

Church of the Holy Name

1900:   2 sanctuary windows of 1 light each.

Convent of Mercy:

1896:   sanctuary window of 3 lights & tracery; 8 aisle windows of 1 light each.

St Michael's Church

1914:   window over altar of 3 lights & tracery; 14 aisle windows of 2 lights & tracery; 12 clerestory windows of 2 lights & tracery; window of 3 lights & tracery over entrance; window of 1 light over door; 2 windows of 1 light & tracery on either side of choir; 2 windows of 1 light each for baptistery & staircase.

1915:   6 clerestories; 3 aisle windows; 2 traceries over side entrance.

1916:   3 aisle windows.

St Stephen's Church

1895:   centre apse window of 2 lights & tracery.

ROCHESTER (N.Y.)

St Mary's Church

1915:   window of 2 lights & tracery

SAN FRANCISCO (California)

St Patrick's Cathedral

1914:   16 windows of 2 lights & tracery.

1915:   2 windows of 1 light & tracery, adjoining sanctuary; 2 front windows of 1 light each; 5 apse windows, lancets.

1920:   window of 1 light between tower & balcony.

1921:   16 clerestory windows of 1 light.

St Patrick's Seminary

1904:   14 nave windows of 1 light & tracery.

1914:   2 windows of 1 light & tracery.

St Patrick's Chapel, Menlo Park

1923:   14 round-headed widows of 1 light.

SANTA BARBARA (California)

Episcopal Church

1917:   window of 2 lights & tracery.

SHARON HILL (Pennsylvania)
Convent Chapel
1888:   2 lancets on either side of sanctuary.

SHENECTADY (N.Y.)
Christ Church
1915:   traceried rose window over high altar.

SLEEPY HOLLOW (N.Y.)
Cemetery Mortuary Chapel
1922:   one 3-light windows & two windows of 2 lights each.

SOUTH BETHLEHEM (Pennsylvania)
South Bethlehem Church
1904:   replacement window.

STAMFORD (Connecticut)
St John's Church
1907:   window of 2 lights.

SYRACUSE (N.Y.)
St Paul's Church
1907:   window of 2 lights & tracery.

TAUNTON (Massachusetts)
St Mary's Church
1900:   east window of 5 lights & tracery; 2 side windows of sanctuary; 2 lights & tracery; rose window over St Joseph's altar.
1901:   5 aisle windows of 3 lights & tracery.
1902:   11 aisle windows of 3 lights & tracery; 2 vestibule windows.

TORRESDALE (Pennsylvania)
Convent Chapel of the Sacred Heart, Eden Hall
1888:   2-light window & tracery.
1890:   2 x 2-light windows & tracery.
1894:   2 windows of 2 lights & tracery.

TROY (N.Y.)
Miss Sarah Tracy's Mausoleum, Oakwood Avenue
1902:   9 windows of 1 semicircular light each.

UTICA (N.Y.)
St Elizabeth's Hospital
1917:   window of 3 lights.

WACO (Texas)

First Presbyterian Church:

1912:   window of 2 lights.

1913:   window of 2 lights.

WASHINGTON D.C.

St Paul's Church

1896: single-light window over side altar.

1897: south aisle window: 2 lights & tracery.

St John's Church

1933: 1 rectangular light.

WATERBURY (Connecticut)

Trinity Church

1901: 2 windows of 1 light each.

WHITE PLAINS (N.Y.)

Memorial Chapel: Convent of the Divine Compassion

1897: 6 round-headed windows in apse.

Church of St John the Evangelist

1892: 14 aisle windows of 2 lights & tracery; 14 clerestories of 2 lights & tracery.

WILKES BARRE (Pennsylvania)

Presbyterian Church

1889: window of 3 round-headed lights.

WILLIAMSTOWN (Massachusetts)

Williams College Chapel

1904: centre light of 5-light window & tracery; 3 aisle windows of 3 lights.

1905: 4 lights for 5-light window in south elevation; Aisle window, 3 lights transomed; east transept window of 5 lights, transomed & tracery; 4 aisle windows of 3 lights each, transomed & tracery; west transept window, five lights, transoms & tracery; tower window of 1 light; 2 windows in transepts looking north: 3 lights & tracery.

1906: Ornamental work & tracery for existing windows.

YONKERS (N.Y.)

St Joesph's Seminary

1896: 10 windows of 1 light each; 2 rose windows.

GLOSSARY OF ECCLESIASTICAL TERMS

AGNUS DEl — Literally 'Lamb of God', it is a an artistic representation of Christ shown as a Lamb bearing a flag with a Cross upon it. A gnus Dei is also a devotion said during Mass.

ALB — A full-length, close-fitting vestment (q. v.) of white linen worn by clergy under the other vestments, and also on its own by lay assistants at the Eucharist.

ANGLO— CATHOLIC — A term used from the later nineteenth century onwards to describe members of the Church of England who stressed the continuity of the Anglican Church with the medieval Church, and laid stress on the Sacraments and ritual.

ALTAR — The most important item in a church. Made of stone or wood, it is the place where the Holy Sacrifice of the Eucharist is offered. On the surface of the altar (the mensa) five crosses are incised, representing the Five Wounds of Christ. The principal altar is known as the High Altar.

AUMBRY — A small cupboard set in the wall close to the altar, used for the keeping of sacred vessels. In medieval times, and currently in many Anglican churches, an aumbry is used for the Reservation of the Blessed Sacrament.

BAPTISTERY — The area of the church - normally at the west end - where the font is situated, and sometimes defined by structural screenwork.

BENEDICTION — A service of devotion to the Presence of Christ in the Blessed Sacrament. A blessing is given by the priest, using the Sacrament enclosed in a vessel known as a monstrance (q. v.).

BENEDICTION ALTAR — An altar and reredos (q.v.) with a large central niche above the tabernacle (q.v.) on which the monstrance is placed for Benediction.

CHALICE — A cup made of precious metal used to contain the wine at Mass

CHANCEL — The eastern limb of a church containing the altar; usually separated by an arch – 'chancel arch' – from the nave, and defined externally by a different roof–level.

CHANTRY — An altar, often enclosed within a small chapel or by screens, at which Mass was said for departed benefactors who had made gifts and endowments for this purpose

CHASUBLE — The principal priestly vestment worn at Mass. It is found in two main styles; "Gothic" which is very full, and "Latin" which has the sides cut away for ease of movement.

CHRISMATORY — A vessel for Chrism, a mixture of olive oil and balsam, used in the rites of Confirmation and Ordination. Sometimes used as a geenral term for a set of vessels containing also the Oil of the Catechumens (used in Holy Baptism) and the oils for anointing the Sick.

CIBORIUM — A vessel chaped somewhat like a chalice, but with a domed lid; used for holding quantities of communion wafers. It is also the term for a stone or wooden canopy over a free-standing altar, carried on four columns

CLERESTORY — A row of windows running above an arcade and below the roof-level to admit light into the nave or chancel.

COMMUNION RAIL — A rail placed in front of altar to enable communicants to kneel reverently when receiving Holy Communion, and to protect the altar. The use of such a rail is an Anglican invention of the seventeenth century. It was generally unknown in medieval times.

COPE — A semi-circular full-length cloak, often elaborately embroidered, worn in processions and at Benediction. It is fastened across the chest with a clasp known as a morse.

CORONA | or corona lucis. A circle, or crown, of ornamental metalwork, often adorned with enamelled or engraved texts, and suspended on chains. Candle—holders were attached to the corona to form the 'crown of light', and coronae could be made of two or three tiers.

CRUETS | Jug-shaped vessels used to contain the unconsecrated wine and water used in the Mass

DALMATIC | A vestment proper to the order of Deacon, and also worn by a bishop under the chasuble. It consists of a knee—length tunic with elbow—length sleeves, worn over the alb.

DOOM | A representation of the Last Judgement showing Christ in glory surrounded by angels and saints, welcoming the Blessed and condemning the wicked. In medieval times the Doom was painted over the chancel arch

FONT | A large stone vessel containing the water for Baptism. Font means, literally, a source of water. The font—bowl usually stands on a carved pedestal, and there is often a wooden cover or a more elaborate canopy carried on a pulley.

FRONTAL | A cloth, often richly decorated and embroidered, which completely covers the front part of the altar, either hanging loose or stretched on a frame. In the Church of England the so—called 'Laudian frontal' was devloped in the seventeenth century - a cloth which completely envelops the altar, reaching to the floor on all four sides.

GASOLIER | A piece of lighting equipment consisting of a metal standard, hanging corona, or chandelier, but carrying gas—jets rather than candles. The development of electric lighting led to the creation of 'electroliers' of similar design.

HOST | A large wafer of unleavened bread which is consecrated in the Mass. The word derives from the Latin hostia (victim), signifying the Body of Christ.

LANCET | A tall, narrow window with a pointed top, but without tracery; characteristic of the Early English (q.v.) period of Gothic architecture.

LECTERN | A book-rest supported on a column to hold the books used in services of worship.

LITURGY | An alternative name for the Mass or Eucharist (q.v.) but often referring to the ceremonial which accompanies it.

MASS | The name given to the Church's principal act of worship in which the Last Supper is recalled, and in which bread and wine are consecrated to be the Body and Blood of Christ. It is also known at the Eucharist ('Thanksgiving') and Holy Communion. The word Mass (Missa) is derived from the concluding words of dismissal in the Latin Rite, Ite, missa est. High Mass is celebrated with music, incense, and elaborate ceremonial. Low Mass is said rather than sung, and the priest is usually attended by only one server (assistant).

METROPOLITAN CROSS | A cross—staff carried by an archbishop and also called a crozier. Not to be confused with the crook-shaped pastoral staff of a bishop.

MISSAL | The book containing the texts of the Mass, used by the priest at the altar.

MITRE | The ceremonial headgear worn by a bishop.

MONSTRANCE | An ornate vessel, often of precious metal, for the exposition of the Host (q.v.) for veneration and the rite of Benediction.

MULLION | A vertical element, usually of stone, dividing a window into two or more lights.

OGEE | An S-shaped double curve, one convex and the other concave. A feature of Decorated and Perpendicular Gothic architecture, and used frequently in the canopies of tombs and niches.

ORPHREY | A rich band of material of contrasting colour and often embroidered, used orignally to conceal seams on the chasuble (q. v.) but later used as decoration, and also applied to other garments such as the cope.

PARCEL GILT — Gilding applied to part of a vessel or ornament made of silver, e.g. the inside of a chalice bowl

PASCHAL CANDLESTICK — A tall free—standing candlestick for the large candle used in the Easter Vigil ceremonies, and subsequently lit for services between Easter and Pentecost.

PASTORAL STAFF — A ceremonial staff carried by a bishop. Shaped in the form of a shepherd's crook, it is a reminder of the bishop's office as 'shepherd of Christ's flock'. It is sometimes mistakenly referred to as a crozier,. a term which should only be applied to a metropolitan cross (q.v.)

PATEN — The plate, usually of precious metal, on which the Host is placed at Mass.

PAX — (or paxbrede) An ornamental metal plate engraved or enamelled with the figure of a saint or some appropriate symbol, and with a handle at the back. Anciently the pax was passed between members of the congregation at Mass as a visible sign of God's peace ('pax') being shared among them.

PISCINA — A small recess in the sanctuary wall near to the altar (usually on the south side) containing a basin for the washing of the sacred vessels after Mass (see Sacrarium).

PEW — A privately-owned seat in a church, usually enclosed, and with its own door. Also known as a box-pew. They were generally replaced in the nineteenth century with open benches which are commonly - but incorrectly — referred to as 'pews'.

PONTIFICAL — A term relating to vestments and other ornaments used specifically by bishops. Also a book containing details of rites and ceremonies performed exclusively by the bishop.

PYX — A metal container for the reservation of the Host, and for carrying the Reserved Sacrament to the sick and dying.

PULPIT — An elevated platform or desk from which sermons are preached, and normally situated on the north side of the chancel arch.

RELIQUARY — An ornamented vessel, sometimes in the shape of a casket, containing relics (often body—parts) of saints.

REREDOS — A picture, sculpture, or hanging placed behind the altar.

ROOD — A large crucifix, often flanked by figures of Our Lady and S. John, and carried on a beam or rood-screen spanning the chancel arch.

SACRARIUM — A recess in the wall close to an altar, with a shelf for the cruets (q.v.), and a stone basin (piscina) for washing the vessels amd the priest's hands.

SACRISTAN — A person appointed to take care of the vessels and vestments used in church services, and to ensure than everything needed for a service is in its proper place.

SACRISTY — The place in a church where the sacred vessels and vestments are kept.

SANCTUARY — The eastern end of the chancel, where the altar stands; often enclosed by a communion rail (q.v.)

SANCTUARY LAMP — A hanging lamp suspended before an altar. A lamp showing a clear white light signifies that the Blessed Sacrament is reserved nearby. Blue is used at altars dedicated to Our Lady, and red elsewhere.

SEDILIUM(A) — The seat, or seats of the Sacred Ministers (Priest, Deacon, Subdeacon) at Mass; normally on the south side of the sanctuary.

STATIONS OF THE CROSS — A set of fourteen (sometimes fifteen) pictures or carvings depicting the journey of Christ from his condemnation to his crucifixion and entombment, and placed around the walls of a church for devotional use.

STOLE — A priestly vestment resembling a narrow scarf, often embroidered. The stole is also worn cross—wise by deacons over the left shoulder and tied under the right arm.

STOUP — A vessel placed near the door of church, containing holy water used to make the sign of the cross by those entering, as a reminder of their baptism.

SURPLICE   A long white garment with wide sleeves worn by clergy, choristers and others for the offices of Morning and Evening Prayer. In the Anglican Church it is sometimes worn with a stole by the celebrant at the Holy Communion, instead of the full vestments. A shorter version of the surplice, with a square neck—opening' and less ample sleeves, is known as a cotta.

TABERNACLE   A small safe fixed centrally at the altar, and used for the Reservation of the Blessed Sacrament

THURIBLE   Also referred to as a censer: the vessel in which incense is burned, usually suspended on chains and carried by a liturgical assistant known as a thurifer.

TRACERY   Ornamental stonework in the head of a Gothic window. In stained glass, 'traceries' refer to pieces of glass cut to fit into the often complicated spaces created by the stonework.

TRACTARIAN   A name given to those who followed the teachings of Oxford scholars such as Newman, Keble and Pusey in the 1830s and '40s as contained in a series of publications called Tracts for the Times. 'Trac tarian' later became synonymous with Ritualist, although the scholars of the Oxford Movement were concerned with the doctrines of the Church, not with ceremonial.

TRIPTYCH   A carved or painted panel, often a reredos (q.v.) which has two folding panels enabling it to be closed up.

TUNICLE   A vestment worn over the alb by the sub-deacon at Mass, and sometimes also by the crucifer (cross–bearer) in processions. It is identical in shape to the dalmatic (q. v.) but has less decoration.

VESTMENTS   The collective name used of any garments worn by the priest at Mass, and including also those proper to bishop, deacon and subdeacon.

SELECT BIBLIOGRAPHY

Aldrich, M., *Gothic Revival*, London: Phaidon Press, 1994

Andrews, B., *Creating a Gothic Paradise; Pugin at the Antipodes*, Hobart: Tasmanian Museum & Art Gallery, 2002.

Anthony, E., *The Architecture of Ralph Adams Cram and his office*, Norton 2007

Atterbury, P., and Wainwright, C., Pugin: *A Gothic Passion*, New Haven and London: Yale University Press, 1994.

Belcher, M., A.W.N. Pugin: *An annotated critical bibliography*, London & New York: Mansell, 1987

  Birmingham Gold & Silver 1773-1973. Catalogue of an exhibition celebrating the bicentenary of the Assay Office: Birmingham: City Museum & Art Gallery, 1973.

Brooks C., *The Gothic Revival*, London: Phaidon 1999.

Bury, S.. In Search of Pugin's Church Plate, *The Connoisseur*, vol. 165, no. 663, May 1997.

Bury, S. 'Pugin and the Tractarians, *The Connoisseur*, vol. 719, january 1972.

Champ, J.F. (ed), *Oscott College 1838-1988: A volume of commemorative essays*, Oscott 1988

Cheshire, J., *Stained Glass and the Victorian Gothic Revival*, Manchester: Manchester University Press, 2004

Cooke, R., *The Palace of Westminster*, London: Burton Skira 1987.

Crook, J. M. *William Burges and the High Victorian Dream*, London: John Murray 1981

Crook, J.M., *The Dilemma of Style: Architectural Ideas from the Picturesque to the Post-Modern*, London: John Murray, 1987.

Doolan, B., *The Pugins and the Hardmans*, Birmingham: Archdiocese of Birmingham Historical Commission, 2004.

Feeny, P., 'The Heraldic Glass in the Houses of Parliament', *Journal of the British Society of Master Glasspainters*, vol. xii, 1955-59.

Fisher, M.J., *Alton Towers: A Gothic Wonderland*, Stafford: M.J. Fisher, 1999

Fisher, M. J., *'Perfect Cheadle '. St. Giles Catholic Church, Cheadle, Staffordshire*, Stafford: M.J. Fisher, 2004

Fisher, M.J., *Pugin-Land*, Stafford: M.J. Fisher, 2002.

Fisher, M. J., 'Pugin's Candlestick Maker', *Country Life*, 21 September 2006.

Gwynn, D.R., *Lord Shrewsbury*, Pugin, and the Catholic Revival, London: Hollins & Carter, 1946.

Harrison, M., *Victorian Stained Glass*, London: Barrie & Jenkins 1980.

Hill, R., *God's Architect: Pugin & the Building of Romantic Britain*, London: Allen Lane, 2007.

Hodgetts, M., *Erdington Abbey 1850-2000*, Erdington, 2000.

Martin, C., *A Glimpse of Heaven*, Swindon: English Heritage, 2006.

Meara, D., *A.W.N. Pugin and the Revival of Memorial Brasses*, London: Mansell 1991.

Meara, D., *Victorian Memorial Brasses*, London: Routledge & Kegan Paul, 1983

Muthesius, S., *The High Victorian Movement in Architecture*, 1850-1870, London & Boston: Routledge & Kegan Paul, 1972.

O'Donnell, R., *The Pugins and the Catholic Midlands*, Leominster: Gracewing, 2002. Port, M.H. (ed.), The Houses of Parliament, New Haven & London, 1976.

Pugin, A.W.N., *An Apology for the Revival of Christian Architecture in England*, London: John Weale, 1843

Contrasts; or a parallel between the noble edifices of the Middle Ages and corresponding buildings of the present day; shewing the present decay of taste, London: C. Dolman, 1841 (2nd edition).

Glossary of Ecclesiastical Ornament and Costume, London: Henry Bohn, 1844

Some remarks relative to ecclesiastical architecture and decoration, London: Charles Dolman, 1850. Reprint: Leominster: Gracewing, 2004

The True Principles of Pointed or Christian Architecture, Reprint, Oxford: St. Barnabas Press, 1969.

The Present State of Ecclesiastical Architecture in England, London: C. Dolman, 1843,

Spencer-Silver, P., *Pugin 's Builder: The Life and Work of George Myers*, Hull, University of Hull Press, 1993.

Timmins, S. (ed.), *The resoureces, products and industrial history of Birmingham and the Midland hardware district*, London: Robert Hardwicke, 1866. Reprint, London: Frank Cass, 1967.

Webster, C. & Elliott J., *'A Church as it should be': the Cambridge Camden Society and its influence*, Stamford, Shaun Tyas, 2000.

Webster, C. (ed.), *'Temples worthy of His presence': the early publications of the Cambridge Camden Society*, Reading: Spire Books, 2003.

Wedgwood, A., *Catalogue of the Architectural Drawings in the Victoria & Albert Museum: A.W.N. Pugin and the Pugin Family*, London, V&A Museum, 1985.

Wedgwood, A. (ed.), *Pugin in his home . Two memoirs by John Hardman Powell, Ramsgate:* The Pugin Society and Thanet District Council, 2006

INDEX

John Hardman & Company

Established 1838

Lightwoods House ✦ Lightwoods Park

Hagley Road ✦ Birmingham B67 5DP

England

tel. 0121 429 7609

Master craftsmen in stained glass
working from the original Hardman archive

Suppliers & purchasers of church furnishings